GUNSMITHING:
THE TRICKS OF THE TRADE

By J. B. Wood

DBI BOOKS, INC., Northfield, Illinois

STAFF

Editor
Harold A. Murtz

Associate Editor
Robert S.L. Anderson

Cover Photography
John Hanusin

Production Manager
Harold A. Murtz

Publisher
Sheldon L. Factor

DEDICATION
This book is dedicated to the careful
amateur and the beginning gunsmith:
May you never break off a tap in a blind hole!

ISBN 0-910676-46-1   Library of Congress Catalog Card #82-072294

CONTENTS

Acknowledgements

My thanks to these people, who
helped to make this book possible:
James Mongello, Jerry Bernstein,
Kenny Davis, Harold Murtz, Steve
Robbins, Jim Blanford, A. D.
Jenkins, Sr., George P. Whittington,
Lawrence Payton, Don Hatten,
Sheriff Larry Markham, Tom
Thornber of Colt, Harry Sanford of
AMT, Dave Ecker and Charlie Gara
of Charter Arms, Bob Sconce of
MMC, Frank and Bob Brownell of
Brownells, Dan Bechtel of B-Square,
Spike's Gun Shop, and Jim, John
and "Big John" of Lock & Load Gun
Shop.

J. B. Wood

Intro-duction

This is not an ordinary gunsmithing book. I've noticed that most of the books in this category are often either too general or too specific. The general approach of previous volumes frequently fails to give the answers that may be needed on a particular piece of work, while the specific books are usually helpful only for the gunsmithing specialist.

For those who want to learn the proper way to glass bed a rifle action in a stock or to reblue a handgun by the heat-bath process, there are excellent books that detail these operations. *This is not one of them.* The "tricks" referred to in the title are simple small-shop operations that I've been using in my work as a "practicing" gunsmith for more than 30 years. Though some of them might be called "shortcuts," they all have proved to be effective and durable repairs.

When time and money are not important factors, the old, traditional gunsmithing methods are best, especially when working on a high-quality gun or a collector piece. Sometimes this is the only way. When the gun is an ordinary practical shooter, the object is to restore it to working order, and there's no need to do it the hard way.

There's also another factor involved: The beginning gunsmith and the knowledgeable amateur seldom have complete machine shops at their disposal. They have to operate without the advantages of such main shop tools as a lathe, welding torch, and drill press. For the beginner or the advanced amateur, the simple alternatives described here can help until the time comes when they do acquire heavier and more sophisticated equipment. A number of the "tricks" can even be used in a fully-equipped shop, on jobs that don't require the traditional approach. In those cases, this book can also serve the professional.

For purposes of illustration, a wide variety of guns will be shown and mentioned here. It's not my intention, though, to describe the repair of any particular gun. All of these operations can be applied to firearms other than the ones shown, if the mechanism is similar. When, for example, I show the replacement of a broken blade spring with a round-wire type in a certain revolver, it follows that the same repair will work on any other gun having the same spring arrangement.

A note on the drawings: The non-photo illustrations in this book are not intended to be exact representations of the parts that are described in the text. For purposes of clarity, spaces are shown between surfaces that are actually tightly fitted.

One point should be stressed: Any original part, new factory replacement, or repaired part can break. So, as with anything mechanical, the operations described here can't be absolutely guaranteed. To put it into formal language, *neither the author nor DBI Books Inc,. will be responsible for any accidents related to the information in this book.* As always, in any aspect of firearms handling, *be careful.*

J. B. Wood
Raintree House
Corydon, Kentucky

Tools

Some of the tools that I've been using for a long time in my shop are ordinary carpenter's or mechanic's items, but all of them have been modified in some way. In its original form, hardly any tool is right for firearms work unless it was made specifically for that purpose. In that category there are hundreds of fine items offered by Brownells, B-Square, Tom Menck, and others.

The illustrated list that follows this brief dissertation is by no means complete. It was included mainly to show a few of the specialized gunsmithing tools, along with a number of helpful shop-made items. In addition to these, there are quite a few other necessities that the advanced amateur or beginning gunsmith will definitely need. Let's check a few of these un-illustrated items.

Vises: If you'll have only one vise, be sure it's a heavy one with 3″ to 4″ jaws and full rotational capability. It should bolt to the workbench, not simply clamp on the edge and it should have either double guide rods, or a single heavy rectangular bar. Don't buy a cheap vise—get the best you can afford. Years ago, while straightening a barrel, I actually managed to break a cheap vise. On my workbench at the present time I have two vises; the larger one has

3½″ jaws, and the smaller one measures 2½″, and both are fully rotational. The small vise was made by Millers Falls, and I've been using it constantly for more than 30 years. Again, it just doesn't pay in the long run to buy a cheap vise. It should be noted that there are special purpose vises, such as the Versa-Vise and PowRarm, that will swivel to any position. Both are excellent, but there will still be times when a good, solid, bench vise will be needed.

Saws: This is one item that can be purchased at your local hardware store—a good hacksaw. Also, get a supply of blades in both lengths (if your saw is adjustable to them), and in various tooth-counts, to adapt the use to different thicknesses of metal. Generally speaking, a tubular-frame saw is stronger than one with a flat-formed frame. My own main hacksaw is an ancient tubular-type marked "Bluepoint," which I bought years ago in used condition. I also use a small English-made metal saw with 6″ blades. Brownells have the equivalent of these two saws in their "Challenger" and "Little Hacksaw," and they are not expensive. For those who intend to get into gripmaking for handguns, a good coping saw can be purchased at almost any local hardware store.

Drills: For the full-time serious gunsmith, a drill press will be an absolute necessity. A good one will not be inexpensive, though, and for a time, with care, an electric hand drill can be made to do some remarkable things. We'll go into this further in the "Tool Use" section. If you're restricted to using a hand drill, I'd suggest two of them, one in ⅜″ capacity, the other in ¼″. The smaller drill will usually have a higher RPM speed, useful in some applications, and its chuck will grip smaller diameter drills and rod stock with more precision. The brand name is not important, as long as the drills are of good quality. My own ¼″ is a Sears Craftsman, and my ⅜″ is a Black & Decker. In some cases, reversibility and variable speed may offer some advantage, but probably not enough to justify the extra cost.

Stones: There are some jobs, like those involving super-hard parts which must be given a mirror-finish, where files are useless. For this, you will need a set of good stones in assorted grades and shapes. A good example of this would be the work that is popularly termed a "trigger job." Altering the depth and angle of a sear step, and giving it the required high polish, can be done only with a succession of fine India stones. There is no point in my recommending the shapes you will need, as you will eventually meet a situation requiring the one I didn't mention. Get a wide assortment of shapes, in grades from coarse to fine.

Before we get into the illustrated tools, I'll list here the sources of some of the specialized items, with their addresses:

Brookstone Co.
127 Vose Farm Road
Peterborough, NH 03458
Phone: 603/924-7181

Brownells, Inc.
Route 2, Box 1
Montezuma, IA 50171
Phone: 515/623-5401

B-Square Co.
P.O. Box 11281
Fort Worth, TX 76109
Phone: 817/923-0964

Chapman Mfg. Co.
Route 17
Durham, CT 06422
Phone 203/349-9228

T.W. Menck, Gunsmith
5703 South 77th Street
Ralston, NB 68127
Phone 402/592-5810

MMC (Miniature Machine Co.)
210 E. Poplar
Deming, NM 88030
Phone: 505/546-2151

Pin-Pal
1626 Wilcox, Suite 636
Hollywood, CA 90028

For several reasons, not the least of which is inflation, I've decided not to list prices of the tools shown. The big annual catalogue from Brownells is available for $3.25 at the time this is written, and price lists from the others mentioned are available on request. When the tools shown are available only from a particular source, this will be noted after the description.

1. When bought as a complete set, the Magna-Tip screwdriver comes with 12 regular screw bits, 10 for Allen screws, and 3 for Phillips types. The bits are held in place by a strong magnet inside the socket, and this transfers magnetism to the bits, an often useful feature. The tips are very hard. With enough force, you might manage to break one, but they'll never bend. **Brownells**

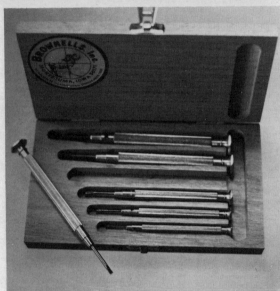

2. This set of small screwdrivers carries the arrow trademark of F. Dick, and they are German precision and quality all the way. The smallest one in the set is really too tiny for gun work, but the others will be used constantly. **Brownells**

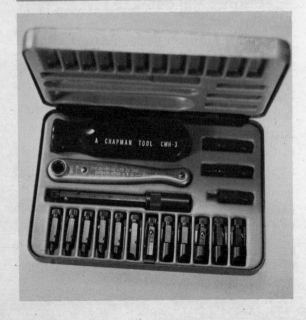

3. The Chapman screwdriver set, like the two described above, has the hollow-ground bits that are necessary for gun work, and the quality is excellent. There are 12 regular bits, 2 Phillips-type, and one tiny Allen bit, intended for a screw on the handle which will lock any of the bits solidly into the handle socket, or lock the extension in place. For normal use, this will not be necessary, as the extension and each of the bits has a spring-powered ball bearing detent which snaps them into place. The Allen bit also happens to be the right size for the screws on most trigger shoes. There is also a reversible ratchet wrench which can be slipped onto the shaft for extra leverage. This Chapman set is well known, and rightly so. **Chapman, Brownells**

4. You will need a wide assortment of good quality pliers, and the two types shown are just a small example. The larger ones are by Bernard, and have parallel jaws that are smooth and unhardened, to avoid marring parts. The smaller pair have curved smooth tips and the hinge is a box joint. They are by F. Dick of Germany. **Brownells**

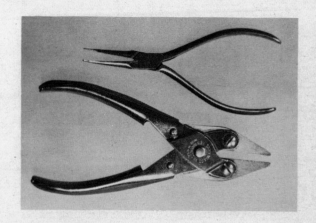

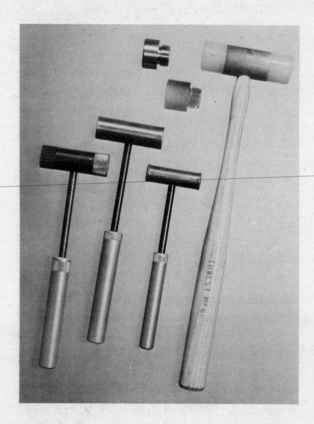

5. The larger hammer shown has faces of nylon in place, but it can be had with any combination of nylon, brass, or plastic faces. All screw into the head, and can be replaced as they wear. The solid brass hammers come as a set, and have perfect weight and balance for pin drifting. The shafts are steel, and the handles are alloy. The hammer at left, about the same weight as the larger one in the set, has knurled replaceable head faces of brass and steel. (Note the peened-over faces on the small brass hammer—it is one of my most-used tools.) **Brownells, B-Square**

6. There are situations where reach and accessibility are beyond the capabilities of fingers and even sharp-nosed pliers. For these, you will need heavy-duty tweezers, such as these. They are nickel-plated, and very strong. **Brownells**

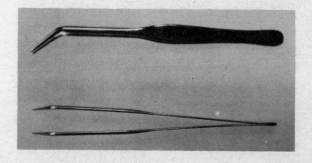

7. For pistols of the U.S. Government Model pattern (Colt 1911, etc.), tight muzzle bushings will often require a wrench of the type shown here. The smaller one was made by Micro. The larger one also has provision for removal of the ejector/ratchet piece from Colt revolvers. **Brownells**

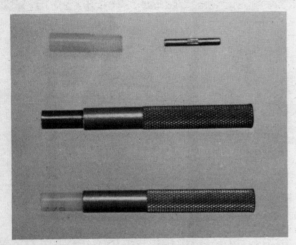

8. This inexpensive little "soft" drift punch is one of the most-used tools in my shop. The tips are replaceable, and I keep two of these punches on hand, one with the brass tip, the other with nylon. The nylon tip has an internal steel pin for extra strength. **Brownells**

9. A good set of steel drift punches is absolutely essential, and these, made by Mayhew, are of fine quality. The straight-tapered types on the top are for starting pins, and the others, available in two weights and lengths, are for pushing the pins through. **Brownells**

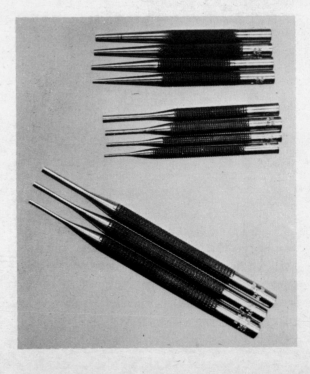

10. Many modern guns use hollow "roll pins," and using a regular drift punch on these will often deform them. Mayhew makes a special set of roll pin drifts, the tips having a small projection or "teat" which fits the hole in the roll pin. **Brownells**

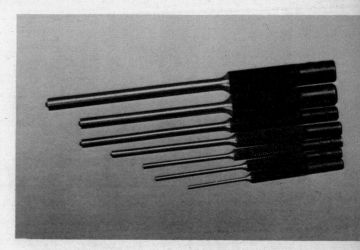

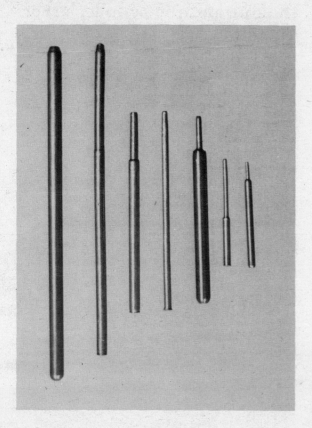

11. These punches were made in the shop from various sizes of welder's brazing rod. Soft and non-marring, they won't harm the gun even if they slip.

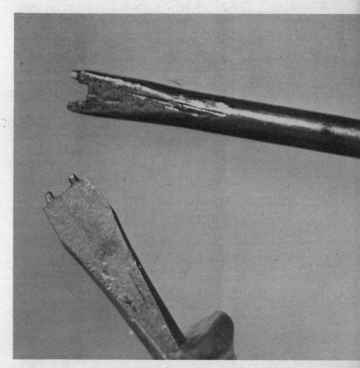

12. Also in the category of shop-made tools are these two-point wrenches, made from old screwdrivers. They are used on adjustable sights, firing pin retainers, and the magazine release buttons of some auto pistols.

13. This little double-ended wrench covers two sizes of ejector spring retaining nuts in early pattern Colt revolvers. Without it, removal of the retaining nut is quite difficult, and may result in damage to the nut and the cylinder arbor. **Brownells**

14. This wrench is specifically designed for use on the barrel retaining nut of the Winchester 150/250 and 190/290 series of 22-caliber rifles. Without it, removal and replacement of the barrels will usually result in some marring. **Brownells**

15. This special heavy wrench is designed for removal and replacement of the barrel retaining nut on Remington Model 742 and Model 760 rifles. It's a quality tool, made from 01 steel, hardened to Rockwell C 46-48. **Brownells**

16. These stock and fore-end wrenches make a bothersome job much easier. The longer one at the top is for general use on any gun that has through-bolt stock mounting. The two at the left are for the stock and fore-end of the Remington Model 870 shotgun. The one at lower right is for the stock of the Remington Model 1100. **B-Square, Brownells**

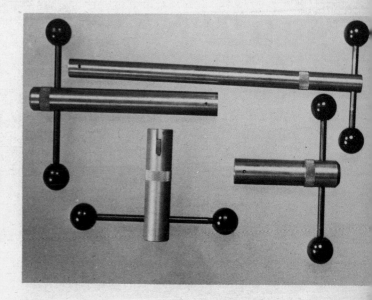

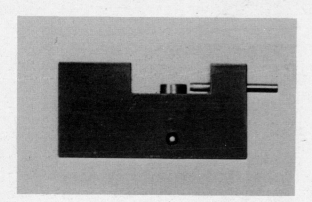

17. In most Remington centerfire rifles, the extractor is mounted inside the front of the bolt by a tiny rivet, and this makes replacement quite difficult. With this special tool, the new rivet can be set with a minimum of trouble. **B-Square**

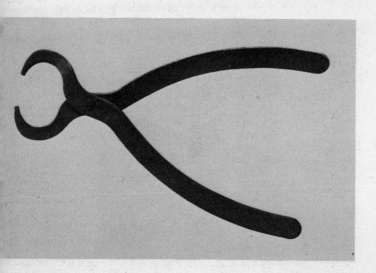

18. These extractor pliers are used in both the removal and replacement of Mauser and Springfield-type extractors. They can make a sometimes difficult job much easier. **Brownells**

19. These wrenches are for removal of the piston nut on the U.S. 30 M1 Carbine and its commercial copies. The single-end wrench is from a military surplus source. The double-end wrench fits both the three-point military nut and the two-point commercial version. Both are available from several sources.

20. Most military surplus dealers can supply this Carbine bolt disassembly and reassembly tool. Without it, takedown of the Carbine bolt can be a tedious job.

21. Many quality shotguns, especially the European double guns, have firing pin retainers which require a large two-point spanner, or wrench, for removal. You can make one for each job, but this tool will make things a lot easier. The pins which fit the holes in the retainer are adjustable from ³⁄₁₆″ to ⁷⁄₁₆″ spacing. If they become worn or snap off, they are replaceable. This is a beautiful tool. **B-Square**

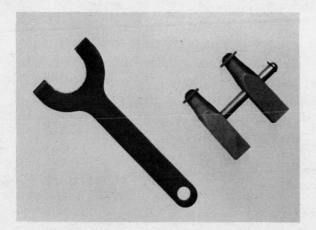

22. The Brownells wrench on the left is for removal of the fore-end cap on a Winchester Model 12 shotgun, but it is adaptable to several other guns. The Menck fore-end cap wrench on the right is fully adjustable for any gun, and is designed to be held in a vise. **Brownells, Menck**

23. Staking the shell stops in place inside the receiver of a Remington 870 shotgun is an awkward job, unless you have one of these tools. The one on the left is from B-Square, the one on the right from Menck. They both work well. **B-Square, Menck**

24. Some Savage slide-action shotguns have an un-slotted fore-end cap, and if it's tight, removal without marring can be difficult. With the Menck wrench shown, it's easy. The endpiece has two faces, to accommodate both 12 and 20-gauge diameters. **Menck**

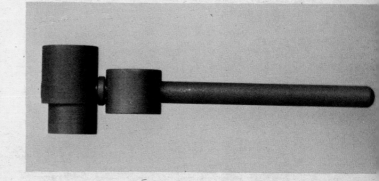

25. This wrench is for adjustment of the barrel sleeve on Winchester Model 97 and Model 12 shotguns, and it will do the job without the danger of damage to the outer threads. **Menck**

26. Replacement of the plastic magazine throat on the Winchester Model 1200/1400 series of guns is an interesting job, to say the least. This heavy tool is designed to encircle the magazine tube and drive the throat into place. **Menck**

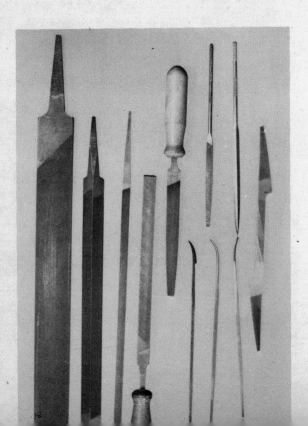

27. An assortment of good files is indispensable in any shop. Some can be bought at the local hardware store, but the more esoteric shapes must be obtained from special sources, such as Brownells. They offer one set of small Swiss files that is particularly nice. For a good medium round file, get a chainsaw sharpening file from your hardware store. They come in two diameters, and they're very hard.

28. For anyone who does much work on the Government Model pistol and its various commercial copies, this "Pin-pal" tool is absolutely the best accessory made. It easily removes the mainspring housing cross-pin without hammering, and also replaces it. It also has a muzzle bushing wrench, and provision for releasing the firing pin retainer. **Pin-Pal**

29. Here's one item you can get almost anywhere—a good pair of Vise-Grips. Be sure you get the genuine brand-name type, and not a cheap copy. Note that on the ones shown, used in my shop, the outer edges of the jaws have been hollow-ground to allow clearance into tight places.

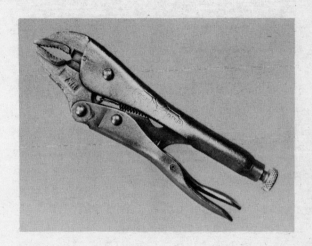

30. For polishing chambers, magazine tubes, or any other cylindrical interior surface, a simple shop-made tool is a split-end brass rod with a rectangle of emery cloth clamped into the slot. The larger type shown was made from an old cleaning rod, with a screw installed to hold the abrasive cloth in the slot. The other tool has adjustable tension and fine stones on its arms for fine polishing. It's an auto brake cylinder tool, and can be bought at auto supply stores.

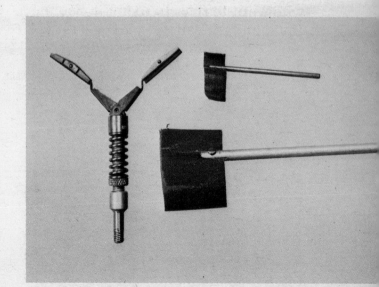

31. The tool shown here is an antique, but its modern equivalent is available from Brownells. It's a spring-winder, and when used with winding rods of different diameters, it will produce a wide variety of coil springs. Coil springs are best bought in assortments from Wolff, but when you encounter odd sizes that are not in any of the Wolff packets, this tool will make them.

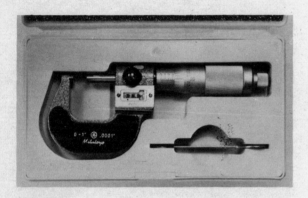

32. If your eyes are no better than mine, and you find it difficult to read a "mike" without a magnifying glass, then this Mitutoyo direct-readout micrometer would be an ideal shop accessory. For those who want to refer to them, it also has the standard calibration scale on the barrel and thimble. **Brownells**

33. Also by Mitutoyo, this dial-type inside caliper has many shop uses. I've found it to be invaluable when polishing out the choke on a shotgun from "Full" to "Modified," as it allows very precise measurements. **Brownells**

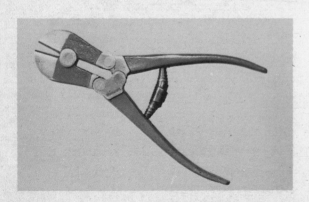

34. If you try to cut spring wire ("piano wire") with ordinary cutters, you'll just dent the edges of your tool. These large cutters have edges that are induction-hardened, and will snick off spring wire up to .080″ and larger. I've been using the one in the photo for about 15 years. **Brookstone**

35. I keep my taps in small envelopes along with the proper size of drill bit, both marked on the outside of the envelope for easy reference. Taps in ordinary sizes can be bought at any hardware store, but in commonly-used firearms sizes, such as 6-48 and 8-40, they must come from special sources. I buy all of my taps and number-drill bits from Brownells. My tap wrenches are by L.S. Starrett Co. of Athol, Massachusetts.

36. Anyone who tries to do gunsmithing work without some sort of hand grinder is doing it the hard way. The best known of these are the Foredom and the Dremel tools. They are of equal quality, but the Foredom is capable of heavier work. The small Dremel shown is one that I keep in the drawer for emergency use, in case one of my heavier tools is temporarily out of commission. Shown with the tool is a small portion of the wheels, mandrels, and other accessories that are used. There's no such thing as having too many. The Dremel and the Foredom, and all of the accessories, are available from Brownells.

37. Even if you don't specialize in the Colt Government Model auto, every gunsmith (and many shooters) will eventually be faced with the job of replacing the front sight. Usually, this involves installing replacements for both front and rear sights, changing to those with better visibility. With the tool shown, the otherwise difficult job of clenching the front sight inside the slide can be done neatly and with very little effort. **MMC, Brownells**

As noted back at the start of this section, these are just a small part of the tools that are needed for gunsmithing work. To show them all would fill a book of this size. In fact, this has been done. See *The Gun Digest Book of Gunsmithing Tools and Their Uses*, by John E. Traister, also available from DBI Books.

Tool Use

Even when all of the tools are exactly right for the job, it's still possible to make a mess of things if they're not handled properly. It's also possible to hurt yourself, which will heal, or mar the finish of a fine gun (depending upon the seriousness), which won't heal. In the interest of perhaps preventing this sort of thing, I'll set down a few observations here, and if they're too elementary for some old hands, those folks can ignore this section.

First of all, when working on any gun, **wear eye protection**. Brownells has several excellent types of eye protectors, but they can also be obtained at your local hardware store. Even if you wear prescription glasses, you need a safety shield, the type that completely encloses, with sides and lower edge touching the face. I know of a case in which a small grinding wheel shattered, and one of the fragments hit the cheek, rebounded to the inside of regular glasses, and glanced into the eye. Though this is an unusual case, there is always danger from released springs and spring-powered assemblies. Many injuries from firearms are not from accidental shootings, and, like those, they won't happen if you're careful.

Speaking of accidental firings, it may seem totally unnecessary to insert the old warning about being sure the gun is unloaded, especially to the readers of this book, but it needs to be repeated. As "gun people," you will have learned this long ago. Take care, though, that your familiarity doesn't make you careless. For example, I know of a gunsmith of many years experience who took out a shop window while working the action of a rifle when a round "hid" in a tubular magazine, and was jarred loose at just the wrong time. So, check, and then check again.

Getting back to personal injuries to the gunsmith, the damage that even small hand tools can inflict is amazing. Here's an example: A part is being held tightly in a pair of ordinary pliers, forcing it into place against spring tension. The part slips, and the pliers close suddenly, catching the skin at the base of the index finger between the handles behind the hinge. If enough pressure was being applied, the result is a painful blood blister, at the least. In this particular operation, Vise-Grips should have been used.

Other injury-avoidance can be even more obvious. Never put your other hand in the way of a sharp tool when exerting pressure. Even a screwdriver can do a lot of damage, and puncture wounds are always dangerous. Keep your fingers away from drills and saw blades. When starting a saw cut, pre-cut the starting groove with a file or a cutting disc in the Dremel tool. Extensive filing can abrade the hands. Install handles on your files, or wrap a shop cloth around the holding end. A large portion of safe tool use needs no specific rules, other than care and common sense.

Aside from the safety factor, there are other points about tool use that can be noted, including some unusual applications of ordinary items. The first illustration is an example of the latter.

1. In the small shop, any electric hand drill can double as a lathe. This use is limited to the capacity of the drill chuck, of course, and will work well only on short items, such as firing pins and screws. To use a drill this way, pad the jaws of a large vise with two squares of heavy leather or some other suitable material, and clamp the body of the drill firmly in the vise. With the part to be made se-cured in the chuck, files can be ap-plied to shape the part. If the reduc-tion is extensive, as in taking the end of a ¼″ rod down to .060″ for a firing pin point, the friction vibration may tend to loosen the chuck, so it should be checked occasionally for tightness. This use also puts an unusual strain on the motor of the drill, and too long a work period will cause it to overheat. When the body of the drill becomes too warm to comfortably lay a hand on it, stop and allow it to cool. When turn-ing narrow edges, such as screw-heads, always use a fine file. A course one will tend to bite deeper as the slot in the head passes, and the head will be oval-shaped. When turning har-dened parts, it is possible to use the Dremel tool in conjunction with the drill/lathe, holding a grinding wheel against the part. The speed of the Dre-mel is a lot higher than most hand drills, so this operation takes a lot of practice. One of the best uses of the Dremel in this situation is with a cut-ting disc, to make a starting cut which is then worked down with a file.

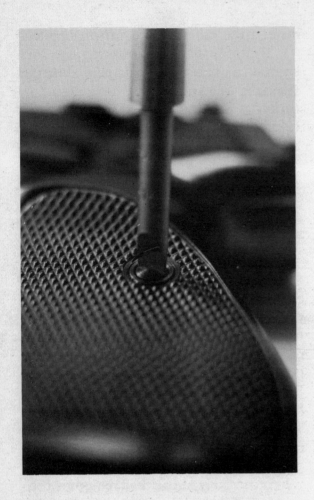

ened by setting the blade in the slot and giving the handle a light tap with a small hammer. Don't overdo this, though. If a light tap doesn't free the screw, apply a good penetrant, such as Break-Free or WD-40, and give it time to work. When installing a screw that tensions a spring, take special care that the threads are properly engaged before turning it into place. As noted in the Tool Section, never use a regular tapered screwdriver blade on gun screws. Some that I use are not only hollow-ground, but have been further altered to be absolutely flat and parallel at the tip.

2. The main piece of elementary advice on screwdrivers is to be sure that the blade exactly fits the slot of the screw. This applies to all three dimensions of the slot, the depth, width, and its span across the screw head. If you don't have a blade that fits perfectly, grind or file one to mate with the slot. It's better to ruin a screwdriver blade than a screw on a fine gun. When applying the blade to a screw, guide the tip into the screw slot with the fingertips, and if the screw is not extremely tight, keep them there to control the blade against slipping out of the slot as the head clears its recess. A tight screw can often be loos-

3. There is one punch not shown in the Tool Section that should have some comment here. This is the center punch, which has a hardened, pointed end, and is used to make a starting indentation for hole drilling. In this operation, I usually use two punches, the first one very slim, made from an ice-pick end. The slim punch makes it easier to properly locate the point, and it is tapped very lightly. The point of the regular center punch is then fitted into this dent, and it is struck with more force.

Starting punches have a straight taper from handle to tip, and the tip is flat. These are used to make the initial movement of tightly-fitted pins, the stronger tapered shafts being less likely to bend or break under heavy stress. The drift punch, which tapers

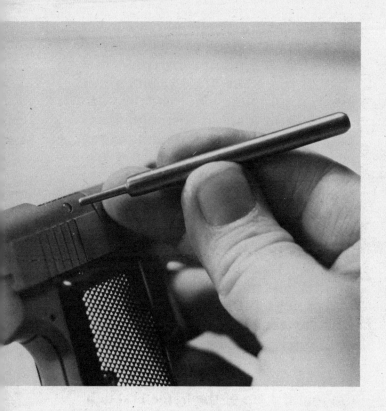

pin, holding the punch in position. The removal of roll pins seldom requires a lot of force, and these special punches can be used for the entire operation. Regular drift punches should not be used on roll pins, as they tend to deform the ends, and make re-installation more difficult. One last point, and a very important one: Whatever type of punch is used, always be sure that its diameter is as near as possible to the size of the pin on which it is used. Otherwise, the punch, the pin, and the assembly can be damaged.

sharply to a long tip of uniform diameter, is then used to push the pin on out of the assembly. With either type, several light taps with the hammer will be better than one or two heavy blows. When the pin is in an exterior surface that might be marred, it's best to start with a shop-made punch of brass or bronze. If one of these slips, there's no more than a smear of brass on the surface, which is easily removed. When setting the punch in place on the pin, guide it with the fingertips, and hold it in position for the starting taps. After the pin has begun to move, the drift punch can be inserted into the hole to push the pin completely out of the hole.

Roll pin punches are particularly easy to use, as the projection at the tip will fit into the hole at the center of the

4. From long habit, I use several models of the Dremel power tools, but this should not be taken to mean that the excellent Foredom or some other brand will not do as well. Since most of my work has been on handguns, the lighter-duty Dremel tools happen to suit my purposes. It should be noted that the use of any power tool of this type requires some practice. Whatever tip is in the tool, centrifugal force will tend to move the tool in the direction of its rotation, and the user must learn to compensate for this. Before using one of these tools for the first time on a delicate job, it would be a good idea to practice the operation on a piece of scrap material, to familiarize yourself with its action. Of all the various grindstones and other attachments available for the Dremel, the one I keep in place on

5. When a part that is super-hardened has to be cut, this can be done with a stone or cutting disc. When it has to be drilled, though, it must be softened. This is called annealing, and it's just the opposite of tempering. In tempering, the heated part is quickly immersed in oil or water (depending on the type of steel), cooling it rapidly. To go the other way, the part must be cooled slowly. There are several accepted ways of accomplishing this, but the one I have always used is perhaps the easiest. With the part held in a vise, I use a propane torch to bring it to the proper color (this varies according to the type of steel), then back the torch off slowly, just a fraction of an inch per movement, until the color has left the part and just the tip of the flame is touching it. Then, I take the torch away and allow it to air-cool. When the part has cooled enough to be handled, it will be ready to be drilled. Of course, after the work is completed, it may be necessary to re-harden the part, depending on its function.

the variable-speed Model 380 on my workbench is a mandrel holding a thin cutting disc. With practice, one of these can be made to do almost anything. Though these cutting discs can be bought as regular Dremel accessories, I buy mine in large-quantity boxes from a dental supply wholesaler. In this form, they are called "separating discs," and they cost somewhat less, but work just as well. A final warning: *Never use one of these tools without wearing eye protection.*

7. A slave pin is simply a length of rod stock that is shorter than the width of a part, with the ends rounded. It is used during reassembly, inserted in the pin-hole of the part, to hold a spring, or another tensioned part, in place until the original pin can be installed. Although I have a fairly large assortment of slave pins in many diameters and lengths, I find that I still occasionally have to make one. Fortunately, this is very easy. Just select a piece of rod stock (in some cases, a section of nail will do) that is slightly smaller than the original pin. Cut it to a length that is slightly less than the width of the part, and round off both ends. Then, with the part and its spring or attendant part assembled, insert the slave pin to hold everything together. When the part is in position for installation, pushing the original pin into place will force the slave pin out the other side. It should, of course, be saved for the next job having similar dimensions.

6. After a hole has been drilled in any part or assembly, it is always necessary to chamfer the edges. This applies whether the hole is for passage of a pin, or for tapping and screw insertion. In the latter case, if it's not done, it can cause a lot of undue difficulty. With the mechanically-limited reach of a drill press, this is easily done by inserting a larger drill bit. In the small shop, with a hand drill, this should *never* be tried. Instead, use a new, very sharp bit that is larger than the hole, and *with the fingers only*, rotate it against the hole until the edges are chamfered. I have been asked if a regular counter-sink tool would not do this as well. In some metals, it will, but most counter-sinks are not hard enough to work in all cases. Also, their angle is often too steep, making more of a chamfer than is wanted.

Materials

When the subject is metal, there is no such thing as worthless junk. I have, in fact, occasionally gone to what was once termed a junkyard (and now called a "metal recovery installation") for steel in certain thicknesses. In industrial areas, I have sometimes stopped my car and gathered nice little plates of fine nickel alloy off the street! The catch here is that you must be able to tell whether the scrap you find is suitable for the job at hand. Monel, for example, is difficult to work with, and almost impossible when it comes to heat treatment.

For most serious jobs, it's best to obtain just the right type of material from a regular supplier, an industrial wholesale establishment. If, for instance, you are making a replacement hammer for a shotgun, standard 01 carbon steel would be best. It's easy to shape, and easy to give proper heat-treatment. There are a lot of sophisticated alloy steels on the market now, and some of them have amazing strength and other good properties. Unfortunately, most of them require esoteric double-hardening methods, and this needs equipment that's not available in the small shop. Let's look at some of the typical materials that are likely to be needed for gun work, and their sources.

1. In the larger diameters, for making firing pins, strikers, and other heavier parts, drill rod will be needed. This comes in fairly long sections, and is comparatively expensive, so at first it is best purchased as needed, in sizes as near as possible to the parts to be made. Most drill rod is semi-hardened, and in many cases no heat treatment will be necessary. For smaller work, such as making replacements for cross-pins, unhardened ("cold-rolled") rods can usually be obtained in short lengths. Using drill rod in these applications is really

unnecessary, and the cost is prohibitive. When the pin is under no great stress, there is nothing wrong with using a nail of suitable size, turned to the proper diameter. For many years, I've used them to make striker spring guides in true hammerless automatic pistols. The nail head is easily formed to make the spring base flange at the rear, eliminating the necessity of starting with a large piece of drill rod

and turning it down. Also, when a cross-pin needs to be anchored in place by riveting the ends into chamfered areas, a pin made from a nail is soft enough to be easily upset for this purpose. Nails should not be used for pin stock, though, in any application where there is heavy stress or friction. Drill rod and smaller pin stock are available at industrial wholesale supply firms.

2. Bar stock is available at most large hardware stores, and usually comes in 36″ lengths. It is square in section, in various dimensions, and is entirely untempered. It can be bent into the necessary shape, drilled or cut and then hardened, if this is required. Using square-section bar stock will often save a lot of filing and cutting of larger pieces of steel, and it is also inexpensive.

3. Plank steel is different from bar stock in more ways than its shape. It usually comes in sections that are 1″ to 1½″ wide and 18″ long. Unlike bar stock, which sometimes has variable dimensions, these little "planks" are precision-cut, being absolutely true for their entire length. At

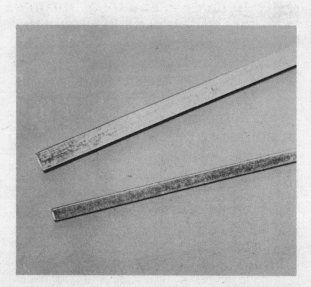

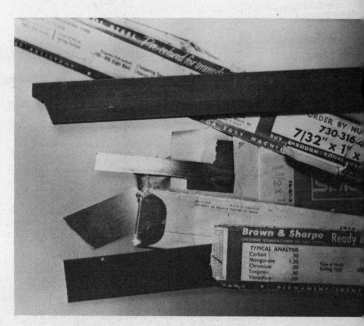

the present time, I have thicknesses ranging from 1/32" up to 9/32" on hand. This stuff is relatively expensive, and is usually bought for a particular job, when a certain thickness is needed. It is also available pre-colored or coated, so that the shape of the part to be made can be scribed right on its surface without first applying cold blue to take the pattern. Steel of this type is sold under several names—"precision tool steel" and "flat ground die steel" are but a few. Buying it in the exact thickness needed saves a lot of work.

4. Spring wire, also known as "music wire" or "piano wire," is one of the items in the shop that can be called absolutely essential. Although it is tempered, it can be cold-

formed into any necessary shape. With a spring-winder (see the Tool Section) you can use spring wire to make coil springs in the shop. With round-nosed pliers, you can make any torsion spring. Spring wire is available in diameters from .006" to .180", both ends of the scale being outside useful sizes for gun work. My own stock of spring wire ranges from .016" to .080", and this covers most firearm uses. Spring wire is usually sold by the pound and fractions of a pound, and the amount of wire will vary with its diameter. For example, a pound of .016" will give you 1,465 feet of wire. In .080", a pound will measure just 58 feet. If the particular diameter is not likely to be used often, I buy it in 1/2-pound or 1/4-pound amounts. Industrial supply wholesalers will usually have spring wire in stock.

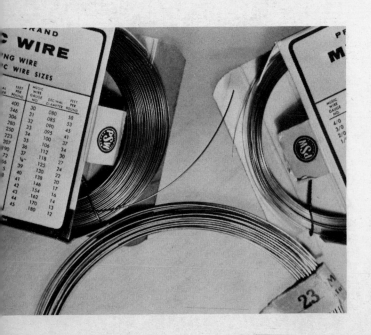

5. In modern guns, flat springs are seldom used. In most of the older ones, this will be the type mostly encountered. Springs of flat tempered stock are also called blade or leaf springs. If these springs are not severely flexed in normal operation, they are no more fragile than the round-wire coil. When they are flexed to their limit, though, as when used for hammer or trigger springs, they tend to break with some frequency. When the gun is not a collector piece, and there is no good reason for replacing with the original type, I will usually replace

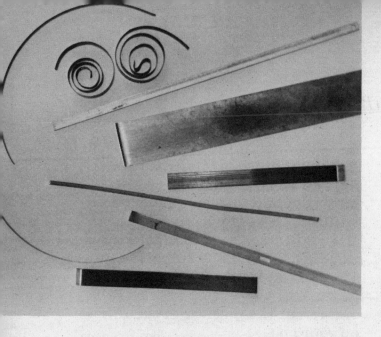

6. A practically limitless assortment of coil springs can be obtained from Brownells or Wolff, in general packages designated "heavy duty," "light duty," and so on, in various lengths. There are special packets of typical recoil springs, striker springs, and complete spring kits for various guns. Any shop that does a fair amount of work should have a sizeable assortment of these packets and kits.

An incidental source of coil springs is salvage from things that are being thrown away. As an example, every Bic cigarette lighter has three excellent coil springs inside, including one very small one that is frequently useful. So before you flick your empty Bic into the trash, tear it apart for the springs. Inevitably, there will be some spring replacement job that will require a coil of a special size and wire diameter that is not in one of the assortments. In that case, you'll have to use a Spring Winder, and make your own. In the Spring Section, I'll show how this is done.

broken flat springs with round-wire types of original design. For the times when this is unsuitable, I either make a flat spring from steel stock (a tedious procedure), or utilize one of the replacements available from the W.C. Wolff Co. (Box 232, Ardmore, PA 19003). One of their great services is making hammer and trigger springs for the Iver Johnson, Harrington & Richardson, and other early top-break revolvers.

No discussion of flat springs would be complete without a comment on the use of clock springs in firearms work. More times than I can count, I've removed from old revolvers trigger springs home-made from the mainsprings of alarm clocks. They are too light for this use, and far too light for use as hammer springs, even when two sections are stacked together. Clock springs, though, do have some legitimate uses. The thinner ones can be cut to shape with metal shears or large scissors, and for smaller springs (sear, cylinder hand, and so on) they work fine. In a few years, this particular paragraph may be obsolete, as the old wind-up alarm clock is rapidly being replaced by quartz and L.E.D. timepieces.

7. Generally speaking, ordinary hardware-store screws should not be used in firearms work, but there are some notable exceptions to this rule. Gun screws will usually have finer threads, and this is particularly significant when they are short, as this supplies a better hold when penetration is shallow. Where regular machine screws are 6-32, the types used in firearms will be 6-48. The first figure refers to the screw size, and the second indicates the number of threads per inch. Brownells has the best gun screw assortment I've seen, and I'd advise buying the longer ones. They can always be cut to length. Also available are blank screws, for applications where the screw is also a pivot. On these, just the tip can be threaded with a die. These are also available from Brownells.

When the penetration of an assembly will allow enough thread bite for security, regular hardware screws can be used. If, for example, you have an older shotgun that is missing the through-bolt that retains the stock, finding an original replacement may be next to impossible. In this case, determine the length necessary, and the size and thread count, and get a carriage bolt or stove bolt at the hardware store. If the exact thread count can't be matched, get the nearest available, and re-cut the receiver to the thread on your bolt.

As with the other materials, be alert for good screws in discarded junk piles. I once found a large quantity of fine Fillister-head 5-40 screws in a telephone terminal box, when a local firm scrapped its old switchboard and put in pushbutton phones. By the way, one item that I should have shown in the Tool Section, and will illustrate here, is a Screw Checker, available from Brownells. It will tell you the size and thread count of any screw instantly, and is an almost indispensable item. It's also inexpensive, and there is a metric model.

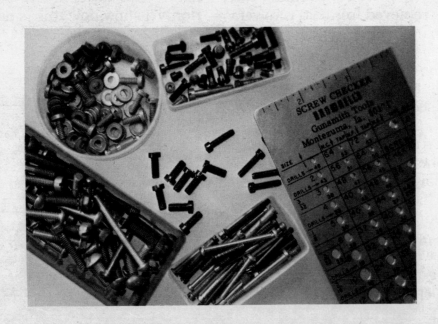

Extractors

L-Shaped Extractors

In firearms of recent manufacture, one of the most common extractor designs is an L-shaped part, with the short arm of the "L" hooked into a recess in the bolt or slide, and the extractor both retained and powered by a plunger and spring. The plunger fits into a notch at the upper rear of the extractor. While this has come to be a popular design, the concept is not new. A variation of it was used in Searle's design of the Savage pistol in 1905, though in that case the short arm was a lateral pivot, and the extractor beak was on the side of the long extension. A more recent example, in a gun that is now discontinued, was the double extractor arrangement in the 22 semi-auto Stevens Model 87A rifle. Parts for this gun are no longer routinely obtainable, and when I have made replacement extractors for it (and for others of similar extractor pattern), I usually made them from small rod stock. The type used was un-tempered, to allow cold-forming (bending) without the necessity of using a torch.

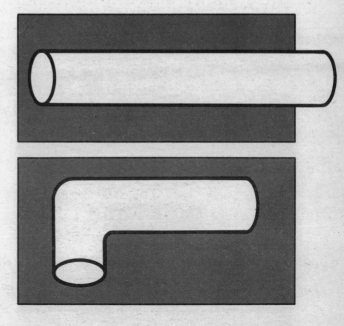

1. Select a length of rod stock with a diameter equal to the width of the original extractor. If the original is missing, check by inserting the rod into the extractor recess in the bolt or slide.

2. Grip the rod vertically in a vise, with about ½" protruding above the jaws, and use a hammer to bend the tip of the rod into a right angle.

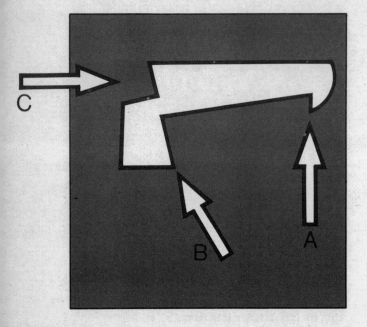

3. The rod is now ready for shaping into an extractor. The shaping should be done with a file, preferably a triangular-type with one blank face (Brownells has these, as sight-dovetail files). The initial cuts should be at the beak (arrow A) and at the front face of the short arm (arrow B). The distance between these two points is critical, so work slowly, with frequent fitting checks. Keep an empty cartridge case at hand, to try the beak engagement with the rim. As the beak and the retaining lug are being shaped, the underside of the shaft must be slanted, from rear to front, and the front face of the beak must be curved or sloped.

The final cut can now be made, the notch at the upper rear for the spring plunger (arrow C). If the original broken extractor is not available for use as a pattern, the exact depth of this cut will have to be determined by experiment. Its shape will be close to the one shown in the illustration, but both angles may require slight adjustment, depending on the particular gun. When the shaping is complete, and the installed extractor works properly when the action is cycled by hand, it can be removed and heat-treated if necessary. This depends on the steel used, as some types will have sufficient hardness as is.

4. In some guns with this type of extractor system, the extractor beak must have more reach than is possible with the simple L-bend of the rod, or the cartridge used may require a stronger extractor. In that case, make a double bend in the rod, forming it into a shallow U-shape.

5. This will allow the beak to be shaped from the other short arm, with no tapering of the shaft. The underside of the shaft (arrow) is parallel to the outer surface, and with more steel to work with at the front, the beak can be extended as far as necessary. This pattern is somewhat stronger than the one described earlier. The shaping is done as described in step 3, above, with the exception of the taper.

Pivot-Type Extractor Repair

One of the most common extractors is the type that is pivoted on a pin, with a tailpiece extending to the rear and bearing on a coil spring. This type is often used on automatic pistols, but it is also frequently seen on other guns. While extractor breakage usually occurs at the beak, the part contacting the rim of the cartridge, the tailpiece also snaps off with some frequency. When this happens, and the front of the part is undamaged, there is a way to make an effective repair without replacing the entire extractor. When the gun involved is an older one, and parts are entirely unobtainable, this can be a valuable alternative to making the entire part.

1. This side view shows a typical extractor of the type, with the tailpiece intact and the spring in place.

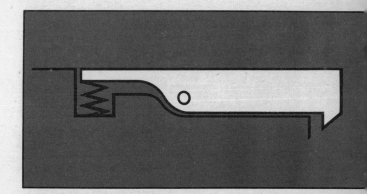

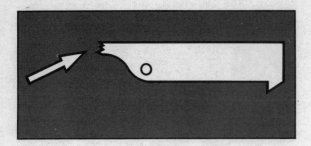

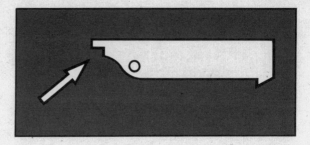

2. The tailpiece will usually break at about the point indicated. As long as there is some extension to the rear beyond the pivot point, the repair is possible.

3. Square off the broken end, and file a shallow step on its underside, as shown.

4. Cut a strip of .043″ to .045″ thick steel, with a width the same as the extractor recess. For this purpose, I have often used the large staples that are often found on large shipping cartons. Illustration 4A shows a side view of the shape into which the strip is formed, the step at the right designed to contact the step that has been filed on the extractor tail. The length of the upper arm and the length of the vertical guide must be adjusted to each installation, of course. If the spring well is too small

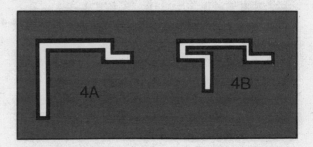

to accommodate the guide arm and a smaller spring, then you can go to the connector shown in illustration 4B, bending the guide arm back to the center, its width reduced to enter the coil spring.

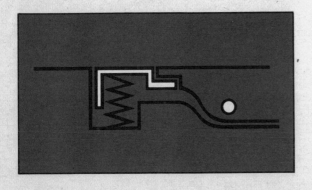

5. Shown here is the 4A-type connector installed. In addition to supplying tension to the extractor, it also fills the gap left by the broken tail. The rear edge of the connector can be rounded to match the rear of the extractor recess, and it can be polished or blued, depending on the bolt or slide in which it is used.

Magazine Repair

As most shooters know, the magazine is the heart of the feed system of any repeating firearm. When the magazine is a detachable box-type, it is susceptible to damage while it is out of the gun. Even a slight deviation in the shape of the feed lips can cause misfeeding, and any dents in the magazine body can interfere with the proper travel of the follower, the platform that lifts the cartridges. The box magazine design is used in rifles, shotguns, submachine guns, and pistols, but the first three are not as likely to sustain damage as the pistol magazine, because they are usually made of somewhat heavier materials. Though the procedures that follow are concentrated on the auto pistol magazine, some of the information can be applied to the others.

When an auto pistol magazine sustains damage, or the gun begins to malfunction for some unknown reason, the amateur will often reach for the magazine and a pair of pliers. This approach has ruined a large number of magazines. Some magazines, such as the early Colt-types, have the upper portion hardened, and these are particularly intolerant of adjustment. When these must be repaired, it's necessary to anneal them first, to prevent breakage. The one tool that should never be used is a pair of pliers.

1. To properly reshape the feed lips of a magazine, a forming tool is needed. The larger one shown here, for 32-caliber magazines, was made from a piece of bar stock. The smaller 25-caliber tool was made from a broken pin punch. Note that the rear tip is slanted to match the back of the magazine, and the recess is to clear the front opening.

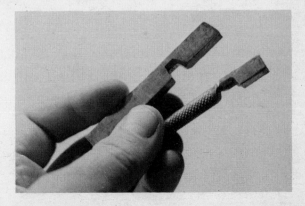

2. To use the forming tool, the tool is inserted into the top of the magazine, and the magazine top is clamped gently but firmly in a padded vise, with the top of the tool aligned with the feed lips. A small hammer is then used to tap the lips into the proper angle.

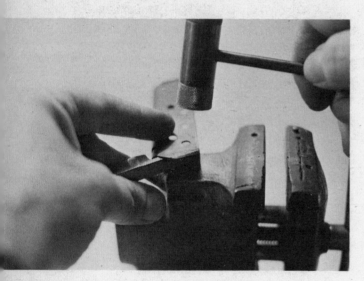

3. The tool, or any piece of bar stock of the proper dimensions, can be inserted into the magazine to level a dent in the side of the magazine body. The tool is positioned on the dent, and the outside of the magazine is struck with a small hammer until the dent is eliminated. During this operation, the body of the magazine is held firmly on a flat surface of steel, such as a vise anvil.

4. When the dent is in the front rounded portion of the magazine, a piece of drill rod of the right diameter is clamped solidly in a vise, and the magazine is then tapped with a hammer at the dent until the shape is restored.

5. A dented or deformed floorplate can be repaired by resting it on a flat steel surface, and using a flat-ended punch to restore its shape. When doing this, always use the largest-diameter punch possible, to avoid creating reverse dents. Always take care that the track-edges of the floorplate are not struck and damaged, as they are difficult to open again to fit the mounting flanges on the magazine body.

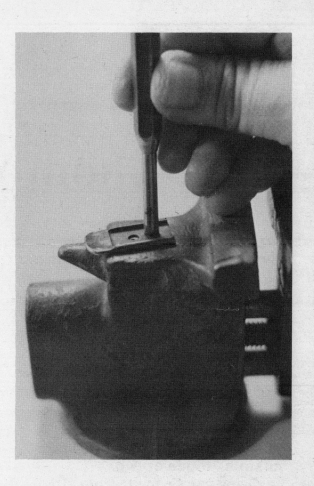

6. In magazines which have a plain, stamped follower, it is sometimes necessary to alter the angle of the top section. For this, clamp the tail of the follower firmly in a vise, and if the angle is to be opened, insert a screwdriver tip beneath the top section and lift it gently. If the adjustment is in the opposite direction, tap the top section with a small hammer, striking at the rear, near the vise jaws. On this type of follower, there is one place where pliers *can* be used—for minor adjustment of the slide stop projection on the left side. For this operation, the *top* section should be gripped in the vise.

Grips

Make Them Yourself

With all of the regular factory replacement grips that are available, and the custom and semi-custom specials that are offered, why would anyone want to make a set of grips? Well, if the gun is long out of production, and the grips have not been commercially reproduced, and the custom makers don't supply it, there's no other choice. Also, as in the two examples shown here, making them yourself allows a "custom" touch or two.

Grips can be made from almost any workable material, of course, but the easiest to use is a good, dense-grained wood. For the guns shown here, the grips for the Savage are of rosewood, and the one-piece unit for the Tokarev is walnut. The initial problem is finding slabs of the preferred wood in thicknesses of $\frac{1}{4}''$ to $\frac{3}{8}''$ (or, for revolvers, a little thicker). If your local lumber company has a millroom, they can reduce the thickness of any larger piece you might obtain. High school wood shops are also usually equipped to plane down thicker pieces of wood if the lumber yard can't do it.

1. The first step is to cut a piece of stiff paper, such as an index card, into the shape of the grip to be made.

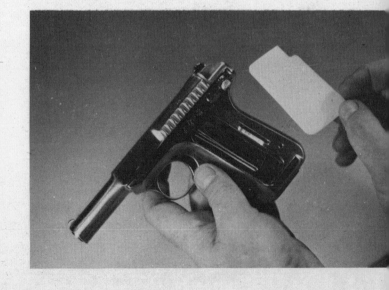

2. On the Savage pistol shown, the original grips were narrower than the template, and flexed to lock into a recess on the frame. It was decided in this case to bring the grip panels all the way to the edge of the backstrap, and secure them with screws.

3. After the card is perfectly shaped and fitted to the grip frame, it is laid on the wood and outlined with a pencil. The panel is then cut out of the wood with a power jigsaw or a coping saw. The next step is to locate the screw hole, by placing the card on the frame and piercing the card at the hole. The location is then transferred to the panel blank, and the hole drilled.

4. The finished grip is shown, in comparison with the pattern card. To make the screw-head recess, use a drill bit the same size as the screw head, and turn it *by hand,* not in a power drill. The recess can be finished this way, but for a professional touch, stop just before the desired depth, and use a flat-faced milling tool in the Dremel to level the bottom of the recess. Proceed carefully, to avoid going through. Usually, one light touch will do it.

5. The finished grips are shown in place on the gun. In the case of this Savage, the upper and lower edges of the panels are beveled, the grip sliding in from the rear. With the screw, this serves to stabilize them against turning. On most other guns, the grips are stabilized by a stepped panel on the inside, or by a protruding pin which enters holes in the back of the panels. If there is no separate pin in the design, one of the existing pins, such as the magazine catch pin, can be extended to serve this purpose.

6. In this example, a one-piece grip was designed for a Tokarev pistol.

7. With the card fitted to the pistol, note the extension at lower rear. This was bridged, between the two panels, by a block of walnut which was secured with epoxy glue. The sides of the insert block were angled slightly, to tilt the panels inward at the front for a tight fit.

8. The rear insert block was then drilled and recessed for a large screw, and the lower rear of the grip frame was drilled and tapped for it. Note that the grain of the wood is *across* the insert block, and vertical on the side panels. This arrangement is stronger, and makes splitting from recoil impact unlikely. With fairly frequent use, this home-made grip has lasted on the gun shown for the past eight years.

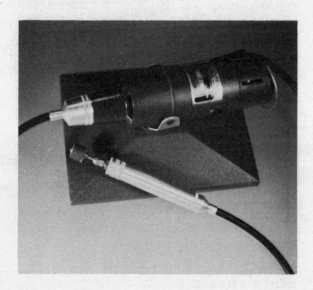

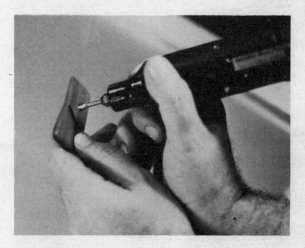

9. When working inside a one-piece grip such as on the Tokarev, a slim cable-driven tool is almost a necessity. The Dremel Model 232 is shown, with a #407 Drum Sander in the handpiece.

10. Levelling the bottom of the screw head recess like this, with an end-cutter in the Dremel Model 380, requires great care, but it can be done with just a touch. It does a very clean job. If you go all the way through, though, it's time to start over.

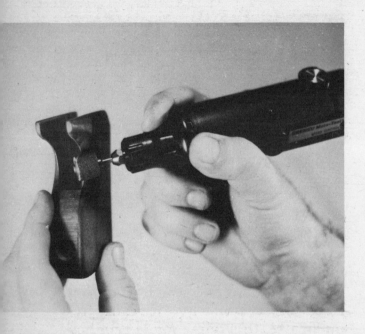

11. A sanding drum and the Dremel can be used for initial shaping, but it works too fast for final sanding. This should be done by hand.

A final word on grip screws: Many guns, especially most revolvers, have the grips retained with a single screw, with a recessed nut on the opposite side, and often with an escutcheon for the screw head. If the original can't be salvaged from broken grips, screw sets are available, complete with escutcheon, from Brownells, and they are very inexpensive.

When making grips that are held by separate screws, take care when cutting the screw head recesses that the inside tip of the screws don't protrude to interfere with the magazine or some other part of the mechanism. If the new grips are thinner, and this penetration is unavoidable, be sure to trim the screw ends to clear.

12. A small "flap wheel" is also good for shaping, but the same advice as with the sanding drum applies. These things can remove a surprising amount of material in a short time, and it's easy to go too far.

Repairing Old Hard Rubber Grips

In earlier times, one of the most preferred materials for handgun grips was hard rubber. This mouldable substance could be cast into exact shapes, and the addition of trademark symbols and "checkering" was easy. Its drawback was a tendency to become brittle with age, a characteristic that is evident on many of the older guns. When the grip panel is broken clear across, cleanly, I have had some repair success with the new cyanoacrylic glues, the ones that will cement your fingers together if you're not careful. More often, though, the hard rubber grip will chip at the edges. One gunsmith of my acquaintance fixed this sort of damage by using a torch to melt pieces of scrap hard rubber grips into the chipped areas. This worked, but there was usually some deformation of the unbroken area in the vicinity of the chip.

My own repair method was an outgrowth of my experiments with epoxy front sight inserts, and the materials are exactly the same. I use Devcon 5-minute epoxy glue, colored with black model airplane enamel, or a mixture of black and brown. When the chip is large enough to extend beyond the frame's inner edge, the gap can be bridged by stretching a sheet of aluminum foil over the grip frame, then installing the grip to hold it in place. In the example shown here, on a Forehand & Wadsworth "British Bulldog" revolver, the chip was small enough that the frame edge could be used to contain the epoxy.

1. A chip of this size, in an edge location, is relatively easy to repair. Except for the imperfect left grip, the gun shown was in excellent collector condition.

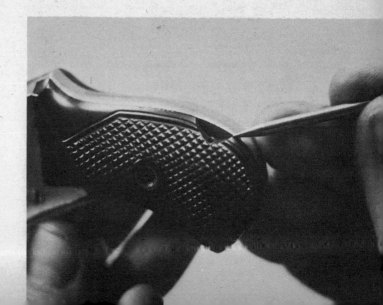

2. As noted earlier, the materials for this repair are much the same as those used in the installation of front sight inserts: Devcon epoxy, Testor's model enamel, and two opened paper clips to mix and transfer the prepared filler.

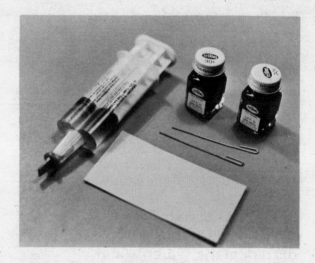

3. Inside the chipped area, two angled holes are drilled, to anchor the epoxy in place. The exact diameter of the drill used is not a critical point, but it should be of larger diameter than the paper clip. The depth of the holes should be about ⅛" or less. Avoid extreme pressure on the drill, keeping in mind that aged hard rubber grips are quite fragile. Also, note that this material will drill very easily—take care not to go too deep.

4. If your vise does not have tilting accommodations, find a way to position the gun so the chipped area is level, so the liquid epoxy will be retained. In the example shown, the gun is held by leather pads in a small vise that has been removed from its swivel-mount, tilted by resting it on a brass bar.

5. Age had "browned" the surface of the grip, so in mixing the epoxy, two parts of brown had been added for every part of black. The epoxy mixture is added a few drops at a time, and the end of the paper clip is pushed into the two previously-drilled holes, to insure that the epoxy enters. The mixture is added until the surface is just a little above the surrounding area.

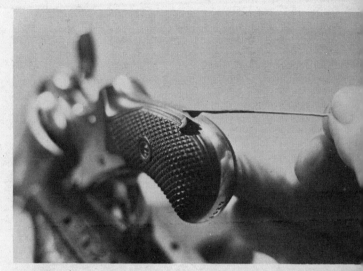

6. Though this epoxy will set up in just 5 minutes, I usually allow it to cure overnight, or for a few hours, at least. A small file is then used to bring the surface down even with the surrounding area. Care must be taken to avoid cutting into the undamaged portion of the grip.

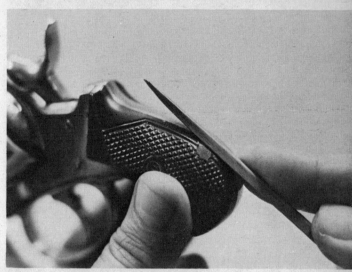

7. A tiny knife file is then used to match the lines at the edge and the checkering, blending the epoxy addition into the pattern of the grip. For this work, a headband binocular magnifier is an advantage, even if your eyes are good. Just cutting the lines is not enough—the side-angles of the grooves must also be matched.

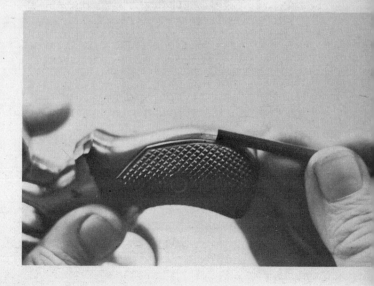

8. A final polish with a soft buffing wheel treated with a fine abrasive will match the original tone of the grip surface.

9. Here is the finished repair. During polishing, a tiny bubble in the epoxy became apparent, near the upper edge of the area. Had this been a customer's gun, a repouring would have been necessary. Since it's my own, well, I'll get around to it someday.

Strikers & Firing Pins

Replacing Indicator Pins___

Several of the true hammerless automatic pistols have striker/firing pin units that have an integral cocking indicator. When the striker is in the cocked position, the combination spring guide and indicator protrudes slightly at the rear. Of the guns that have this system, two that come to mind are the Mauser Model 1910/34 and the Beretta 1919/318 in 25 ACP.

When the guide/indicator breaks off, the separation is usually at the front, deep inside the striker hollow. There is really no feasible way to rejoin the original guide/indicator to the interior of the striker, and parts for most of these guns are difficult to find. If the striker is otherwise undamaged, though, there is a way to replace the guide/indicator.

1. This sectioned view shows an unbroken striker, with the integral guide/indicator intact.

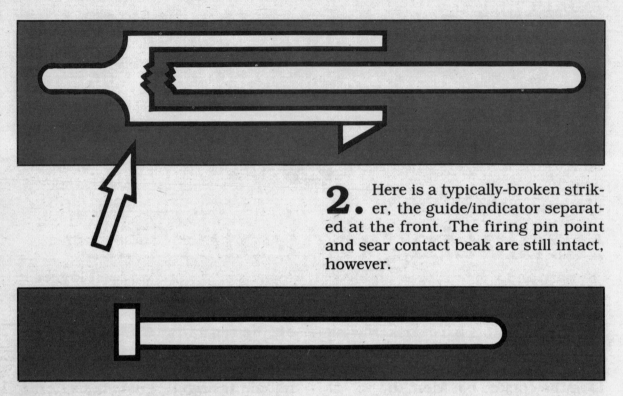

2. Here is a typically-broken striker, the guide/indicator separated at the front. The firing pin point and sear contact beak are still intact, however.

3. A new guide is made, with a collar at its forward end that is a snug fit in the striker hollow. Allowance is made for the size of the collar, keeping the over-all length the same as the original, so the rear protrusion will be the same. The edges of the collar are bevelled very slightly, to ease entry.

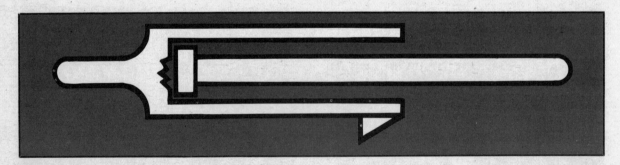

4. The finished replacement is driven gently into place, and the repair is complete. Depending on the space allowed for the original spring, the spring may have to be shortened by two to four coils. This is an important point, as the extra space occupied by the new collar can cancel the spring space allowance in the original design. In that case, if the spring is not shortened, either the spring or its base on the frame can be damaged with the first shot.

Repointing Auto Pistol Strikers

The true hammerless auto pistols usually have hollow strikers that travel in a tunnel in the slide, and the firing pin is integral with the front of the striker. The striker spring extends into the hollow interior of the part, and a detent beak on the underside contacts the sear. When the firing pin point is broken off, and the striker is otherwise undamaged, the point can be easily replaced. When semi-hardened drill rod is used for the new point, and no further heat treatment is done, the replacement will likely last longer than the original point.

1. The firing pin point usually breaks off as shown, leaving a semi-conical front surface on the striker.

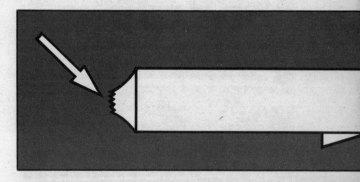

2. The first step in re-pointing is to file the coned area flat, back to the front shoulder of the striker. Some strikers are quite hard, and the front area must then be spot-annealed before it can be filed. (See the Tool Use section for this operation.)

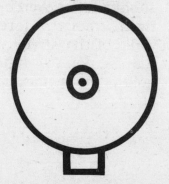

3. After filing the front surface flat, use a centerpunch to indent the exact center of the front face.

4. Check the diameter of the firing pin hole in the breech face, inside the slide, and use a drill of the next smaller diameter to drill a hole in the center of the front face of the striker, all the way through to the inside. To do this with a hand-drill, grip the striker horizontally in a leather-padded vise. This position allows better control, as the hand holding the drill can be rested on the workbench to steady it. If the drilled hole is not absolutely straight, a slight adjustment can be made by a small reduction of the point diameter after installation, and a very slight bending of the point.

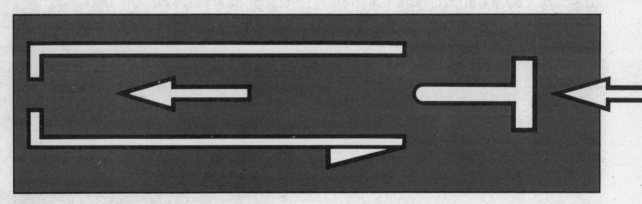

5. From drill rod or any other suitable rod stock, turn a new point with a collar at the rear, the diameter of the collar being a tight fit inside the striker. Use a hand drill gripped in a leather-padded vise as a lathe, as shown in the Tool Use section. An allowance must be made for the thickness of the front wall of the striker, making the point extension of sufficient length for proper protrusion from the breech face. Remember that in some pistols of this type, the firing pin point is also the ejector, and it has to protrude farther than just ignition distance. It is best to leave the point a bit long so you can use the "cut and try" method for determining the proper length. An empty fired case or a dummy round hand cycled through the action will be the only way to find this dimension. Tapering the point and bevelling the edges of the collar will allow the replacement point to be driven into place tightly, but this should not be overdone. If the fit is too tight, the extra force can crack the walls of the striker. Also, take care that the point is aligned with the front hole as the replacement is driven into place.

6. When the point is in place, the striker should be tried in its tunnel in the slide, to check for the centering of the point and its protru- sion from the breech face. At this time, no test-firing or ejection testing should be done, as this could loosen the point.

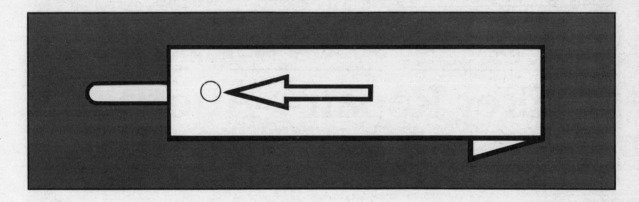

7. Although a properly-fitted re- placement may seem to be quite firm, the repeated impact of shooting will loosen it in time. It is possible to anchor the replacement point in place by staking the sides of the striker body at four equidistant locations, just to the rear of the point collar. These raised dents on the inside will bear on the collar, holding it in place. A better way, though, is to cross-drill the striker just behind the collar, and install a small cross-pin to hold it in place. The cross-pin holes on each side of the striker should be cham- fered (bevelled), and the pin should be of non-hardened stock. A small nail, turned to size, is ideal. The ends of the pin should be peened or riveted into the chamfered areas, and then contoured to match the curve of the striker exterior.

This is begun by filing the peened ends of the cross-pin, then the striker can be gripped in a drill and rotated while a file and emery cloth complete the contouring. Be sure that the cross-pin ends are not protruding from the outside of the striker, as even the smallest amount can inter- fere with its free movement in the slide. While the striker is turning in the drill, check the point for any deviation from center, and carefully bend it until it is straight. This can be done by lightly tapping at sides of the point with a small hammer. Be sure the new point has enough clearance in the breech face hole to prevent binding. If it is not moving freely through the hole, it can be slightly reduced in diameter at this time. Make the tip of the point a round shape, not a sharp cone, or it may pierce primers.

Installation of the new point will have reduced the total space inside the striker, so the striker spring and its guide must be altered to compensate for this. If this is not done, the first shot will damage or break off the striker spring base on the frame. Insert the spring guide in the striker, and be sure its entire length will be accommodated. If not, shorten it accordingly by removing a small section from its forward tip. Be sure to round the edges after this is done. Put the spring and guide in the slide tunnel, use a tool to compress the spring, and note whether any coils of the spring are still outside the striker body when the spring is fully compressed. Remove exactly that number of coils from the spring, and reverse the spring, putting the cut end inside the striker. This completes the re-pointing operation.

Striker Repair—Another Way

This striker, from an Ortgies 7.65mm pistol, was not re-pointed in my shop, but the method used is interesting and worth mentioning here. Apparently, when the firing pin point fractured, the front face of the striker body was also broken. The front of the striker was cut off, and a plug made which had a main section the same diameter as the body of the striker. The rear portion of the plug was rebated to fit inside the striker, and the unit was cross-pinned in place. The only problem with this method is that it drastically reduces the space inside the striker, and a shorter and more powerful spring must then be used. I must note, though, that it was found in a gun which was working perfectly.

Solid Firing Pin Points_____

A broken solid firing pin is generally easier to re-point than a hollow striker, as a simple straight piece of drill rod or rod stock can be used, without the necessity of turning a collar to fit inside dimensions. It should be noted, though, that with some firing pins, those having very slim forward sections, re-pointing is not possible. In those cases, an entire new firing pin will have to be made.

1. Most firing pin points have a concave-cone shape, and breakage of the tip will usually occur in the manner shown.

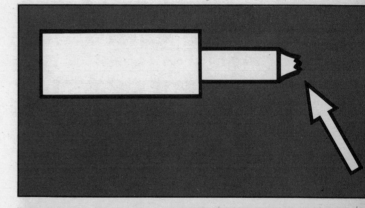

2. The first step is to cut off the tip back to the shoulder, leaving a flat front face. The exact center of the face is then marked with a punch.

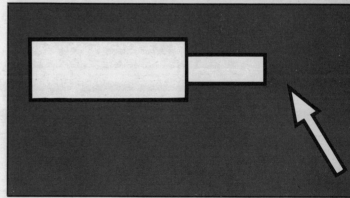

3. Using a drill of a diameter that will pass through the firing pin hole in the breech face of the gun, drill a hole in the center of the forward section of the firing pin, to a depth of about half its length. The smaller forward section will tend to heat up quickly, so proceed slowly, and apply cutting oil frequently. Otherwise, you'll ruin a good drill bit.

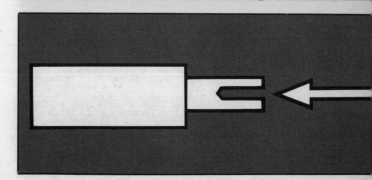

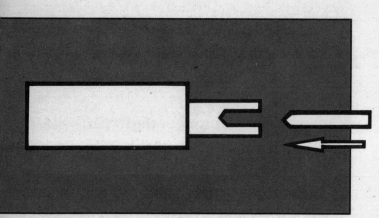

4. Turn a piece of drill rod for a snug fit in the hole, giving it a slight taper, and coning the end to match the bottom of the drilled hole. Be sure to allow enough length for proper protrusion from the breech face, and for shaping of the end, as some length will be lost in that operation. Mark the side of the new point equal to the depth of the hole, so you'll know when it is fully in place, and drive it in.

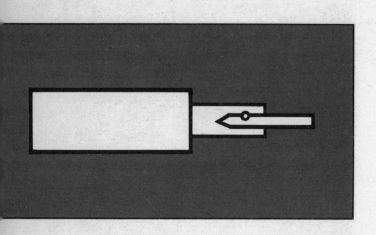

5. Punch a mark on the side of the forward section of the firing pin at a point that will give a cross-pin a half-bite in the installed piece of rod, and drill a small hole through the forward section and across the rod. Start the drilling straight into the side of the forward section, then adjust the angle to cross the rod, taking care that it is not drilled directly and separated. Chamfer both ends of the drilled hole, and install a small crosspin, peening the ends of the cross-pin into the chamfered areas.

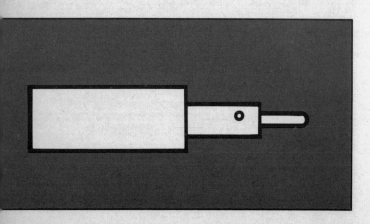

6. File the riveted ends of the cross-pin to match the contour of the forward section, then insert the entire firing pin in a drill chuck and turn and polish the forward section. Trim the end of the rod and round the point, and the job is complete.

Hammer-Type Firing Pin Repair

Many older revolvers have firing pins that are integral with the hammer, and when one of these breaks, the amateur will usually try to build up the broken-off portion with weld, then recut the point to shape. This method rarely holds, and the welding process will soften the rest of the hammer. There's a better way, and if it's done carefully, it won't drastically change the original appearance of the hammer.

1. The Smith & Wesson Model 1880 top-break revolver, in 32 and 38 caliber, is typical of guns having this type of hammer and firing pin. The one shown here is unbroken.

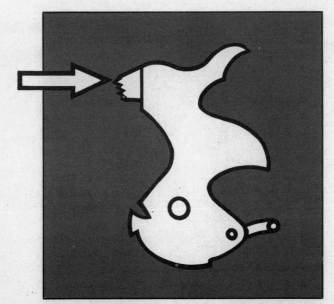

2. Typical breakage is as shown, near the tip of the flat triangular firing pin.

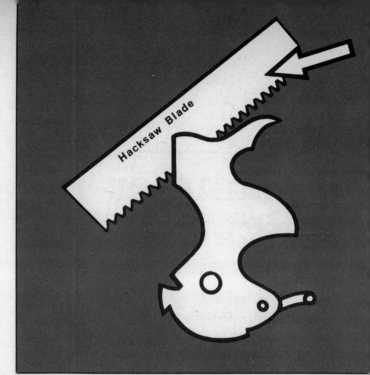

3. The first step in repair is to cut or grind off the broken firing pin point, even with the front face of the hammer. This is most easily done with a cutting disc and the Dremel tool, but a sharp hacksaw will usually do it as well. These hammers are surface-hardened only, and once the "skin" is broken, the cutting will proceed easily.

5. The saw will usually leave the bottom of the slot slightly rounded, and the slot will not be quite as wide as the original firing pin point. A small file is used to bring the slot to the proper width, and to square its bottom edges. A small rectangle of good steel is then fitted into the slot, being sure that its lower edge is solidly against the bottom of the slot. A small hole is then cross-drilled through both the hammer and the inserted plate, and the outer edges of the hole chamfered on both sides. A cross-pin is installed, and its ends peened (riveted) into the chamfered areas. The ends of the pin are then filed down even with the sides of the hammer.

4. When the point is removed, its remaining outline on the hammer face will serve as a guide for the centering of a vertical slot. Start the cut, at the top front of the hammer, with a file or cutting disc, then use a sharp hacksaw, as shown, to make a vertical slot about as deep as the one in the drawing. Take care that the blade does not touch and mar the checkering on the hammer spur. A piece of heavy tape wrapped around the spur will help to guard against this.

6. When shaping the plate into a firing pin point, do the top first, and leave some extra material at the front to leave room for reach adjustment. When doing the final fitting, insert the hammer in the gun often, and use particular care when shaping the lower edge of the firing pin. Be sure the point protrudes from the breech face enough for reliable ignition, but not so much that primers are pierced. When the shaping and fitting are complete, I usually do a quick heat-coloring of the upper portion of the hammer. This will also have a slight surface-hardening effect, and will not affect the hardness of the lower portion.

Nambu Striker Fix

1. The problem here is the striker from a Japanese Type 14 Nambu pistol, with a broken point. An original unbroken striker is shown for comparison.

2. After the base of the broken tip is levelled, a center-punch is used to indent the center of the front face of the striker. The repointing then proceeds as outlined in the drawings in this section.

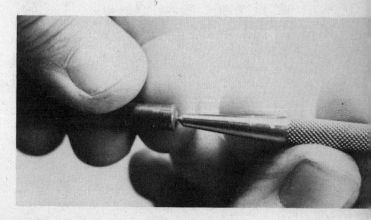

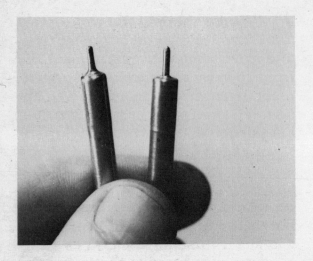

3. After installation, the new point is cut to the proper length and its tip is shaped. The striker on the right has the replaced point.

Marlin Model 17 Firing Pin

1. The Marlin Model 17 shotgun, obsolete since about 1908, has a long firing pin that is mechanically involved with the bolt locking system. Its large rear section has various planes and recesses that must be precisely fitted to the locking block inside the bolt, and this makes producing an entire replacement firing pin quite difficult. Original parts are, of course,

practically impossible to find. Repointing, though, is easily done.

2. The Marlin Model 17 firing pin is shown, with the tip broken in the usual manner. The first step in repointing is to file the broken tip back level with the shoulder of the forward section.

3. As shown in the drawings earlier in this section, the front of the firing pin is drilled and a new tip inserted and cross-pinned in place. It is then cut to length and shaped. The replacement will probably last longer than the original tip.

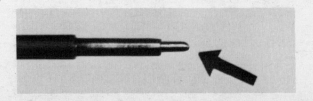

Making a New Striker Spring Guide

One of the most frequently-lost parts in striker-fired auto pistols is the small guide at the rear of the striker spring. This often occurs during amateur disassembly, when the little guide is flicked out by the compressed striker spring, never to be seen again. It should be noted in passing that during takedown of a striker-fired pistol, the striker should always be in the fired position.

When the gun with a missing striker spring guide is an out-of-production piece, and replacement parts are difficult to find, making a replacement is not difficult. You can, of course, start with a section of drill rod of the same diameter as the head or flange of the guide, and reduce the shaft to fit inside the spring, but this is the hard way.

Before I outline the easy way, one important point: Be sure to measure the interior length of the striker to determine the proper length for the guide. In most pistols, the spring is completely compressed when the gun is cocked, and the guide must fully enter the striker. If the guide is too long, the first shot will damage the spring base on the frame, the guide, or both.

Since the guide is normally under no great stress, the replacement can be conveniently made from an ordinary nail. A nail has the advantage of already having a "flange" at its end, and this saves a lot of work. Select a nail that has a shaft somewhat larger than the required size of the guide shaft, as it will be necessary to reduce it enough to eliminate the wood-anchoring serrations found on most nails.

1. If necessary to shorten it, remove a section at the point of the nail, and grip it in the chuck of your drill/lathe. Use a medium file to reduce the head until it will enter the striker freely, and then remove enough material from the shaft until it will enter the spring. After making the initial cut on the head, check it for roundness and concentricity with the shaft, and make adjustments where necessary, with the drill stopped. Few nails have heads that are round and concentric. Check several nails and pick the one that comes closest to being "true."

2. As the guide nears its proper shape, use the striker to check the head flange, and an outside caliper to check the diameter of the shaft. Remember that the shaft must enter the striker spring and move freely, with no binding. A tight fit is *not* what you want.

3. Use the Dremel tool and a cutting disc to mark the shaft at the cut-off point, then make the cut with a triangular file, bevelling the tip of the shaft as the finished guide is removed. After it is cut off, slightly flatten the point of the shaft with a file. Before the guide is cut off, I usually polish it with emery cloth, as this is easily done while it's turning.

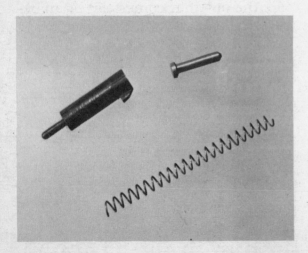

4. Double check the finished guide for length, and for free movement inside the spring and the striker. It is now ready for assembly.

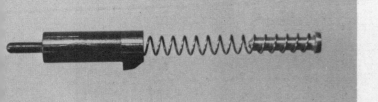

5. The guide is shown installed in its proper position at the rear of the striker spring. Without this little guide, the spring would soon be deformed, and the gun would begin to misfire.

Broken Striker Spring Base

A familiar feature of many true hammerless striker-fired auto pistols is the "doll's head" protrusion at the upper rear of the frame that forms the base for the striker spring and its guide. This usually consists of a cylindrical top piece on a rectangular neck, with the front face of the top recessed to accept the striker spring guide. In some guns, the center of the top piece is drilled through for passage of a cocking indicator. The striker spring base is sometimes removable, a part of the takedown system. We are concerned here, though, with those that are integral with the frame, and not routinely removable.

The base has to sustain only the tension of the striker spring, and in normal operation breakage is not common. Nearly all of the breakage I've seen was the result of amateur installation of a replacement striker, spring, or guide of non-standard size. When any of these parts are too long, the first shot after installation will cause the base to be badly bent or broken off. With the slide at the full rear position, there is a certain minimum of space in the striker tunnel, and any replacement parts for that area must be kept to exact dimensions.

1. The base can break anywhere in the neck area. The one shown in the drawing is fairly typical. When the broken-off extension is found and saved, it can be rejoined to the frame with silver solder or by welding. In most cases, the base is lost as breakage usually occurs when the gun is fired, and the striker spring will send the broken piece quite a distance.

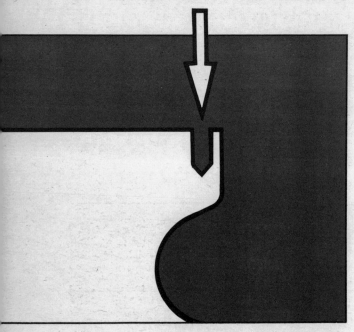

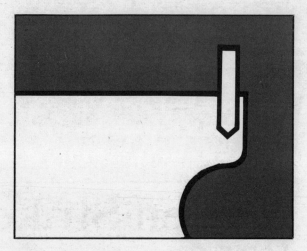

2. When the broken portion is missing, file off the remaining rough edge of the neck, even with the top of the frame. With a drill that is about two-thirds the diameter of the lengthwise measurement of the neck, drill a hole vertically into the frame, as shown. Most pistols will have enough solid steel in that area to support this.

3. Turn a piece of drill rod to be a tight fit in the hole, taper the end slightly, and drive it into place. Be sure that it has enough length to extend to the top of the striker tunnel in the slide. The diameter of the pin may or may not be larger than the original neck of the base. If so, its sides can be cut later on to move freely in the track-slot in the underside of the slide.

4. Turn a short piece of drill rod to a diameter that will allow it to move freely in the striker tunnel, and cross-drill it for a snug fit on the top of the vertical pin mounted in the frame. After this is tapped onto the pin, and the sides of the pin are cut to match the width of the slot in the slide, the rear of the base head is contoured to match the rear of the slide. If there is room in the length of the tunnel for the extra front protrusion of the base head, the guide recess can be cut, and the base used as is. There will be a gap at the rear, between the head and the frame, but if the function is more important than the appearance, it will work.

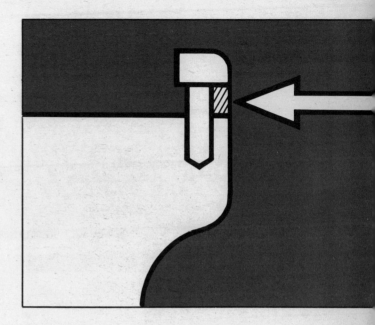

5. To do a really complete job, if you have access to a welding outfit, steel can be added in the area indicated by the shaded portion and then be cut to match the slot and the rear of the slide. This also serves to permanently anchor the new base to the frame, and adds strength.

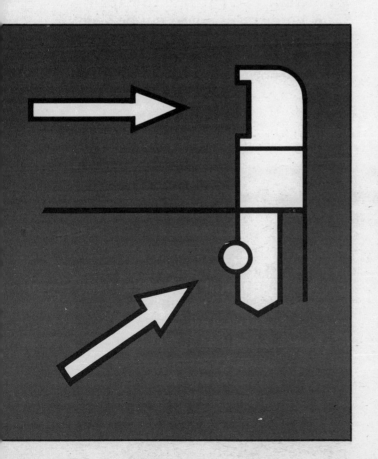

6. Another way to retain the base on the frame is to cross-drill for a pin to bite into the vertical post of the base. Actually, a properly-fitted base will need no extra retention measures, as the slide will keep it in place when the gun is assembled. The lower arrow indicates the cross-pin. The final step in fitting the new base is to cut off the forward projection of the head, and cut the recess (upper arrow) for the spring guide. I usually do this with a small grindstone in the Dremel tool. The recess doesn't have to be very deep, just enough to center the head of the spring guide.

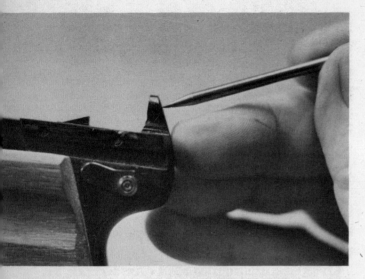

7. Here is a finished striker spring base, done by the method described above, on a Stenda auto pistol. Since this gun has a pronounced slope at the rear of the slide, the base is slimmer than the one shown in the drawings.

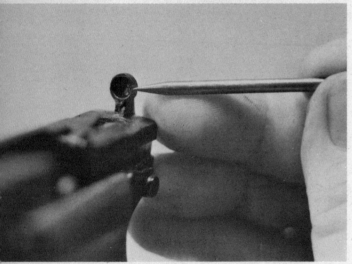

8. As noted earlier, the spring guide recess need not be deep. Its function is to keep the head of the guide at the center, to prevent kinking of the spring.

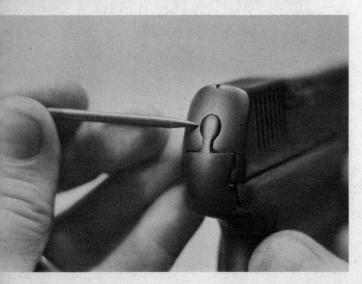

9. At the rear of the slide, the base is contoured to match the shape of the surrounding area. When the gun is refinished, as this one has been, it's difficult to tell that the base is a replacement.

Broken Striker Spring Base—Another Way

The best way of replacing a broken-off striker spring base is described in the preceding tip. There are some guns, though, in which the upper rear of the frame does not have a sufficient amount of solid steel to allow the usual method to work. If that is the case, it may be possible to do the repair as described here. It should be noted that space limitations in some guns make this way impossible, and this will have to be determined on an individual basis. Check the movement of parts before you begin, to see if this arrangement will work. Also, keep in mind that this particular repair requires cross-drilling the slide at the rear, and if the gun is a collector piece, this will reduce its value.

1. The first step is to select a piece of drill rod that is slightly larger than the diameter of the striker tunnel in the slide, and cut a piece about 1″ long.

2. With a drill and file, about ½″ of the rod section is reduced in diameter to be a snug fit in the striker tunnel.

3. A point is marked on the slide which will allow cross-drilling to pass through the center of the spring base plug.

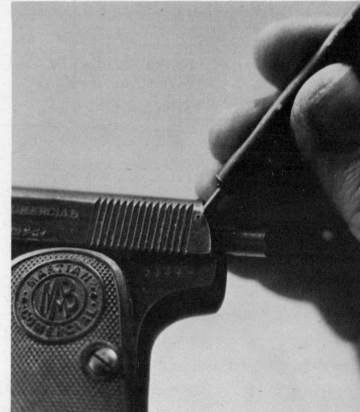

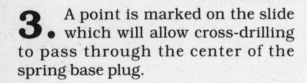

4. When drilling the cross-hole, take care that the drill goes straight across. If you have access to a drill press, this will be no problem, as the slide flat will keep it straight.

5. A slightly tapered cross-pin is made, to be a snug fit in the hole.

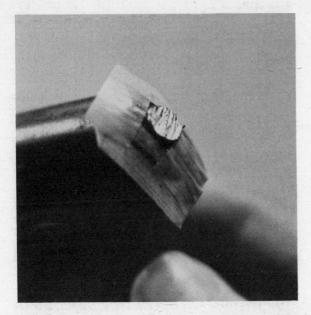

6. Nylon-filament tape applied to the rear of the slide will protect the surface while the plug is sawed off at an angle that matches the rear slope of the slide.

7. The rear end of the plug is then shaped with a file to conform to the rear of the slide. Avoid filing it flat. Keep the rounded contour. Note that there is still a small gap below the plug, originally filled by the stem of the spring base.

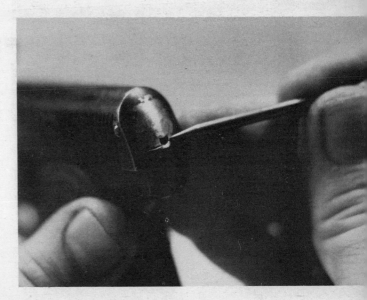

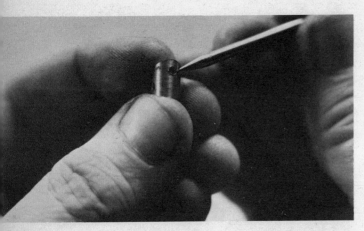

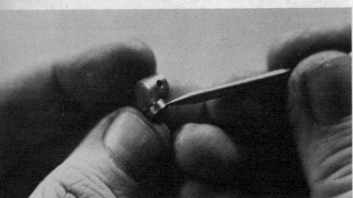

8. With the plug still in place in the slide, it is marked on the underside near the rear edge for drilling of a vertical hole about ⅛″ deep. Be sure that the mark is far enough from the rear edge that a hole of this depth will not go through the rear outer slope.

9. A piece of the remaining drill rod is turned to make a short tip that will fit the hole in the underside of the plug. This can be tapered and driven into place, but a better method is to tap the hole and thread the tip, screwing the spacer into place. Be sure to chamfer the hole, so the spacer piece can be snugged tightly against the plug. The sides of the spacer are then cut away, and its rear edge filed to match the rear curve of the plug and slide.

10. The completed striker spring base and the rear of the slide can be cold-blued, if the entire gun is not to be refinished. Also, the inside face of the new base can be recessed for the head of the spring guide. It may be necessary to adjust the length of the spring by a coil or two. If the striker point, the firing pin, also serves as the ejector, ejection may be slow, and it may be necessary to install a slightly heavier striker spring, or drill the frame top just behind the magazine well and install an angled pin to be a separate ejector. In most cases, I've found that this is not needed. On the gun shown, the system worked perfectly. Let me stress again, though, that this particular method will not work in all cases.

Cleaning & Lubrication

Time-Tested Tips

Since self-loaders of all types have long been my special field of interest, I've observed what may be one of the "Great Truths of Gundom:" At least 75 percent of malfunctions are caused by dirt in the action. This is not restricted to semi-autos, though—it will also hold true for any type of repeating action, and this includes revolvers. All guns have some allowance for build-up of powder residue, wax, unburned powder grains, and so on, but there is a limit. I am sometimes amazed at the condition of guns brought in for "repair" which prove to be simply clogged by dirt. In one memorable case, a gun was brought in by a gentleman who used it for hunting, trap, and Skeet. He was puzzled when I told him it needed only a thorough cleaning. "Can't understand it," he said, "gave it a good cleanin' a couple of years back . . ."

Aside from the possibility of dirt in the action causing malfunctions, there is another factor to consider. Any porous substance that is next to the internal parts can absorb moisture from the air, and cause oxidation (a fancy word for rust) at the point of contact. This is what has given many a bright bore those tiny dark spots that are so difficult to remove. If the prevailing climate is moist, the problem is intensified. I live in the western Ohio River Valley, and I clean my guns each time they are fired.

Some of my cleaning methods are of the time-tested type, and some may be unique. We'll go through a few guns of different types here, and add a few words on lubrication at the end.

1. It wasn't too many years ago that the only gas-operated guns familiar to us were the U.S. Garand and Carbine. Now, we have shotguns, sporting rifles, and even a few auto-

matic pistols. One of the finest of the latter is the Heckler & Koch P7, known earlier as the PSP. Its gas cylinder, located below the barrel in the frame, is easily cleaned with a cylindrical bronze brush. A 32 caliber fits it nicely. The finned gas piston, attached to the slide, tends to accumulate gas scale between its rearmost flanges, and this is easily taken off with one of the little stainless-steel brushes available from Brownells, as shown. I use these brushes constantly, catalog number 4D00PKL, and at the time this is written they sell for only $2.20 each.

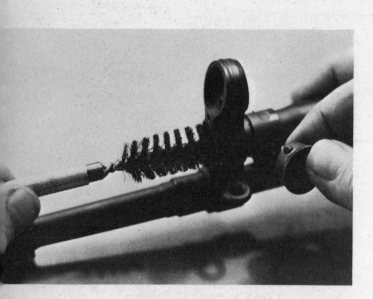

2. Where gas scale is concerned, I *never* use a cleaning solution—all brushing is done dry. The reason for this is the difficulty in removing the solution after the cleaning is done, and no liquid of any kind should *ever* be left in a gas system. In areas where the handled brush can't reach, a cylindrical bronze brush will do the job, as on the gas tube of this Heckler & Koch HK91 A-2. Be sure that a *bronze* brush is used—the nylon and fiber types are totally useless for this.

3. While gas scale is usually thought of in relation to gas-operated systems, there is some deposit that is at least similar around the chamber area in other guns. On stainless steel guns, regular steel wool will tend to "transfer" to some extent, darkening the stainless. Brownells has some special stainless steel wool which works well for this, and leaves no discoloration. The stainless steel brush can also be used here.

4. There are too many excellent cleaning solutions and solvents to fit into one photo, so here are just a few. For removing excess oil, a degreaser (such as the short can shown) is necessary. I often use a Birchwood-Casey product called "Gun Scrubber" for this purpose.

5. Most of my initial cleaning, though, is done with a dry bronze or stainless steel brush. In the chambers of a revolver cylinder, use both a straight push-through and a turning motion.

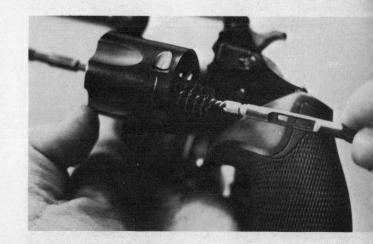

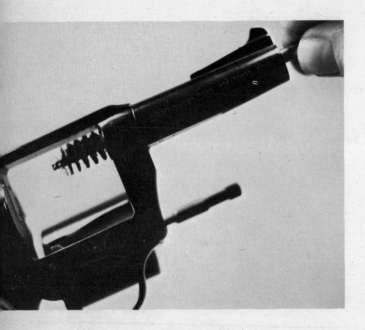

6. The usual recommendation is that bores be cleaned from chamber to muzzle, but this isn't always possible, especially with a revolver. One rule that I do follow, whenever it's feasible, is to use a brush that is one size larger than the caliber of the gun. Many of the "proper size" brushes barely touch the bore.

7. No matter how close the cylinder/barrel gap, there is always quite a bit of residue deposited in that area. The little stainless-steel brush from Brownells is perfect for removal of this from around the inner top strap and the adjoining places.

8. Though the breech face will not get as much residue as the cylinder face, it should always be included in the cleaning operation. This area is easy to get at so there's really no excuse for not doing it.

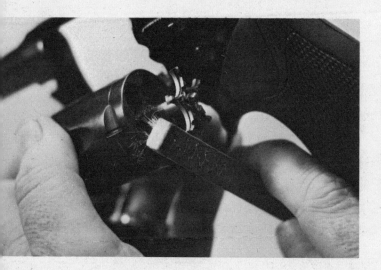

9. Unburned powder grains and other residue can build up under the ejector and in its recess, and if this is severe, it can even impede cylinder rotation. Some powders are more likely to cause this condition than others, but keeping this area cleaned is always a good idea.

10. When cleaning the barrel in automatics, remember to brush the chamber entry ramp. If cast-bullet handloads are being used, this is particularly important because lead residue can build up to the point where the gun won't feed reliably.

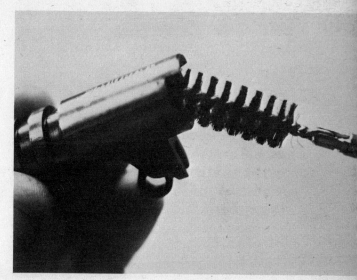

11. The ramp area on the frame is another site for lead and powder deposits, and the surrounding area should also be brushed or wiped clean. Anything you can do to smooth-up this area will help the feeding process.

12. The breech face in the slide should be brushed during each cleaning, and attention should be given to the inside of the extractor beak. In guns such as the GM, with the extractor easily removable, this should be done regularly.

13. Some residue will eventually accumulate in the grooves on the underside of the breech block section of the slide. I routinely brush this area during each cleaning. It's an easy and quick process.

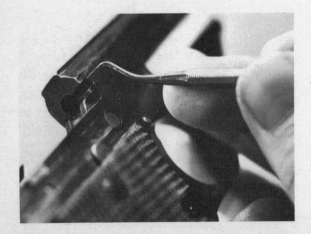

14. The extractor recess at the chamber edge should be scraped out occasionally. A dental tool is shown, but this can also be done with a small screwdriver.

15. In 22-caliber automatics, some slight shaving of lead at the edge of the chamber is inevitable. This should be removed with each cleaning.

16. Just as with the cartridge guns, I usually use the next larger bore brush in shotguns, especially for chamber cleaning. With some tight Full-choke barrels, it's not always possible to use the larger size for the bore. Several of the cleaning solutions, such as the G96 Nitro Solvent shown in #4 above, are formulated to remove the acid residue from plastic shotshells. If not removed, this can cause surface rust in the chamber, and retard extraction.

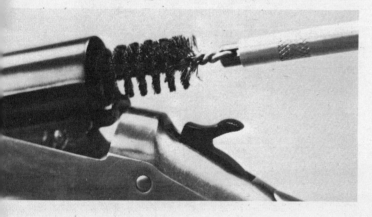

17. For application of cleaning solvents to the bore of a shotgun, these swabs are even better than regular patches. The one shown was made by Gunslick, but several brands are available.

18. Any gun chambered for 22 rimfire cartridges is especially susceptible to an accumulation of residue. During routine cleaning, in addition to brushing out the inside of the receiver, be sure to clean the face of the bolt.

19. Dirt and residue can build up under the extractor beak, sometimes to a point that it can interfere with its operation. In the absence of a dental tool, as shown, a small screwdriver will do the job.

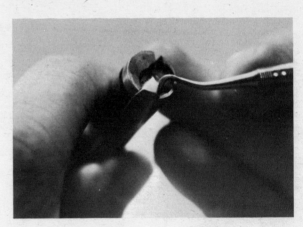

20 The ejector groove in a 22 bolt will often pick up a lot of residue. Again, a dental tool or screwdriver is used to scrape it out. Unless the groove is quite shallow, a brush will usually be ineffective on this stuff.

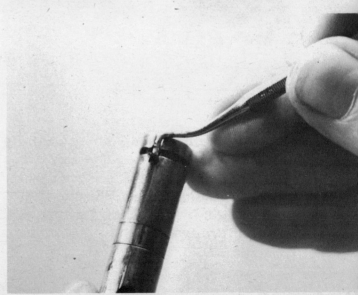

21. When the extractor is removable without much difficulty, more effective cleaning is possible. The area inside the beak should get particular attention.

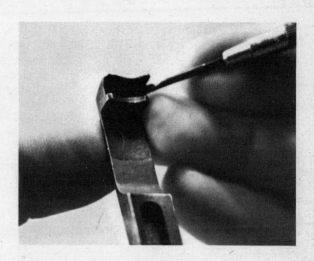

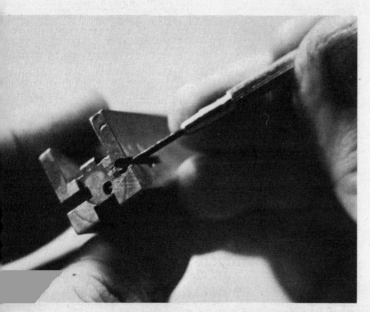

22. With the extractor removed from this 22-caliber semi-auto rifle breech block, a surprising amount of "gunk" can be removed from the extractor recess. In all cleaning, keep in mind that any groove, recess, or tunnel probably will have some deposits.

23 Too much oil in a gun can do more harm than no oil at all. Just a drop or two on the site of mating surfaces will do the job perfectly. There are a large number of good lubricants, and just a few are shown here. The new "space age" types such as Break-Free and Dry Slide are excellent, too.

24. Several special lubricants have been developed especially for use in stainless steel guns, and one of the best of these is "CS Lubricant." I even use it in guns made of regular steel, particularly in the areas of engagement in double action trigger systems.

Rust Removal

Just as rust can range from a light sprinkling on the surface of a gun to the heavy incrustation found on "dug-up" battlefield trophies, the methods of removal are very different. This depends on not only the extent and depth of the rust, but also on the status of the gun. If it's just a gun for practical use, a "shooter," then any means that does not damage the surface of the steel is acceptable. If the gun has potential collector value, though, rust removal becomes an exacting operation that must be done with extreme care.

Every gunsmith and collector can recall horror stories of both rust removal and refinishing, the latter being the logical next step. I

remember one instance in which an owner decided to "save part of the cost" of refinishing by "knocking off the rust" himself. Using a bench-mounted rotary wire brush, he had totally removed 100 years of even brown patina from the steel parts of an otherwise perfect Harper's Ferry musket. Wait for the bottom line: He wanted it nickel plated!

In cases such as that, the proper treatment of the surface is to simply rub it with a cloth containing a good preservative lubricant, such as RIG. This will stabilize the patina, keeping it from growing a fur of surface rust, and will preserve the nice "antique color." If an originally blued piece has one very bad spot of deep rust, and if the gun has sufficient collector value, a complete restoration might be considered. This is done by only a few specialists and it is expensive, but it will bring the gun back to its original factory condition. Certain parts will be blued, color-casehardened, "strawed," or polished, as when the gun was new, and really bad rust pits will be filled.

1. This British Webley 25 ACP automatic was almost "as new," except for a few small areas of light surface rust on top of the slide and along the upper right edge. Very fine (0000) steel wool was used to *gently* rub the affected areas. There are two schools of thought on this, using the wool dry, or with oil. Generally, I prefer the dry method, because the oil sometimes interferes with checking the progress of the operation.

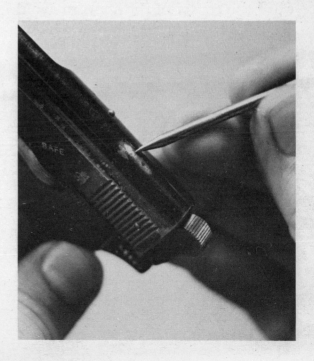

2. Here is the little Webley after the steel wool treatment. As you can see, the spots are visible, but the surface rust has been entirely removed. If this were an ordinary blue finish, it could be touched up with cold chemical blue. Since there is no way this deep English-type blue could be matched, in this case the spots will be left bare and kept oiled.

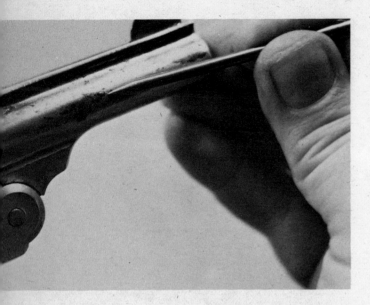

3. When a gun is to be re-nickeled, the original plating is "stripped" by a method that is an electronic reversal of the application process. When refinishing is not intended, and there are just a few small areas of peeling and surface rust, it's possible to improve the appearance by just treating the individual spots. A peeled, rusted area is shown here, before anything was done.

4. Steel wool can be tried, but for really stubborn areas a fine rotary brush in the Dremel tool may be necessary. Under no circumstances, though, should a heavy rotary wire brush be used. At the edges of the peeled area, the brush should be applied so its direction of rotation is toward the center of the spot, to avoid further peeling of the plating.

5. After all traces of rust have been removed, very fine emery cloth or paper is used to blend the bare steel surface into the existing plate.

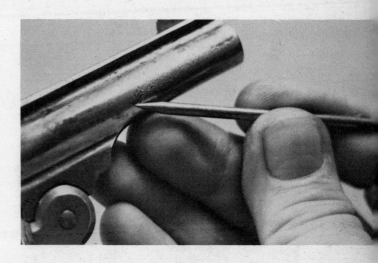

6. A difference in color will be discernible between the plating and the steel, but the appearance will be greatly improved.

7. When the rust is far more than just a light sprinkling on the surface, and complete refinishing is intended, a chemical rust remover can be considered. There are several on the market that will do a good job. The one I use is shown—OR-1 by TDP, Inc., P.O. Box 277, Zieglerville, PA 19492.

8. There are many ways of applying rust removers. I have used small containers for soaking individual parts, a glass medicine dropper, or cotton swab, as shown. It should be noted that most of these solutions contain acid in some proportion, so extreme caution in handling is advised. In cases of very heavy rust, more than one application may be necessary.

9. Depending on the solution used, the item being cleaned will have to be left to soak for some time, usually specified in the directions on the container. When the bare metal is visible (it will have a grayish color from the chemical action), the job is done. On the gun shown, just a spot was cleaned, to show the contrast with the uncleaned portion.

Using the Lewis Lead Remover

Anyone who reloads with cast bullets knows that if a fair amount of shooting is done, there will be some leading of the bore, no matter how hard the alloy used. In revolvers, there will also be some deposits in the cylinder and the forcing cone of the barrel. Generally speaking, the more powerful the load, the more likely there will be an accumulation of lead, and removing it is a problem. Long scrubbing with a bronze brush will take out light deposits, but a really heavy accumulation will just be polished by the brush. The best and easiest way to get the lead out is to use a

device that has been around for quite some time, the Lewis Lead Remover.

1. The Lewis tool is a simple device, consisting of a rod with a T-handle and two different end-pieces—a solid cone-shaped one for the forcing cone in revolver barrels, and a compressible rubber piece for cylinders and auto pistol barrels. Three different sizes are available, for 38, 41, and 44 or 45 calibers. The

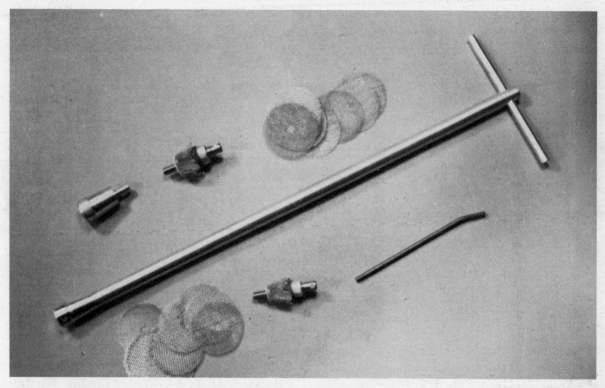

"brass cloth" patches come in corresponding sizes. A basic set in one caliber costs about $10, and the tool is available from L.E.M. Gun Specialties, Inc., P.O. Box 31, College Park, GA 30337.

2. To clear lead from the forcing cone of a revolver barrel, the first step is to fit a screen patch onto the threaded shank of the solid conical tip. Depending on the size of the hole in the patch, it can be pushed through or turned into place on the threads.

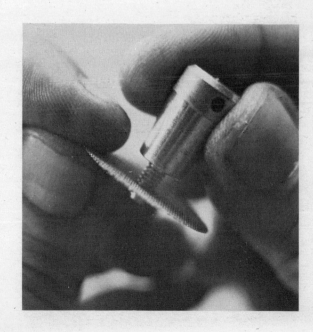

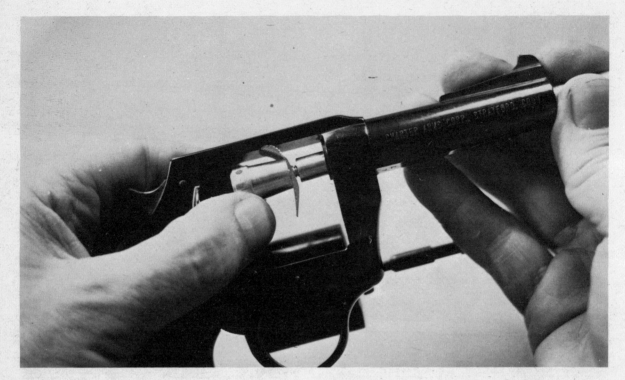

3. With the rod and handle inserted through the barrel (the cylinder swung out, of course), the conical tip and its brass cloth patch are installed on the end of the rod.

4. With the gun held firmly, either in the hand or in a padded vise, the conical tip and its patch are pulled up tight into the cone of the barrel, and turned clockwise (front view). If the cone is badly leaded, it may be necessary to back out the tool and flick the flakes of lead from the patch, then repeat the turning.

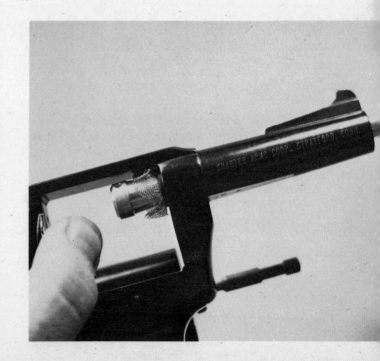

5. For leading in the barrel itself, the adjustable rubber tip is used. Before this assembly is pulled through the bore, it's important to be sure the knurled nut is backed off slightly, about a half-turn, away from the rubber. This allows space for the rubber to expand lengthwise as it is compressed by the bore. As the tool is pulled through the barrel, it must be allowed to turn, following the twist of the rifling.

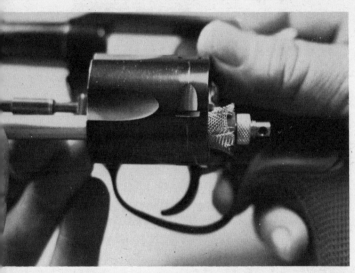

6. The rubber tip is also used to clear lead from the cylinder. When the brass patch engages the step in the chamber, the tool is turned clockwise, while even pressure toward the front is maintained. According to the instructions furnished with the tool, it may be necessary to snug the rubber tip against the handle to prevent stripping of the patch. However, I've never had this problem.

7. Both the cone tip and the rubber tip are cross-drilled to allow the use of the pin-wrench supplied, if necessary.

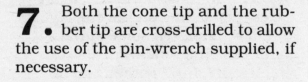

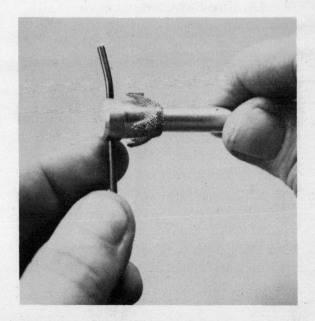

Repair Tips

Bluing Touch-Ups and Heat Bluing

Nothing, absolutely nothing, can match the depth and luster of heat-bath bluing on steel. The same can be said for its older equivalents, the slow-rust process, and the English "charcoal" blue. These latter two are used today only by restoration specialists. There are times, though, when none of the above makes any sense, as when a small worn area needs to be touched-up, or when very small parts are to be colored on a gun that otherwise doesn't need refinishing.

Double-barreled shotguns (and this includes the over-unders) are a special case. Because of the soft-solder construction used in most of these, immersion in a bluing tank will leave you with four separate parts: The two barrels, and the upper and lower ribs (or side ribs). When a double is reblued, the barrels are usually done with cold chemical blue, and keeping it even is not easy. The barrels are slightly warmed under a lamp, a large swab is used, and application must be done quickly, moving the entire length of the barrels.

Cold chemical blue can be used for small parts, but when the hardness of the part is not an important factor, I seldom use it for this purpose. Instead, I use the torch-and-oil method. This is practically impossible to illustrate as heat colors in steel do not photograph well, so I'll just describe it here: Using a propane torch and an old pair of pliers (the heat will eventually ruin good pliers), hold the part in the flame until it goes to bright orange, then immediately quench it in oil (motor oil works fine). Shake off the excess oil, and hold the part back in the flame until the oil is burned off. Lay the part aside on a vise or metal plate to cool. With a little experimenting, you can even vary the color of the blue, and in most cases (depending on the steel) you will have imparted some surface-hardness. The finish will also be much more durable than can be obtained with cold chemical blue.

On large assemblies, barrels, receivers, and so on, cold chemical blue is good for touch-up work, but it must be used with care. Its strength and color vary widely among the various brands, and it's often difficult to blend it into the existing finish. For large areas, or entire parts, Q-Tips are often used. Brownells has some long-handled swabs (wooden handles) that are very good for this. I use a stainless-steel swab-thing that was given to me by my doctor. It tapers to a very thin square tip, and when twisted into a piece of cotton, it makes an instant swab. The cotton won't come off in use, but it is easily removed. One of the great things about it is that the size of the swab can be varied, from very large to the tiniest wisp. Medical supply houses should have them for sale, you could make one yourself, or you might be able to talk your doctor out of one. Either way, there're handy.

There are several points to remember about applying cold chemical blue: Be sure the surface is clean and dry, with no oil left on it. Swabbing the area with denatured alcohol is advisable. Warm the surface or part under a lamp to speed the bluing action. Use the chemical sparingly, keeping it off the existing blue, and re-apply the solution until the desired color is obtained. When very small spots or nicks are to be done, don't use a swab. Instead, use the method described in the illustrations which follow.

1. This Remington Model 3200 barrel was "spotted" by some unknown substance in one small area, but the rest of the gun was perfect. Since the gun was for sale, the owner decided against complete re-bluing.

2. Using a round wooden tooth-pick and cold chemical blue, each spot was touched and rubbed individually. The wood absorbed the chemical, just as a swab would, and excess liquid was easily shaken off before application.

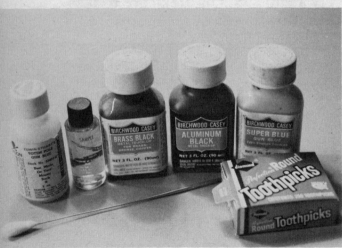

3. After application, the spots can still be located, in the right light, but they are no longer "white," and are much less obtrusive. After all the spots were treated, an application of oil made them difficult to find except on very close inspection.

4. There are a number of brands of cold chemical blue, and all do a good job. Also shown here are Brass Black and Aluminum Black, the latter good for touching up spots on parts made of alloy that won't take cold blue. Its use is much like cold chemical blue, except that it will usually take several more applications for durable coverage. Brass Black can be used to "age" brass when replacements are made on antique arms. One blackpowder shooter I know uses it to darken the brass front sights on his guns.

A final note on hot-bath bluing: I am intentionally omitting this process from coverage here, since those who want to go into full-time refinishing can find detailed instructions on this in several other books. To be properly done, it requires quite an array of specialized equipment as well as a lot of practice. In many areas, one gunsmith will be known as a refinishing specialist, and he will handle this job for the rest. In some ways, this is a good thing. The man who does it in my vicinity is an artist with bluing salts, and can be trusted not to go wild with the buffing wheels, and round off corners, smear lettering, etc.

Rounding Out Barrel Lumps

A barrel lump, or "knot" in a handgun or rifle is sometimes correctable. When it happens in shotguns, and the expanded spot is far enough forward, it's best to just cut off the barrel at that point. It's a rare problem in shotguns, though, as anything more than the slightest of obstructions will usually blow the barrel. In a handgun, the usual cause of barrel bulges is rapid firing with old ammo. The classic case is the war souvenir, and an owner who decides to "try it out" with the original rounds that were left in the magazine, with headstamps that date back to 1943. During rapid fire, one weak "pop" is not noticed, and the next round slams a bullet into the one that stopped in the barrel.

To remove the resulting bulge, the amateur will often resort to filing it down to the original outside diameter of the barrel. However, this creates a dangerous situation as the barrel walls will then be thinned, and a future blowout is likely. Here's the best "trick" to fix that bulge.

1. To properly remove a barrel bulge, rest the swelled portion on a steel block of suitable dimensions, and use a small hammer to strike the barrel on the lump while rotating the barrel in short increments. No heat is necessary, as the steel used in barrels is malleable. This operation requires patience, as the bulge will reduce very slowly. Extreme force should not be used, as this will produce flat spots on the outside of the barrel.

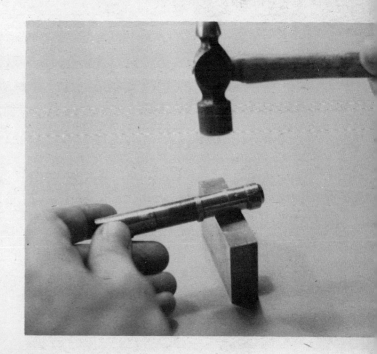

2. When done properly, the bulge will be eliminated, and no filing or other operations will need to be done to the exterior of the barrel. A light application of emery cloth will remove any traces of the hammer marks that may remain. It should be noted that after this repair there will still be a "ring" showing in the bore, but this will do no harm, and will not affect accuracy to any appreciable degree. However, in the interest of safety, the barrel should be Magnafluxed to see if any cracks have developed in the area of the bulge. If it has cracked, the first round through it could be disastrous.

Tightening Top-Break Revolvers

The era of the top-break revolver in the United States lasted about 30 years, and in that time, it isn't surprising that Smith & Wesson made the best ones. The best known is perhaps their model of 1880, which was chambered for the 32 and 38 S & W rounds. Even though these cartridges are of marginal power by today's standards, there are large numbers of the old S & W guns still in use as home and personal protection pieces. All but two of the springs in these guns are flat types. but these are easily replaced. The

hammer spring can be made from an altered Model 10 spring, and those are available everywhere. The cylinder hand spring can be duplicated from a small piece of cut clock spring or regular flat stock. The trigger and sear springs can be made from round wire, as shown in the Spring Section.

Aside from spring breakage, the three main mechanical ailments of the Model 1880 are looseness in the barrel latching system, breakage of the cylinder stop, and sear wear.

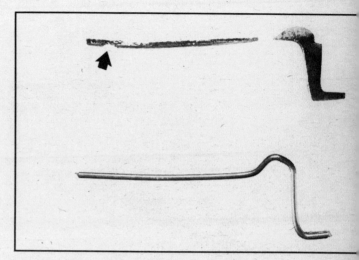

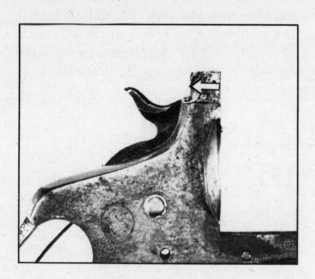

1. The barrel latch is harder than the top lugs of the frame, so it's the lugs that wear. The bearing point is the rear center face of the lugs, so that's where some added surface is needed. Drill a small hole in the back of each frame lug, at about the point shown by the arrow, to about half the depth of the lug. Drive a small tapered pin into each hole, and cut off the pins near the face of the lug. Then, use a file to carefully level the ends of the pins until the latch will close tightly. The upper edge of the pins should be slightly bevelled, so the closing of the latch won't be impeded.

2. Breakage of the cylinder stop usually occurs at the thinnest point, just forward of the operating lug that engages the cylinder slots. Parts have become very difficult to find for the older Smith & Wessons, and making a duplicate of this little horror from plank steel is an all day job. Fortunately, the cylinder stop can be made from flat strip-steel of the proper width. Actually, the one shown in the photo, below the broken S & W original, was made from a section of a large hair-curler pin, available in packets at any drug store. These also have the advantage of being pre-tempered. The one shown is not quite finished. The ends will be squared, and the groove for the retaining cross-pin (arrow, on the original) needs to be cut. The short tail at the rear can be bent up or down for proper engagement with the forward arm of the sear, and the sides of the operating lug can be squared to fit the cylinder slots. If breakage occurs during cold-forming, some heat can be used without destroying the temper.

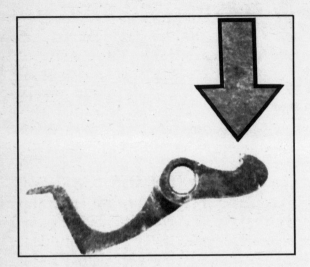

3. On the sear shown, the hammer notch contact beak (arrow) is badly worn and burred. In most cases, if the piece isn't worn too much, simple re-cutting of the beak will restore proper operation. If the damage is too severe, a small hole can be drilled just forward of the beak, vertically, and a tapered pin driven into place. The pin can then be cut with a file or a cutting disc in the Dremel to the proper shape for engagement with the hammer notches.

Tightening Single and Double Shotguns

When the older single and double shotguns become loose in the barrel lock-up, their construction often makes adding steel to the worn locking lugs by welding impossible. In most cases, this much heat will cause separation of the barrels, as soft solder was usually used. A primitive repair of this problem was frequently to use a hammer to upset (or peen) the edge of the main locking lug under the barrel, taking up the slack in the barrel latch. Unfortunately, the first few shots after this was done would usually flatten the peened edge, and the looseness was back. Actually, their idea was not all wrong, but their method was defeated by the soft steel used in the old guns.

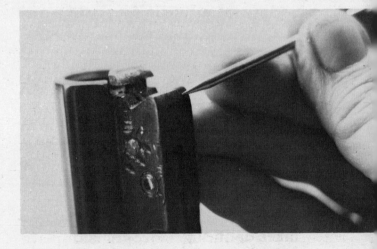

1. The idea here is to raise the surface of the lug, at its contact point with the barrel latch. This can be done by using a tool to impact the lug just *below* the edge, not right on it.

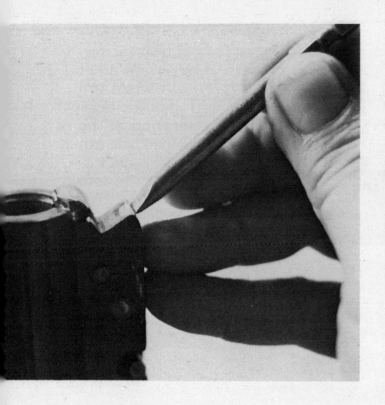

2. The tool I usually use for this operation is an old removable screwdriver blade, similar to the ones supplied with the Brownells Magna-Tip set. Like those, this tool is very hard, and its end makes a nice, rectangular depression that covers about two-thirds of the width of the lug. The tip of this particular tool is .248", or roughly ¼", but this could be varied, of course, in relation to different lug widths. When the tool is held in place below the edge, its end horizontal, it is struck repeatedly with a small hammer. As the rectangular depression is formed, the upper surface of the lug at the latch contact point will begin to arch upward. When enough upset has been done so that the latch will close tightly, stop. The gun should be reassembled frequently during this operation, to check the level of engagement. Remember that some of the older steels are barely more than cast iron, and if you go too far, the edge of the lug could chip.

3. There is often extreme wear not only in the latch, but also in the barrel hinge. This "end play" can be eliminated by drilling a small hole at the center of the hinge bearing area on the front of the barrel underlug, and driving a tapered steel pin into the hole. The pin is then shaped to conform to the curve of the hinge, leaving a slight protrusion which takes up the slack. Before drilling the hole, check the depth of the lug at that point, to avoid drilling all the way through. On some guns, the ejector mechanism comes close to the front of the lug, or all the way through, and in these cases two pins are used, one on each side.

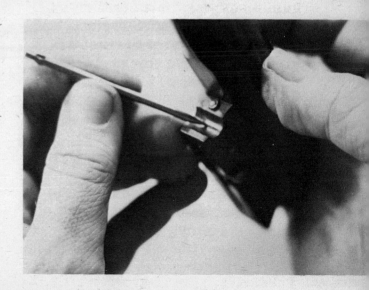

4. Another chronic ailment of single and double guns is loosening of the fore-end latch. Here, again, welding heat that will add steel to the retaining lug will often cause separation of the lug from the barrel or barrels, along with the danger of total barrel separation in doubles. To tighten these latches, drill a small hole in the lug, inside the notch of its hook, and drive a small tapered pin into it. The head of the pin is then cut back until the latch will lock properly.

Repairing Plastic Stocks

It began during World War Two, when most of the walnut for gunstocks was routed to the military. The Savage/Stevens company was one of the first to market guns with stocks and fore-ends of "Tenite." This was, of course, simply a plastic. It worked fairly well on guns with light recoil, such as 22 rifles and small gauge shotguns. On the 12-gauge pieces, it was a disaster, however. Many of these guns are still in use, and in most cases, replacement wood stocks are simply not available.

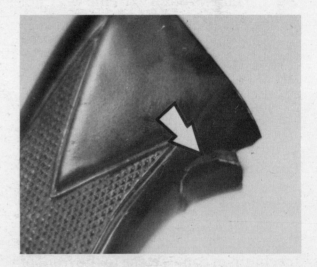

1. The photo shows a Tenite stock with a typical break, at one of the points of heavy stress (arrow).

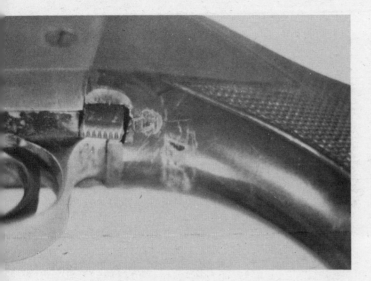

2. Using an ordinary soldering iron, the break was "welded," inside and out. Afterward, the sharp edges were smoothed with a file and emery paper. It's a rough repair, but it's an effective one.

Repairing Alloy Trigger Housings

At one time, under the trade name "Flite-King," "Model 200," and other designations, High Standard made a good slide-action shotgun. Perhaps the largest quantity of these was sold by Sears, Roebuck & Co., as their J. C. Higgins Model 20. As originally made, the gun was all steel, including the trigger group. Unlike most of today's guns of similar design, which use two cross-pins to retain the trigger housing, the Hi-Standard had a single cross-pin at the rear, and projecting lugs at the front on each side which engaged recesses inside the receiver. As long as the housing was steel, this arrangement was quite adequate. Unfortunately, in later years, the trigger housing was made of alloy, and the question then was not "if" the lugs would shear off, but "when." For a while, replacement housings could be bought, but now parts for these guns are becoming difficult to find. Even when a replacement can be located, it will be the alloy type, and in time, it, too, will break. The guns are otherwise well-engineered and are well liked by their owners, so I developed a method of repairing the broken alloy housings.

1. This trigger housing is from a J. C. Higgins Model 20 shotgun, and the tool indicates the area of the broken retaining lug. This is a typical break—the lug on the other side sheared in exactly the same way.

2. After marking with a center-punch, use a ⅛" drill bit to drill a blind hole about ¼" deep, taking care not to go through to the interior of the housing. The housing does not have to be disassembled for this operation. Note that the hole is drilled at a slight outward angle.

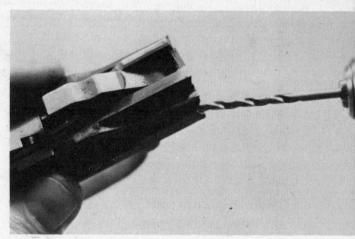

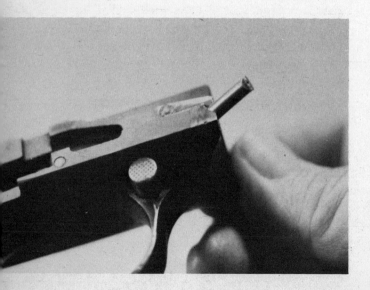

3. Prepare two tapered steel pins, and drive them into place in the holes. Before this is done, mark the pins at the hole depth, so you'll know when they are fully in place. Cut off the forward tips of the pins, leaving about ¼" projection to the front.

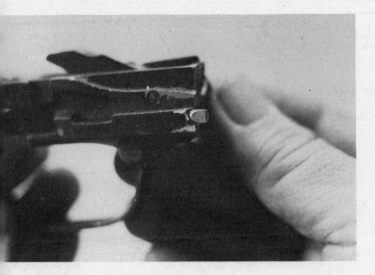

4. The sides of the pins are then cut away, to conform to the side of the trigger housing. Depending on how well the drilled holes have matched the angle of the original lugs, you may or may not have to file the top or underside of the pins for fitting to the recesses inside the receiver.

5. Here is another view of the finished pin on one side. The outward angle of the pins is necessary not only for proper contact with the recesses, but also to be sure of clearance for loading and feeding.

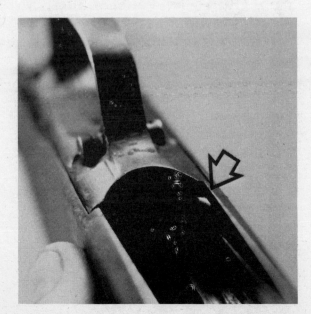

6. The trigger group is shown in the gun, with the pins properly engaged. In time, after long, hard use, the steel pins may loosen in their holes in the alloy. Owners should be cautioned to check them occasionally, if the housing is removed for cleaning. If they do loosen, they can be staked in place. I will note that I have never had a return on this particular repair, so it must be pretty durable.

The H&R Model 922 Revolver

I'm including the older solid-frame Harrington & Richardson revolver here for two reasons. First, because there are so many of them still in use out there, and secondly because their internal mechanism has certain points that parallel the H & R guns of current manufacture. Consequently, some of the information can be applied to them as well. While parts are generally still available for most models, there may be times when it would make more sense to repair, rather than replace.

1. This is a fairly early Model 922, with the then-familiar ham-shaped grip. The gun was of solid-frame design, the cylinder removable by depressing the latch at the front of the frame and pulling out the base pin.

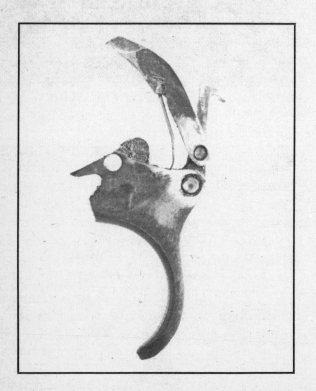

2. The trigger, hammer lifter, cylinder hand, and the combination hand and lifter spring follow an H & R design that has been used for more than 75 years. It is unusual in that the spring is located in *front* of the cylinder hand, its lower tip engaged in a tiny hole in the top of the trigger. The spring is installed on the cylinder hand at the factory, and when one breaks, a new replacement hand and spring come as an assembly. This will often require some fitting, as the replacement may not exactly match the degree of wear in the gun, and the timing will have to be adjusted. If the original hand is undamaged, except for the broken spring, it always seemed to me that it was a shame to waste it. Besides, it *did* match the timing. The spring usually breaks off where it enters the hand, so there's no way to extract its end. Using a cutting disc in the Dremel tool, I cut a narrow slot about ⅛" into the hand at the spring entry point. Then, I double back the same amount at the end of a piece of .020" spring wire, and peen it in place in the slot. Once it is anchored well, the spring can be cut off to the proper length and shaped to function the same as the original.

3. The upper rear extension of the cylinder stop (arrow) can wear in time until it no longer has proper engagement with the stop slots in the cylinder, and this will allow "over-travel," the cylinder rotating past its stopping point, with no lock-up. It's possible to restore a worn cylinder stop, by bending the tip of the upper rear extension upward, and recutting it to square the edges for proper con-

tact. This is a fairly hard part, so heat must be used to prevent breakage. I do this operation by clamping the part firmly in a vise, with the "beak" of the stop protruding above the jaws. Only the rear tip is in the vise, as the two cross-pins must not be damaged. The spring is detached, of course. Using a propane torch to bring the beak up to light orange color, a screwdriver is inserted under the beak, lifting it very slightly. Remember, it's better to have to repeat the operation than to go too far. Even with the heat, it's possible to break it. After the top is recut to restore the edges, the part must be rehardened.

4. In the early solid-frame guns, the ratchet was an integral part of the cylinder. When one of the ratchet teeth is damaged, as on the one in the photo (arrow), it is *possible*, with a very small torch tip, to add some steel weld and recut it to shape. Considering the amount of precision work involved, though, this would be practical only if the gun were a keepsake. It would make more sense to buy a new cylinder.

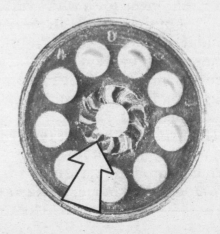

The Remington Model 12 Rifle

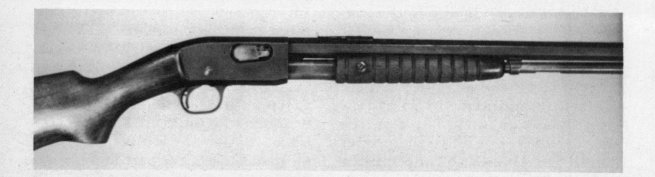

John Douglas Pedersen did several designs for Remington in the early years of this century, and perhaps the best known of these was a little slide-action 22 rifle called the Model 12. It was made from 1909 to 1936, then was slightly redesigned to become the Model 121, and was made in that form until 1954. I don't know the exact total production figure for the Model 12, but it must have been turned out in huge quantity. Any gunsmith who has been in business for a while will have seen a lot of them. Though guns in excellent condition are beginning to be snapped up by Remington collectors, many Model 12 rifles in average condition are still in everyday use.

The firing pin is a flat type with an oblong opening at its center which contains the return spring and plunger. The Model 12 has an internal pivoting hammer. The firing pin also serves as the ejector. A short extension at left rear encounters a receiver-mounted spring as the breech block reaches full rear, pushing the pin out of the breech face to kick out the fired case. The main body of the pin seldom breaks, even though it's cut out for the rebound spring. The thing that usually lets go is the little tab at left rear, the extension that contacts the ejector spring. If the pin is otherwise sound, there's no need to replace it. Just drill a small hole into its rear face near the left corner, and install a stepped tapered pin, driven into place. Then, square the head of the pin, and cut it off to match the original projection of the tab.

The ejector spring mentioned above is the only flat spring in the Model 12, and it receives both impact and compression each time the action is cycled. When this one breaks, it can be replaced with one made of doubled round wire of about .031″ to .035″ diameter, easily mounted with the original screw.

The main problem that occurs in the Model 12 is not one of breakage. The cartridge stop, or retainer, lies in a groove on top of the action slide, and this long, thin part extends through the front of the receiver, between the barrel and the action slide. It is held in place only by the action slide, and when this is removed during total disassembly, the cartridge stop sometimes clings to the underside of the barrel, to later fall out and be lost. Its absence leaves no great gap, and if the person doing the takedown is not familiar with the gun, this may not be noticed during reassembly. It quickly becomes apparent, though, when the gun fails to feed properly.

1. This is the cartridge stop, or retainer. Dimensions: Length —2³⁄₁₆″; width—.140″; thickness— .108″ (maximum vertical measurement). The used-parts dealers may occasionally have one of these, but they are not generally available. At one time, I tried making one of these by forming sheet steel, but the results were not satisfactory. When this part is missing, the only thing to do is mill a piece of bar steel to the proper dimensions, and make a rather complicated series of cuts to bring it to functional shape.

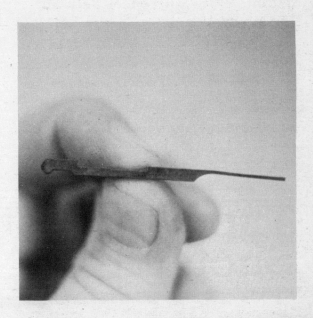

2. The arrow indicates the assembled location of the cartridge stop. During assembly, care must be taken to see that it is properly in place and held there, or it can be damaged as the action slide is moved into the receiver.

3. The cartridge lifter, or carrier, has a recessed track on its right side that mates with a stud on the action slide, and this makes the cross-section rather thin at the narrowest point of this part. While breakage here is not common, it does happen, as illustrated in this photo. A carrier broken in this way can be rejoined with a weld.

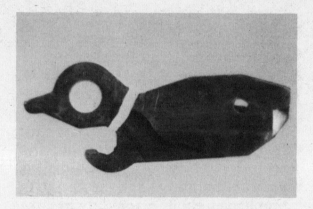

It should be noted that there are definite parts differences between the Model 12 and the Model 121 which succeeded it, and I've even seen one or two transition pieces. The cartridge stop of the Model 121 is similar to the Model 12 version, but its larger rear tip incorporates a feed ramp. The parts of the two models can often be adapted, but they are not routinely interchangeable.

The Winchester Model 97 Shotgun

Between 1897 and 1957, Winchester made nearly one million Model 97 shotguns. Many of them are still in use, which makes this gun a tribute to the design genius of John Moses Browning. An external hammer and absolute reliability are the main assets of the Model 97. Because of the heavy carrier and poor mechanical advantage in the action slide, its operation requires the left arm of "Conan the Barbarian." Considering its popularity, maybe the old saying is true, that there were real men in those days.

The Model 97 does have a few chronic ailments, but most of these occur only after many years of continuous use. The most common of these is a failure to completely lock up when the action is closed. Breakage of the ejector is another. Fortunately, most of the problems that do crop up with this gun are easily corrected.

1. The slide lock bar (arrow) is located in a recess on the left side of the carrier, near its lower edge. It locks into a matching recess inside the left wall of the receiver, and in time this recess can wear at its edges. The locking bar itself is tempered so hard it will almost write on glass, so it seldom shows signs of wear, except for a very slight edge-rounding. The problem is easily cured by reshaping the front half of the bar outward, to bear more positively on the receiver recess. The amateur who has figured out the mechanical aspects of the locking system will often try to do this cold, with the bar still in the gun, and he is inevitably rewarded by hearing a sharp *snap*, as the front half of the bar breaks off.

To do it properly, the carrier must be removed, and the locking bar taken out of it. The bar is then clamped in a

vise, with the pivot hole inside the jaws, and heated to light orange with a propane torch. It is then tapped lightly with a small hammer, bending the forward portion slightly outward. Very little alteration is required, as the length of the part accentuates the bend. After this is done, quenching in oil will restore some of the hardness. Reassemble, and the action will now lock.

2. Another age-symptom of the Model 97 is a failure of the hammer to cock when the action is cycled. This is caused by extreme wear of the upper surface of the bolt guide channels in the receiver. The arrow in the photo is pointing to the rear edge of the right guide channel. A quick cure for this, without subjecting the bolt or receiver to heat, is to use a hammer and a very hard screwdriver blade to make deep stake-marks just above the channel, just inside the receiver at the rear. This will create bearing points on each side, keeping the bolt pushed downward, and compensating for the wear. The hammer will now cock when the action is cycled.

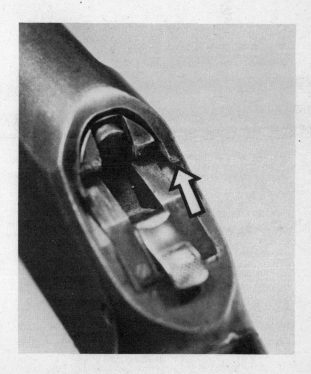

3. The Model 97 was made in both takedown and non-takedown (solid frame) versions, and frequent disassembly of the one with the removable barrel and magazine unit can eventually cause wear of the helical locking lugs, or threads, at the rear tip of the magazine tube. The entire magazine assembly can then pull loose on the forward stroke of the action slide. Because of the thinness of the tube, adding steel to the threads is not feasible, as heat will deform the tube. I usually repair this problem by installing three short screws, one on each side and one at the bottom, at the front of the receiver. These enter holes drilled in the magazine tube, and the tips of the screws are faced off to prevent any protrusion into the inside of the tube. Along with this, the magazine tube hanger screws at the front and their spacer are shortened, allowing the hanger loop to clamp the magazine and barrel tightly. This method does, of course, cancel the easy-takedown, but that may be a good thing, as it prevents further wear on the system.

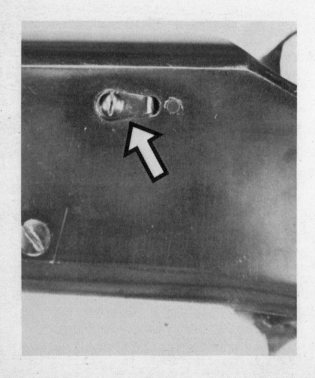

4. The spring-steel ejector is externally-mounted by a single screw on the left side of the receiver (arrow), and this makes replacement easy. Since the ejector is flexed and sustains impact with each cycle of the action (when loaded), breakage is not uncommon.

5. Fortunately, the ejector is one part of the Model 97 that has been commercially reproduced, and they are available from several sources. The one shown came from Triple K, 568 Sixth Avenue, San Diego, CA 92101. In an emergency, when function is more important than appearance, this ejector can easily be made from round spring wire.

The Browning Auto-5 Shotgun

More of these guns are in use than any other autoloading shotgun, and perhaps for this reason, most of the repairs that are done are to correct problems due to wear. Some Auto-5 guns have been in use for nearly 75 years, through three generations of shooters. Even a high-quality shotgun can get a little tired in that time.

One of the most frequently-encountered causes of malfunction, though, has nothing to do with wear. Speaking as a gunsmith who has disassembled more Browning A-5 guns than can be counted, it's a rare thing to find one with a properly arranged set of friction pieces. So, just for those who might look for the information here, they go like this: For medium to heavy loads, the steel

ring should be in front of the recoil spring, its concave side against the bronze friction piece. For very light loads, the ring should be stored behind the spring, with its flat side forward. In most guns that have seen a lot of use, it's best to leave the ring in the medium-to-heavy location for all loads, as in time the recoil spring will take a slight "set," and the retarding effect will be needed, even with lighter loads.

Most of the actual parts breakage that occurs in the Auto-5 involves the three principal springs, all flat types. Unfortunately, none of these can be easily duplicated in doubled round wire. However, all of them are readily available from regular parts sources, including Browning. The three springs are the hammer spring, carrier spring, and the combination spring that powers the trigger and the safety positioning ball. On the last one mentioned, the center arm of the spring that contacts the safety ball will often snap off alone, leaving the twin trigger arms working. The only cure, in all three cases, is replacement with original springs. It should be noted that the Browning hammer spring, which is still available, can be reworked to function in the Remington Model 11.

1. The primary shell stop in this gun is an extension of the carrier latch, and wear is not a problem here. The secondary shell stop, though, is a separate part, its upper arm contacting an inclined surface on the barrel extension. If this contact point becomes severely worn, the inside front edge will fail to release the shell at the right instant, and there will be a spectacular jam. A new replacement part is available, of course, but repair of the original is not difficult.

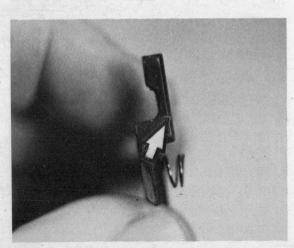

2. With the lower portion of the shell stop gripped in a vise, use a propane torch to heat the upper extension (arrow) to a light orange color, and tap its outer surface with a small hammer to bend it slightly inward. Be careful not to move it too much. After it has cooled, install it and check its clearance. When it functions properly, it can be removed and re-hardened. It will then last for quite a few years before replacement is necessary.

3. On many of the older guns, the carrier pivot screws were hand-fitted exactly on each side. If they are removed during complete disassembly, take care that they are returned to their original positions. If they are switched, this can cause the carrier to bind, and this will affect the feeding. When taking the Auto-5 apart for refinishing, I always scribe a line across the tip of the left screw, for identification during reassembly.

As noted earlier, the Remington Model 11, made from 1905 to 1948, is fairly close to the A-5 design, and several parts can be altered to work in it. Savage also made a series of guns that were externally similar, between 1930 and 1958, but in this case several points in the design were very different, and parts will not interchange.

Marlin Semi-Auto 22s

The earliest versions of the current Marlin 22 semi-auto rifle were designated Model 99, and later variations were called Model 49. The basic gun has also been made on contract as the Western Auto Model 150M and the J.C. Penney Model 2066, among others. As currently made, it is the Marlin Model 60 and Model 990. Mechanically, all of these are very similar, if not identical.

This is a good design, and most of its problems show up only after years of hard use. The disconnector spring, a round-wire torsion-type, may weaken in time, and have to be replaced. All parts are available, so there's no difficulty in obtaining a replacement. In this case, though, the installation can be difficult, especially for the amateur.

On some of these guns, the ejector is an extension of the cartridge lifter spring, its forward tip lying in a groove on top of the left lip of the feed throat. This heavy spring seldom breaks, but it is subject to occasional misalignment and deformation from repeated impact. In most cases, it can be reshaped without replacement.

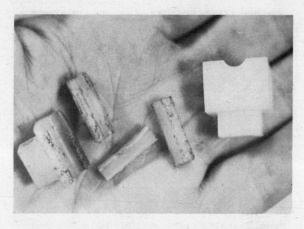

1. The left arrow indicates the carrier spring extension that serves as an ejector on some models. On others, the carrier spring does not extend to this position, and a simple stepped edge on the left lip of the feed throat serves this function. The center arrow points to the disconnector, and the right arrow to a nylon buffer that cushions the rear impact of the bolt during recoil.

2. The nylon bolt buffer is tough, but it will sustain only so many strikes from the bolt before it begins to crack. A shattered bolt buffer is on the left, a new one on the right. While replacements are easily installed, I have often made new buffers for these guns which will last virtually forever, using rubber cut from old auto motor mounts! I've never had one of these returned, so they must work well.

3. The feed throat of these guns is made of a plated alloy, and the surface coating makes them last a

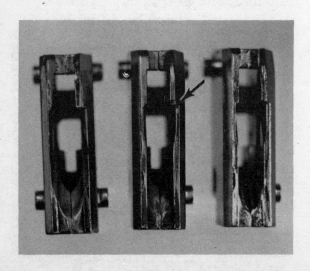

good long while. When the lips do begin to wear, the round being delivered will be misaligned, and will be run into the rear face of the barrel, missing the chamber. On the feed throat at the left, the lips are badly worn. The used one at center and the new one at the right show how the edges of the feed lips should look. When the feed throat wears out, replacement is the only answer, as there's no feasible way to add material and recut to shape. Besides, they're easily available. In the photo, also note that the feed units on each side are of the spring-ejector type, while the center one has the integral ejector surface (arrow).

Iver Johnson Top-Break Revolver

Many "fancy gunsmiths" refuse to do repair work on the old "Owl-Head" revolvers, and I think this is lamentable. The early Iver Johnson top-break revolvers were well-made guns, and in good condition, or properly restored, they still can be dependable home protection guns. One of their main design features, the transfer-bar firing system, has been used in several modern revolvers. In the Iver Johnson, the transfer bar as designed by Andrew Fyrberg was combined with the hammer lifter. The lifter has an upper extension that is interposed between the hammer face and the firing pin only when the trigger is fully to the rear.

As with most of the T-latch top-breaks, a common ailment of the Iver Johnson is looseness of the barrel latch. For a description of one repair method for this, see the information in this section on tightening top-break revolvers. Like the Smith & Wesson, the Iver Johnson was made in both external hammer and "hammerless" versions, and most of them were in 32 and 38 S & W chambering.

In earlier versions of the gun, all of the springs except for the ejector, firing pin, and barrel latch springs are of the flat type. Late guns used round wire springs throughout, and because of this only a few of the parts will interchange. When the flat hammer spring breaks, it can be replaced with one made of round wire, and the same applies to the other flat springs.

1. A typical 32 Iver Johnson top-break is shown. This one is the "hammerless" (actually, internal hammer) version.

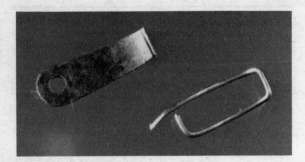

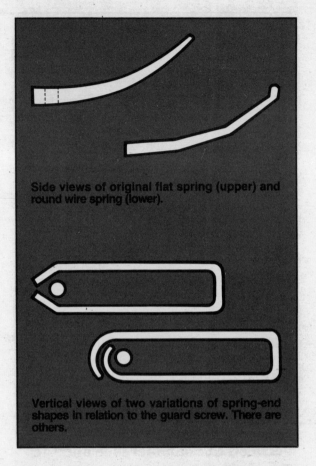

Side views of original flat spring (upper) and round wire spring (lower).

Vertical views of two variations of spring-end shapes in relation to the guard screw. There are others.

2. In most of the early top-break guns, the trigger spring was a flat V-type. The Iver Johnson spring is unusual, as it is a single curved spring with a hole in it for passage of the trigger guard screw. It should be noted that when the trigger spring in an I. J. is weak, it may be due to looseness of the guard screw. Often, tightening the screw will restore the tension. If the spring is broken or missing, it can be replaced with one made from .037" to .039" spring wire, as shown in the photo and drawing. Note that the round wire spring must have a more pronounced curve, and that the forward ends, at the screw, can be shaped in several different ways. In that area, it is important to prevent the spring from slipping forward or back. It must be stabilized to ensure that it remains in proper engagement with the trigger.

3. Shown here are four broken transfer bars (Iver Johnson called this part the "Safety Lifter"), and one (at the far right) intact. The unbroken bar is from a later gun, and its design has more strength than the early type. This part was regularly available for many years, but the supply has diminished greatly in recent times. At this time no one is making commercial replacements. When you encounter a broken safety lifter, the

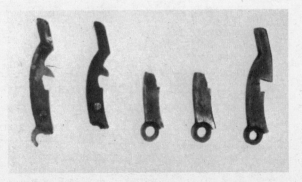

only solution is to add steel weld and recut it to original shape.

4. Late Iver Johnson revolvers will have this type of cylinder hand, its upper lobe drilled for the tip of a round-wire spring that encircles the hand pivot post. A short rear arm of the spring also powers the "safety lifter." The inside of the hand around the pivot is recessed for the spring loop. If this spring breaks, it is easily made from .016″ or .018″ spring wire.

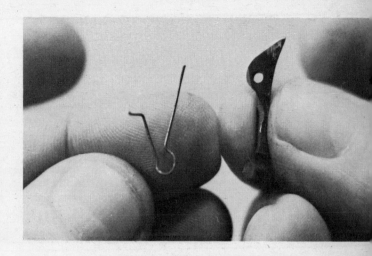

5. Here is the cylinder hand and spring in assembly. If the flat V-type spring of an older gun breaks, the system can be converted to a round-wire-type with very little work. Since the top of the hand is not drilled for the spring tip, the upper end of the spring will have to be shaped into a "hook," to lay over the hand shaft, to keep it from slipping off.

6. The hand, spring, and lifter are shown, assembled on the trigger. This is a late-type assembly, designed for a round-wire spring.

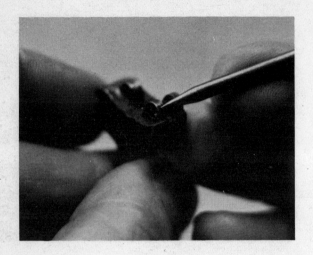

7. When the round-wire system is used on an older gun, the cylinder hand will not have the recess around the pivot post for the spring, so room must be made for it. This is done by thinning the left mounting loop on the rear of the trigger, on its left side. I usually do this with a cutting disc in the Dremel tool, taking off just enough to match the diameter of the spring wire used.

8. Along with the lifter, one of the equally difficult parts to find is the firing pin bushing, or retainer. With the items shown, a replacement retainer can be made. Though this is not a terribly easy job, it's not beyond the capabilities of a careful amateur. Shown are an "I" drill (.2720"), and a 5/16-24 tap and bolt.

9. The "I" drill is used to bring the firing pin recess to size for 5/16" tapping. If a drill press is not available to limit the reach of the drill, turn the bit by hand, to avoid going too far.

10. The next step is to thread the recess to 5/16-24. The tap being used here is a blunt finishing type, but any 5/16-24 tap can be altered to this shape by trimming its end with a cutting disc or carefully grinding off the tip. If this is done, take care to avoid overheating it.

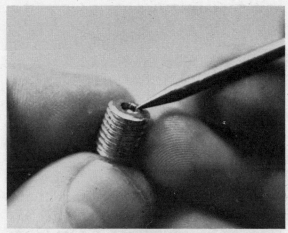

11. A section is cut from the bolt, and it is then drilled through its center, the diameter of the hole matching the firing pin point. Two shallow small holes are drilled on each side of the firing pin aperture to fit the twin-pointed wrench used in installation. The wrench is easily made from an old screwdriver. The bolt section shown is partially drilled. After the hole is all the way through, the end is selected that has the hole most perfectly centered, and the wrench holes are drilled on that end. A thin section is then cut off, its thickness matching the depth of the threads in the firing pin recess in the breech face. The retainer is then installed in the breech face, and its outer surface filed off to level with the surrounding area. Finished, it will be difficult to tell from an original.

12. The "hammerless" version of this revolver has one chronic ailment that is not shared

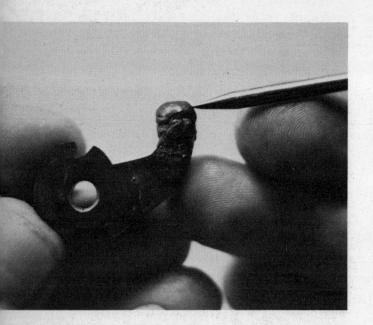

with the external hammer type. The internal hammer has two "ears" at its striking face which flank the safety lifter, and rest the hammer on the inside of the frame when the lifter is in the lowered position. Originally, the hammer is quite hard, and one or both ears break with some frequency. To repair this, a "glob" of steel weld is added to the hammer face. If the shop is not equipped with a welding torch (my own isn't), any commercial welder can do this. Be sure that enough is added to allow for shaping, and that the weld "takes" well in joining the steel of the hammer. This process will slightly reduce the hardness of the hammer, but as these were usually a little over-hardened, this is of no importance.

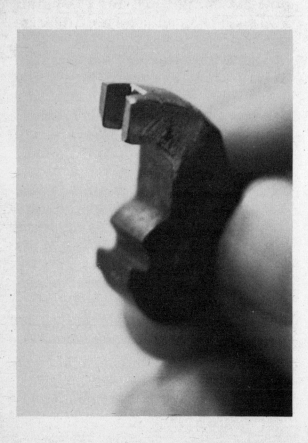

13. After the weld is cooled, tap it lightly with a small hammer to remove any surface slag, and then, as the sculptor said about carving an elephant, cut away everything that doesn't look like the top of an Iver Johnson hammer. Near the finished point, it should look like the one shown. The space between the ears must accept the top of the lifter freely, without any binding. The final adjustment is to file off the front faces of the ears, leaving enough front projection to allow the lifter top to move downward with the hammer at rest, in the "fired" position. This is best gauged by removing the top cover from the frame, and installing the hammer and the trigger/lifter system. With the trigger pulled, the engagement will be visible at the top.

Repairing Broken Parts Without Welding

When a part breaks, and replacements are available, it's usually best to just put in a new part. One exception to this might be when the part is externally visible, and the finish of a replacement can't be matched to the original finish of the gun. In cases of older guns, with parts being either scarce or entirely unobtainable, there are always two alternatives: To make an entire new part from steel stock, or to repair the original broken part. The latter should always be tried first, if the part is repairable. If both pieces of the part are present, they can usually be rejoined with silver solder or steel weld. When only half remains, and the broken extension is not of unreasonable length, a knob of weld can be added and then recut to shape.

In the small shop or home without facilities for heat-rejoining, there is another way which can be used, but only when the part is sufficiently large to support the method. It involves the use of rod stock, either to replace the broken extension or to join the pieces.

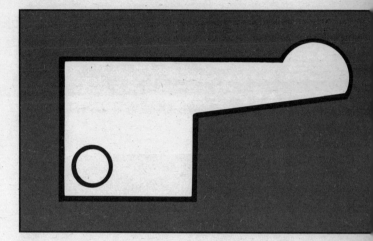

1. The unbroken part shown is not meant to be a component of any actual mechanism, it's just for illustration.

2. Any part with this general configuration will usually fracture at the point where its extension joins the main body, as shown.

3. When the broken-off piece is missing, file off the broken edge even with the face of the part body, and drill a hole at the center of the filed space, as indicated by the arrow in this sectioned view. The hole should be at least two-thirds the size, in diameter, as the neck of the broken extension. Its depth will be variable, but it must be sufficient for the installation of an anchoring cross-pin.

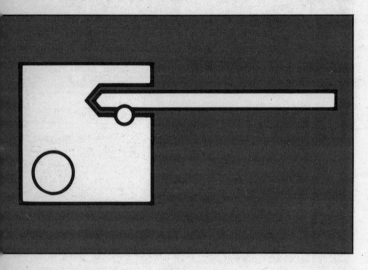

4. A piece of rod stock is selected or turned to fit tightly in the hole, its tip slightly bevelled, and the rod is driven into the hole. The rod must be a little longer than the original extension, to allow for shaping. After the rod is firmly in place, the body of the part is cross-drilled at a point where a cross-pin will contact the rod. The cross-pin is installed, and its ends peened and filed off even with the sides.

5. The projecting portion of the rod is then shaped to perform the function of the missing extension. If drill rod is used, the finished part should require no heat treatment. If the rod is milder steel, it should be hardened after it is shaped and tried for functioning.

6. If the broken-off piece is present, the same method can be used, with the rod acting as a dowel to join the piece to the body, as shown. The difficult point here is getting the two pieces exactly aligned. I do it by drilling the hole in the body first, and placing a free-fit pointed rod in the hole, its point barely protruding. The broken extension is then positioned properly, and tapped with a small hammer, making an index mark for the drill. After the piece is drilled, and driven onto the rod mounted in the part body, it is also cross-pinned. In this repair, the uneven edges of the break are not levelled, but are used to help in keeping the extension from rotating.

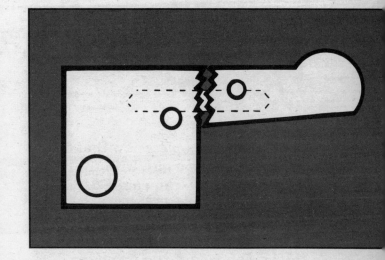

7. When the extension is missing, and if in original form it was externally visible, there may be reason not to use the shaped rod replacement described in numbers one through five above. In that case, the rod-and-double-pin method can be used to install a block of steel, as shown here.

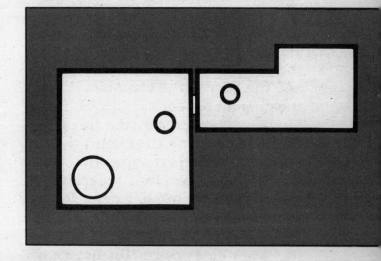

8. The block is then shaped to match the contour of the original extension. It should be noted that the gap between the pieces in the drawings is there only for clarity of illustration. In actual assembly, the two pieces are fitted tightly.

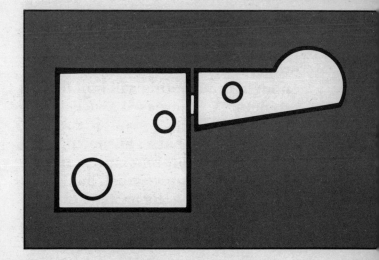

Removing Chamber Edge Dents

Most all gun-people know that dry-firing, snapping a gun with the chamber empty, can cause damage. In the centerfires, if done to excess, it can produce crystallization of the firing pin point or deformation of the breech face at the firing pin aperture. With rimfires, though, the damage will often be more quickly apparent. Rimfire ignition is achieved by "pinching" the rim of the cartridge between the firing pin and the edge of the chamber. When the chamber is empty, and the firing pin has enough reach, the tip of the pin will impact on the chamber edge. Then, it's just a question of which will happen first—breakage of the firing pin point, or a deep dent at the chamber edge. In most cases, it's the latter.

When this occurs, the novice will often use a file or a chambering reamer to cut away the raised portion of the edge that protrudes into the chamber and interferes with proper extraction. If the dent is deep enough, though, this will still leave a problem. The increased space between the firing pin point and the rear face of the barrel at the "pinch point" may result in misfires. It's better not to remove steel, but instead to swage the protrusion out.

1. Here is a typical dented chamber edge, with the upset steel protruding slightly into the chamber. This can affect both feeding and extraction, and, if the dent is deep enough (this one isn't), it can cause misfiring.

2. Select a slim drift punch with a very gradual slope, one that is slightly larger than the cartridge case, and insert it into the chamber.

3. When the punch is fully seated, be sure that there is at least a quarter-inch of smooth sloping area just outside the chamber. If the knurled portion is too close, use a slightly larger punch.

4. Holding the punch snugly in the chamber, tap its head lightly with a small hammer, forcing it into the chamber and swaging the protrusion back into the dent. Don't use too much force, as most barrel steels are fairly soft and you don't want to enlarge the chamber at the rear. During this operation, check the progress of the swaging frequently by inserting a cartridge in the chamber. If the punch becomes stuck, a light tap on its side will free it.

5. When the dent is more severe, as shown in this drawing, the method described above may not work. It should be used initially to get rid of the protrusion, but the remaining deep dent may cause misfires. If that's the case, I've found the following procedure to be effective.

6. After the protrustion is swaged out, use the dent as an index mark, and drill a small hole diagonally, as shown, into the rear face of the barrel. Note the thickness of the barrel, and take care not to go through. The diameter of the drill will be governed by the size of the firing pin dent.

7. Turn a small piece of drill rod to a diameter that will be a tight fit in the hole, and taper it slightly at one end. Drive the pin into the hole, being sure that it penetrates fully to the bottom of the hole.

8. Cut off the outside tip of the pin, even with the rear face of the barrel, and carefully file the portion in the chamber to conform with the curve of the chamber wall. If you have a set of chambering reamers, use them to complete the shaping. If not, it can be done with a fine-cut round file. Finish by light polishing with a split-end bronze rod and #600 emery paper or cloth. The finished job is shown with a cartridge in place in the chamber.

Unlocking the Mauser Broomhandle

The Mauser "broomhandle" has been known by many names, and serious collectors have added even more precise designations. The one shown in photos one and two is a standard war-time commercial gun, from the 1915-1918 period. The gun used in the rest of the photos is an early 1930 model. Aside from being the first commercially-successful automatic pistol, the C96 Mauser is a masterpiece of mechanical design. The internal parts are fitted so ingeniously that it is almost impossible to assemble the gun wrong. I say almost, because there is one notable exception: The rocker coupling. This small, semi-crescent-shaped part is located at the lower front of the sub-frame, and its upper beak supplies tension to the locking block.

Unfortunately, it is possible to install the rocker coupling backwards. Equally unfortunate is the fact that the sub-frame can still be put back in the gun with the coupling in this position. When this is done, not only will the gun fail to function properly, but it will firmly resist all attempts to take it apart. One projection of the rocker coupling will protrude below the sub-frame, and it will lock behind the trigger and trigger spring inside. I have seen Mauser pistols actually

bent and otherwise damaged in attempts to dismantle them after being assembled with a reversed rocker coupling.

One early method of dealing with this problem was to drill a hole just forward of the trigger, inside the guard, for insertion of a punch to force the coupling upward to clear the trigger and spring. After disassembly, the hole was then closed with a steel weld, and the area refinished. I decided a few years ago to try to devise a method for unblocking pistols in this condition, a method that would require no drastic operations. Noting that even a blocked receiver and sub-frame had some movement to the rear, I took out the bolt (this is possible without additional disassembly) and designed a tool that could enter from the top, to unblock the system.

1. The Mauser C96 pistol, field-stripped into its basic assemblies. The sub-frame holds the hammer, rocker coupling, etc., and is shown here above the main frame or receiver.

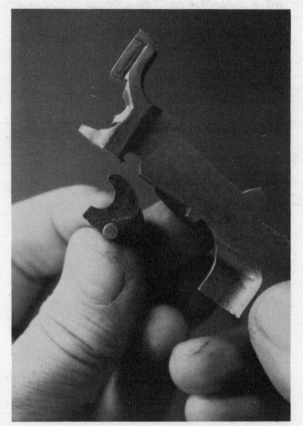

2. Here is the rocker coupling, held just below its slot and pivot recesses in the sub-frame, and in the proper orientation for installation.

3. The rocker coupling is shown properly installed here. If anything is protruding below the sub-frame at the front, it's wrong.

4. When the coupling is reversed, the receiver and sub-frame will move about as far as shown here before meeting firm resistance.

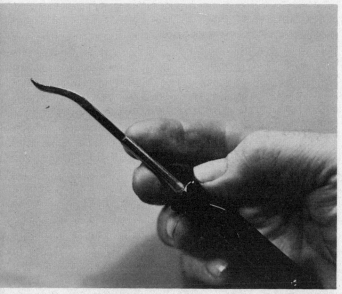

5. This is the tool I designed, made from a screwdriver. Its purpose is not to contact the coupling itself, but to depress the hammer spring plunger toward the rear.

6. The receiver and sub-frame are moved to their rear limit, and the tool is inserted as shown, entering just behind the rear wall of the magazine.

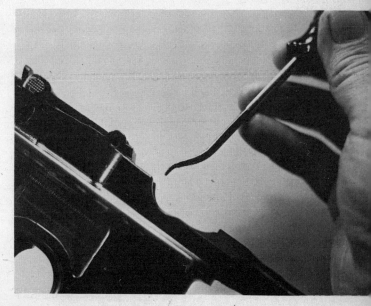

7. With the tool in position, the handle is levered toward the front, and its lower tip depresses the hammer spring plunger toward the rear. This will relieve the tension of the spring on the coupling, and will allow it to rotate, its lower arm clearing the trigger spring and trigger.

8. While pressure on the tool is maintained, the receiver and sub-frame are moved toward the rear, and out of the main frame. With the tool, it's easy. Without it, virtually impossible.

9. The coupling in this sub-frame is properly installed. This view is just to show how the tool engages the front of the hammer spring plunger inside the gun.

Another Mauser Malady

Another "ailment" of the Mauser C96 is not a mechanical thing, but a result of over-zealous enforcement in past years by a certain government agency. At one time, it was routine to weld up the stock attachment slot on Mauser pistols, and many fine collector pieces were defaced during that time. Some Lugers were similarly damaged, and I even remember seeing one beautiful Borchardt with the stock attachment lug crudely ground off. Viewing atrocities of this sort has been known to move grown men to tears. In these more enlightened times, collector pistols with detachable stocks are legally permitted, as long as the stock is of the type originally supplied with the gun. Fortunately, some of the stock attachment systems can be restored, if the welding was not too enthusiastic.

10. I have seen Mauser stock slots that were entirely filled with weld. This one, by comparison, was not so bad, but the side rails were melted in the vicinity of the weld.

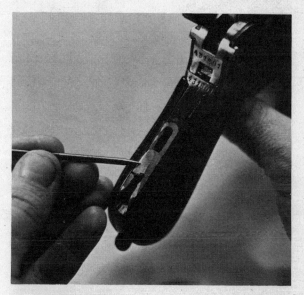

11. The first step in restoring the slot was to use a disc in the Dremel tool to cut a vertical slit on each side, aligned with the edges of the slot, and extending to the floor of the slot. After this, the disc can be used to remove the central block between the slits, if necessary. I had a bit of luck with the one shown. I set a small chisel against the lower rear edge of the block, tapped it with a hammer, and the block snapped cleanly out. It's worth a try.

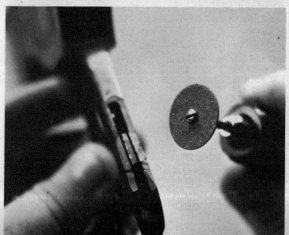

12. After removal of the center portion of the weld, a file is used to level the sides and the floor of the stock slot.

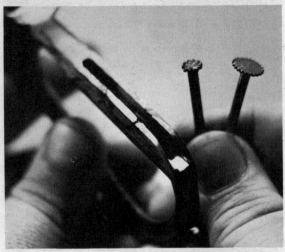

13. To recut the side rails of the stock slot, the *best* way would be to make or obtain a tool that exactly matches the interior dimensions of the slot, set the frame in a milling rig, and make one pass up the slot. Lacking this equipment, you can do as I did. I altered a small Dremel cutter to a diameter that would enter the slot, and recut some teeth on its edge. It was then heated and oil-hardened. An unaltered Dremel #199 cutter is shown on the right.

14. As much as possible, an angled cutting disc in the Dremel was used to cut away some of the weld below the rail. The shop-made milling tool was then used, in multiple passes, to recut the area under the rail in the area of the weld. Care must be taken to avoid cutting into the rail itself. The inside corners can't be perfectly squared with the tool, but most of the weld can be removed.

15. Final shaping of the interior of the slot must be done with a small square file. The one shown was ideal for the job, as its broken-off tip was exactly the right width, fitting the space beneath the rail. At this point, the stock should be tried frequently in the slot, between filings.

16. After the slot is fitted to the stock attachment piece, the surface is polished and finished with chemical blue. If the gun is a collector piece, and not just a shooter, any gaps or bubbles in the original weld can be filled by careful welding, and recut to shape.

17. Another old Mauser is restored to pistol-carbine status.

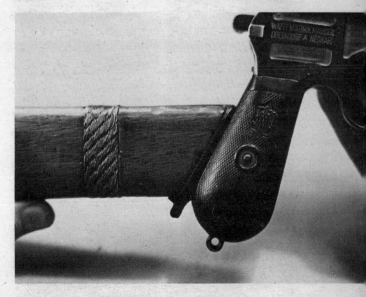

Crowning Muzzles

When a barrel is shortened for any reason, finishing of the muzzle will depend on the type of gun, and on the preference of the shooter. With shotguns, a simple levelling of the front surface and chamfering of the edges is usually all that needs to be done. On rifles, pistols, and revolvers, a bit more work is required. When the barrel is removable, and can be mounted in a lathe, a nice rounded surface can be achieved. Even in lathe-equipped shops, though, the shape of some barrels can make this difficult, or impossible. The alternative is to do the crowning by hand. This is one of those jobs that is easily done if you're careful, and just as easily messed up if you're not.

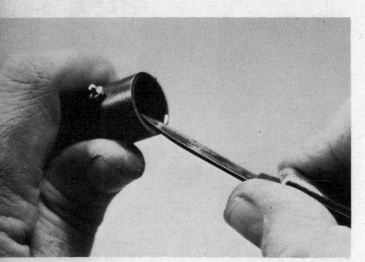

1. Initial inside chamfering of a shotgun barrel can be done neatly with a good knife blade. With the exception of certain chrome-lined tubes, shotgun barrels are of fairly soft steel, and sharp edges can easily be angled with a knife. When doing this, take care to keep the blade edge at an even angle, and keep it from digging in. The outer edge is rounded with a fine file, and both inner and outer edges are then polished with emery paper.

2. On pistol, rifle, or revolver barrels, a simple bevel can be accomplished with an ordinary counter-sink tool, but *only* if the drill in which it is used is a variable-speed type, and *only* if the user has a steady hand. If high speed is used, and if the tool and barrel are not firmly held, the counter-sink will "chatter" and the cut will not be symmetrical. Unless you are really skilled in its use, the counter-sink should be the very last choice for crowning.

3. No matter what tool is used, the advice in regard to holding the barrel and tool firmly applies. For hand crowning, a ball-shaped stone in the Dremel is best. With the stone, the speed requirement is reversed. A slow setting will be more likely to chatter. Use a relatively high speed, and a quick and light touch. The stone can remove a lot of material in a very short time, so use it sparingly. Centrifugal force will tend to pull it to one side, and this must be compensated for. For anyone doing this for the first time, it would be a good idea to practice first on the piece of cut-off barrel.

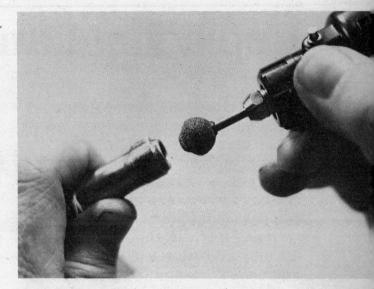

4. After the inner edges are chamfered (bevelled) to the extent desired, punch a hole in a square of emery cloth or emery paper, and attach it to a disc mandrel, as shown. When pressed lightly into the muzzle, the emery will depress at its center, and will polish the inner edges bright. Use it lightly — too much pressure will cause it to wrinkle, and this will make it cut unevenly.

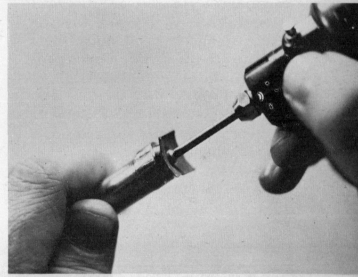

5. Here is the finished crowning. The outer edges have been carefully rounded with a fine file. A final polish for the front face of the muzzle can be done by laying a sheet of emery paper on the workbench, and moving the muzzle in a circle on it. Take care to keep it level.

Replacing Lanyard Rings

Lanyard rings have been a feature of many military handguns for more than a century, especially in Europe, and they were found on many police and commercial civilian handguns as well. When the gun passed into the hands of the average American shooter, though, the lanyard ring was usually the first casualty of "customizing." In its original role, the lanyard ring made a lot of sense. With a cord or strap attached, and its other end either attached to the belt or looped through the jacket epaulet, the handgun would not be lost even if the user fell off his horse. Some military regulations still require a lanyard ring and cord. Not a bad idea, really.

Getting back to the problem, collectors are most unhappy when anything original to a gun is missing, and many otherwise fine pieces will often have absent lanyard rings. In most cases, replacements will not be readily available, so they have to be made. If the ring is a heavy circular type, production of a replacement will be a medium-difficult job. When it's not actually a ring, but a loop of general "U" shape, it will be fairly easy to make. I'm going to show both types here. For the true circular ring, the example is a Mauser C96 pistol. The loop-type is represented by a French-Contract Savage Model 1907 pistol.

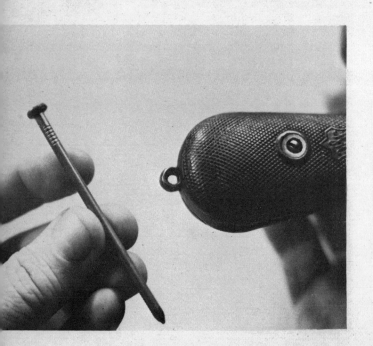

1. In making a replacement ring for the Mauser, a nail was selected that had a diameter nearly the size of the hole in the pistol's ring loop. A common nail is ideal for this purpose, because it can be easily worked and bent cold. It should be noted that some nails are harder than others, and it might be well to "test bend" a spare nail from the same lot before the job is started.

2. Not having a Mauser with ring on hand when this work was done, I used photos to determine the approximate size of the ring. The next step was to bend an ordinary paper clip into a ring of the same comparative diameter, as shown.

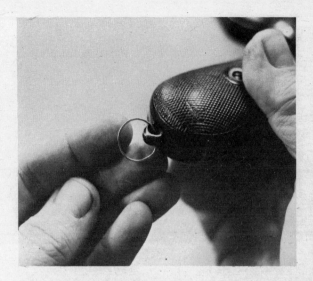

3. The paper clip ring is then unrolled into a straight piece, and the piece is used to measure and mark a section cut from the nail. To compensate for the difference in the diameter of the materials, a small extra allowance is made in length—from about 1/16" to 1/8". Though the nail section is marked for length here, it is not cut off at this point.

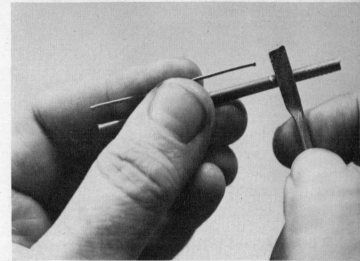

4. Inserted in a drill up to the length mark, the section is now reduced with a file, until its diameter is a loose fit in the ring mount on the pistol. After this is done, the section is cut off at the mark.

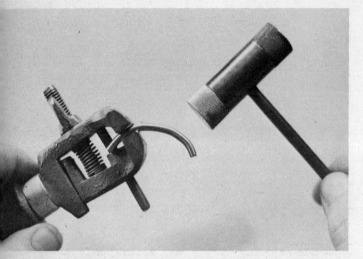

5. In a small bench or a hand vise, the section is cold-shaped with a hammer into a circular shape. Make the initial bends at each end first, then move the piece up through the vise in very small increments. This is very important, as too great a movement will produce a hexagon or an octagon, not a circle.

6. Here is the finished ring, ready to be blued and installed. Note that it is left open, to be closed during installation.

7. The finished loop is gripped with leather pads in a pair of channel-lock pliers, positioned on the mounting loop on the handle, and closed. If the closing alters its true circular shape, it can be adjusted with the pliers, but care must be taken to avoid any stress on the loop.

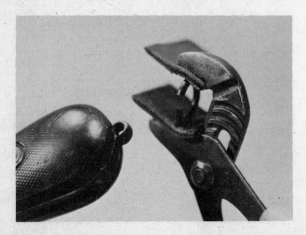

8. Making the "U-loop" for the Savage begins the same way, with a paper clip bent into the approximate shape of the loop. The clip is then opened, to determine the length of rod stock needed. In the case of the Savage loop, cold-rolled rod stock was on hand in the exact size needed. It was also pre-blued, so no finishing was necessary. Because of its smaller diameter, shaping could be done with pliers. The two right-angle ends were formed first, in a vise.

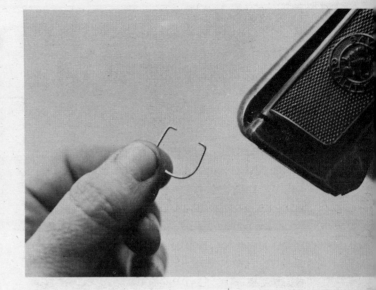

9. Here is the finished loop, ready for installation. Unlike the circular ring, it is not installed by closing it on the gun. Instead, one pivot-tip is inserted in its hole, and pliers are used to carefully lift the other side into place. The natural "spring" of the steel will snug it in place.

10. The Savage loop is shown in place on the gun. As with the Mauser ring, photos of the French contract Savage were used to determine the length and diameter of the loop. Nearly all movable rings or loops on other guns can be duplicated by one of the methods shown here.

Cleaning-Up Deformed Screw Heads

Sometimes, it's just the result of an original over-tightening, or from being rusted in place, and extreme force had to be used during removal. Most of the time, though, it's simply a matter of an inept practitioner using the wrong screwdriver. The effect is the same—a damaged screw slot. You will often see this on guns that are otherwise in good condition, and aside from being esthetically unpleasing, it can also cause a reduction in the value of the gun. If the damage hasn't gone too far, it's possible to rework the screw heads. This process will lower the head a little, in relation to the surrounding area, but even so, this will look better than the gouged edges that were there.

1. Here is a typical deformed screw head. In this case, it appears that general wear was as much a factor as the use of a screwdriver of improper dimensions.

2. The first step is to deepen the screw slot. If this is not done, the reworking of the head will leave the slot too shallow, and this will lead to future deformation, wiping out your work. Shown is a special screw-slot file by F. Dick, but deepening the slot can also be done with a small metal saw, or, on larger screws, with a regular hacksaw. If a saw is used, though, note that it will cut faster than a file. Take care not to go too far.

3. With the screw in a drill chuck, use a file to shape the head. Be sure to remove only enough steel to give a clean, unburred surface. Use a fine file, and if the sides of the head are worked, use very light pressure there. Heavy pressure will cause cutting to be more pronounced at the slot ends, and you'll have an oval screw head.

4. When doing the final polishing of the head, *don't* just hold a piece of emery cloth or paper against the head with a fingertip. This will cause a rounding of the slot edges. Instead, staple the emery to a piece of wood, as shown, and this will keep the edges sharp.

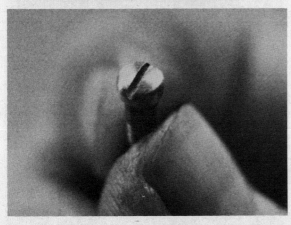

5. Yes, this is really the same screw, and the height of its head has been reduced very little. It can now be blued with cold chemical, or, as I always do on parts of this size, by the torch-and-oil method.

Shaping Screwdriver Blades

As any gunsmith knows, regular "hardware store" screwdrivers have blades, or tips, that are totally wrong for firearms use. Even those that are specifically designed for gunsmithing, such as the hollow-ground tips of the Brownells and Chapman sets, will have to be altered occasionally to fit certain screw slots.

2. The interchangeable blades of the Brownells Magna-Tip screwdriver are hollow-ground, to better fit the square slots of gun screws but even these must sometimes be mated to narrower slots.

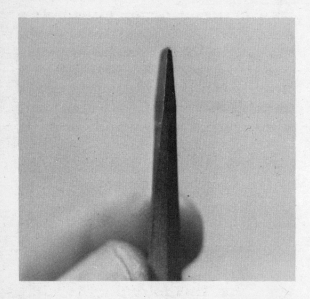

1. Here is a typical "regular" screwdriver. Its V-shaped blade is all right for carpentry or machinery use, but it will quickly deform the slots of gun screws.

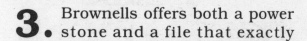

3. Brownells offers both a power stone and a file that exactly

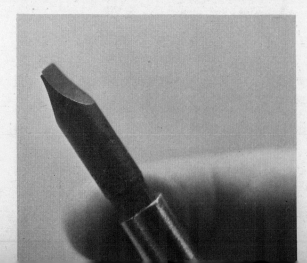

match the hollow-ground curve of the Magna-Tip blades. This one was altered with the file, to fit a narrow slot.

4. B-Square has a neat tool called the "Blade Maker" for hollow-grinding any screwdriver. The smaller block is clamped to the shield-table of any powered grindstone, and the screwdriver shaft is secured in the other block with an Allen screw. The block holds the blade at the proper angle, and it can be moved across on the spindle to keep the edge even.

5. Most of the screwdrivers on my workbench have been either square-cut, like the one shown, or "hollow ground" with a file. The only difficult thing about this operation is keeping the two sides of the blade even as the cut is made. As the file is moved across the blade, it must be kept level, or the finished tip will have an angle.

6. Here are two more file-altered blades, cut to fit screws on particular guns. Before alteration, both of these were regular V-tip screwdrivers.

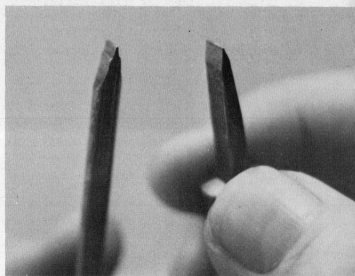

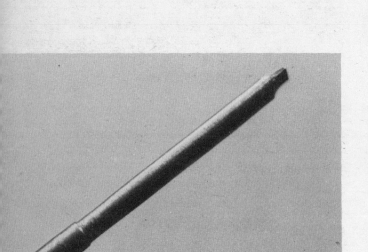

7. Here is an example of a very specialized alteration. On the Winchester Model 1890 rifle, the trigger spring is retained by a vertical screw inside the lower tang of the lower receiver. When a filler screw is removed from the upper tang, this rebated blade tip can be inserted to reach down to the screw. Many other special variations in shape are possible, including tips cut at an angle to reach screws that would be otherwise very difficult to manipulate.

Tuning-Up the F&W 1887 Revolver

In the day of the top-break revolver, the 1880 to 1900 period, four makers dominated the market: Smith & Wesson, Harrington & Richardson, Iver Johnson, and Forehand & Wadsworth. The partners, Sullivan Forehand and Henry C. Wadsworth, were sons-in-law of famous gunmaker Ethan Allen, and their firm was the successor to the Ethan Allen Arms Company. The F & W revolver of

1887 had one feature that made it unlike the others of its time—a rebounding hammer. This is accomplished by the use of a V-type mainspring, its lower arm powering the cylinder hand and trigger, and having a front edge that cams the hammer back a short distance when the trigger is released. During its production life, a few small mechanical changes were made. The points that are covered here refer to the early-production guns.

1. Here is a typical Forehand & Wadsworth revolver. This model was made as a six-shot 32-caliber or a five-shot 38.

2. The F & W has a separate, in-the-frame firing pin, retained by a screw-in-cup-retainer at the rear. When the retainer is lost or damaged, its small size makes reproduction more difficult than the simple front-mounted type, as used on the Iver Johnson revolver. I repair these by cross-drilling the frame and installing a pin at the location shown, to pass through the rear of the firing pin well at just the right point to contact the collar of the firing pin. The head of the firing pin protrudes above the cross-pin, and the cross-pin serves the same purpose as the original retaining cup.

3. When the barrel latch is loose, the best method of tightening is to drill a small hole in the rear face of each latch lug on the frame, and install pins which are then filed off until the latch will close.

4. Originally, the cylinder was retained on its arbor by a small spring-steel catch on the left side, having a hook which engaged a groove inside the cylinder nipple. The catch has a rectangular serrated button as a release, and the catch frequently breaks off just forward of the button. The catch is keyed into the cylinder arbor at the front, so it's necessary to drive out a cross-pin and remove the arbor for replacement of the catch. When pulling out the arbor, take care that it isn't deformed or otherwise damaged. The replacement catch shown was made from flat spring stock, cold-formed. It has no release button, but it is easily released by inserting a tool to push it inward.

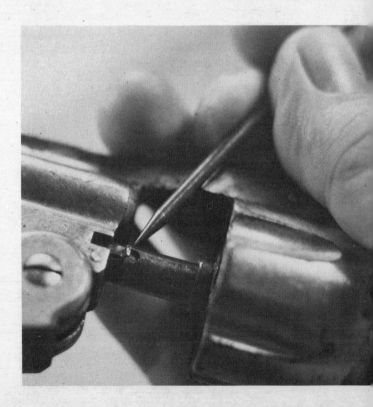

5. In the early guns, the barrel latch was powered by a curved flat spring, retained in a recess on the underside of the barrel extension by a vertical screw. If this screw is rusted in so completely that normal methods of extraction don't work, drilling it out may be the only answer. Since the gun shown was not a collector piece, the extension was drilled through, to allow more thread depth for the replacement screw. Its tip is then faced off level with the top, as shown.

6. When the flat barrel latch spring breaks, it can be replaced with one cold-formed of round spring wire, like the one shown here. The screw shown here is also a replacement.

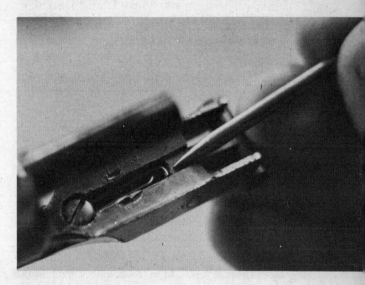

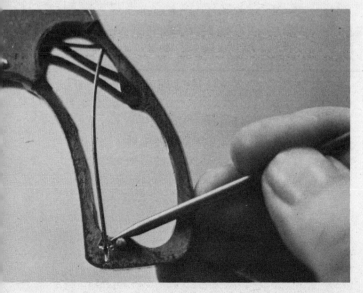

7. A common breakage is the vertical extension at the front of the lower arm of the mainspring, the part that contacts a shelf on the cylinder hand to power the hand and the trigger. In the repair shown, the extension has been replaced by a separate round-wire spring, anchored by staking in a slot at the bottom of the grip frame. With this repair, it is necessary to cancel the hammer rebound by cutting off the front tip of the lower arm of the mainspring, where it contacts the lower rear of the hammer. When the barrel and cylinder assembly is closed after loading, the cylinder must be turned to position the firing pin between two rounds.

8. Without the lower arm extension resting in the shelf of the cylinder hand, the mainspring won't have enough tension to properly power the hammer, so the frame is drilled and tapped just behind the guard for a headless screw, its inner tip bearing on the underside of the lower arm of the mainspring.

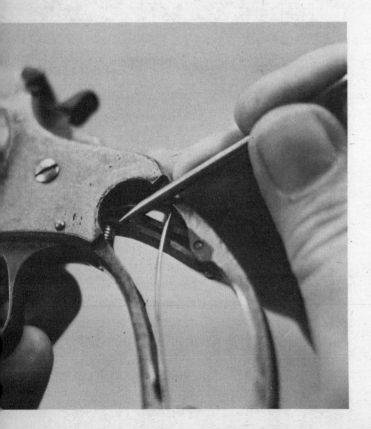

9. Here is another view of the added mainspring tension screw. It should be noted that this method will work only on a gun in which the lower arm has been cut off, and the hammer rebound cancelled. The gun shown here, which has had all of the alterations described above, works perfectly.

Tuning-Up the Hi-Standard Model HD Pistol

This may be a good place to clear up, once and for all, the confusion about the spelling of the company name and the brand name used on the guns. The company, when it was located in New Haven, was the High Standard Manufacturing Co., and later, in Hamden, Connecticut, the High Standard Manufacturing Corporation. Today, in East Hartford, the name is High Standard Sporting Firearms. Through all of this time, the name used on the guns has been "HI-STANDARD." So: When referring to the company, it's "High Standard." When a particular gun is mentioned, it's "Hi-Standard."

The Model H-D (sometimes with, sometimes without the hyphen) also has its share of name confusion. I have seen three different slide markings: "U.S.A. Model H-D," "Model HD - Military," and simply, "Model H-D." Very early Model HD pistols do not have the manual safety lever on the left rear of the frame, but otherwise the guns are all mechanically the same, and all have an external hammer. The gun shown here is a Model HD that was made for U.S. military use, and it carries a "U.S. Property" marking on the opposite side. Incidentally, all of these World War II-era guns were sold as surplus, so

there's no need for the marking to make anyone nervous. (Unless, of course, you know the gun was "liberated" while they were still in use!)

1. Mechanically, the main problem with the Model HD involves user error, and the takedown lever, located on the right side of the frame just to the rear of the grip panel. When this lever is turned downward at any time other than at the proper point in the takedown sequence, it can cause problems ranging from takedown difficulty to actual damage. The lever is shown (arrow) in its correct position.

It must *never* be turned downward unless the preliminary takedown steps have been completed. For those who are not familiar with this sequence, I'll describe it later.

Getting back to the effect of turning the lever down "out-of-order," here are some of the things that can happen: If the slide is operated or the gun fired after the lever is turned, the recoil spring will be deformed and probably crushed, and the slide retainer (factory name: "slide stop") will likely be broken. In any event, completion of takedown and the necessary repairs will probably be beyond the capabilities of the average non-gunsmith.

2. The slide retainer, or "stop," is shown here (arrow) in its original form. The taller pointed projection on its left side contacts the recoil spring guide, and the rest of the part serves as a slide retaining lug. When the takedown lever is operated, this part pivots forward and downward.

3. The tool indicates the slide retainer plunger, which is powered by a coil spring in the frame. The retainer has a recess for the head of the plunger, and this is located at the base of the spring contact extension, right where extra strength is needed. Breakage at that point is not uncommon.

4. Here is a shop-made replacement (arrow) for a broken slide retainer. Note that it is heavier in all dimensions than the original type. Also, the original plunger and spring are left out, and the left pivot-loop at the bottom of the retainer is thinned to allow the use of a round-wire torsion-type spring. This not only makes the retainer stronger, it allows it to be turned down more easily when the lever is operated.

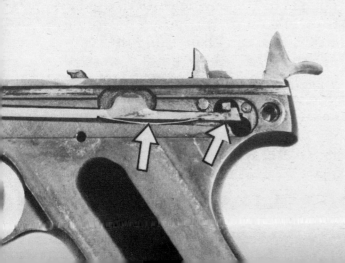

5. There are a few flat springs in the Model HD. The one that powers the trigger bar/disconnector (left arrow) is a simple curved piece of flat spring stock, and is easy to reproduce. The sear hook at the rear tip of the trigger bar (right arrow) occasionally breaks, as does the sear arm that it contacts. In either case, repair will require welding or making an entire new part.

6. Another flat spring powers the slide latch (arrow), and this one is also easy to make. The latch and its attached spring are held in their recess only by the right grip panel, and can be lost when the grip is removed.

7. And now, the proper slide-removal sequence: With the magazine removed, draw the slide all the way to the rear, hold it there, and push down the recoil spring lock button, indicated here by the pointed tool. While holding the button firmly down, ease the slide forward. The recoil spring should be trapped, and there should be no spring tension on the slide. After this is done, don't pull the slide all the way to the rear again, or the spring will be released and re-engaged with its base arm on the retainer.

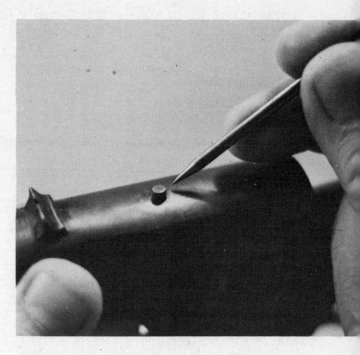

8. With the recoil spring locked out of operation, move the slide all the way forward, and turn the takedown lever on the right side of the frame to its full down position. Hold it there, and move the slide off the frame toward the rear. Depressing the hammer past its full-cock position will make this easier. When replacing the slide, depress the hammer and operate the lever again. Release the lever, pull back the slide until it stops, and the spring will automatically re-engage.

Repairing a Lever-Lock Roller

1. & 2. The Stevens "Crack Shot" rifle was the last of the "boy's rifles" made by that firm in the years before World War II, and its factory designation was "Number 26." So there's no confusion, it should be pointed out that in recent years, the Savage company marketed a modern gun with the "Crack Shot" name, but this one was actually a re-

creation of the old Stevens Favorite, an entirely different gun.

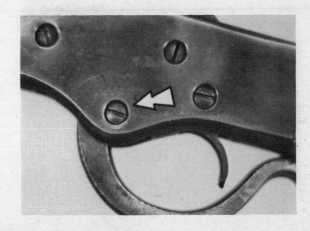

3. When the lever is closed, an inside shoulder locks over a roller which is retained by a large cross-screw (arrow) and which is subject to wear and deformation after long use.

4. The lever lock roller (arrow) is subject to wear and deformation after long use.

5. The upper rear shoulder (arrow) of the lock roller recess in the lever tends to wear. The lever is quite hard, and peening the edge to tighten the lock is risky. The proper repair is to make a new roller, very slightly oversize, to compensate for the wear. This is done by drilling a center hole through a piece of drill rod for the screw passage, then turn its outer diameter down until the lever recess will just snap over it. This is definitely a fit-and-try operation.

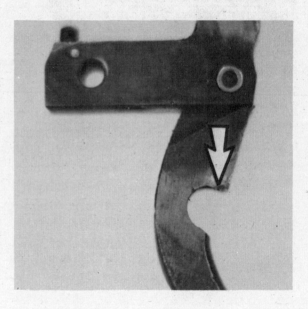

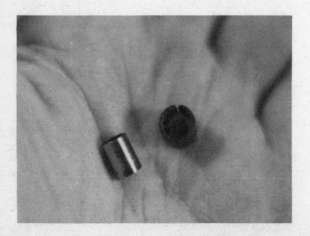

6. Once, when I had a Crack Shot in for repair, I found that I was out of drill rod in the proper size. So, I improvised with a two-piece roller. The smaller inner roller was made from a section of auto pistol striker, and the outer piece is a short length of large roll pin. This combination happened to work perfectly, and there's no reason why it shouldn't be as durable as a solid roller.

The Noble Parts Problem Solved

Prior to its demise in 1972, the Noble company had made a large quantity of shotguns, especially their slide-action, of which the Model 60 is typical. Many of these guns are still in use, and one of their principal ailments is breakage of the forward extension of the connector that joins the bolt to the action slide bar. Original Noble parts are entirely unavailable, except for an occasional gun bought by the used-parts dealers. Even if both pieces of the broken connector are saved, rejoining them by welding is not usually a satisfactory repair, because of the heavy stress on this part and the need for over-all hardening.

In 1973, Smith & Wesson bought the basic design of the Noble gun, and introduced it as their Model 916. Some internal changes were made, however, and the parts for the 916 will not always interchange. In the case of the connector (S & W calls it the "bolt slide"), one of the two bolt contact lugs on its inner face was eliminated. Otherwise, though, the part is dimensionally compatible with the mechanism of the original Noble guns. Here's how to alter the S&W part to make it work in the Noble gun.

1. A new Smith & Wesson connector is shown at the top, a broken Noble original below. Note the small extra lug at the rear (left) edge of the Noble part.

2. The Smith & Wesson connector is drilled at its rear corner to accept a small stud made from drill rod. The stud's diameter should be large enough to slightly overhang the edge. Note that the hole is chamfered, to allow riveting (or peening) of the shaft of the stud when it is installed.

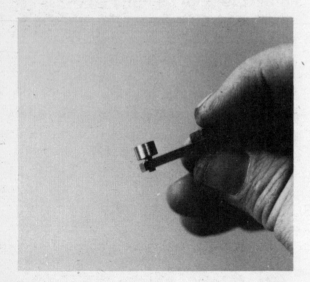

3. The stud is shown inserted through the hole, but not yet tapped into place.

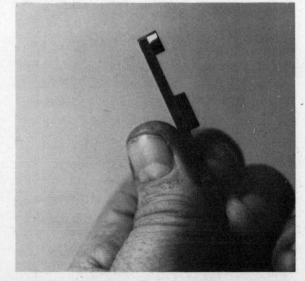

4. Seated firmly against the connector, the stud shaft end is peened into the chamfered area on the other side, then faced off with a file, if necessary.

5. The stud (arrow) is now shaped at the rear to conform to the rear edge of the connector, and its other faces made to properly engage the bolt. I've found that the lug does not have to exactly match the length or shape of the original Noble part.

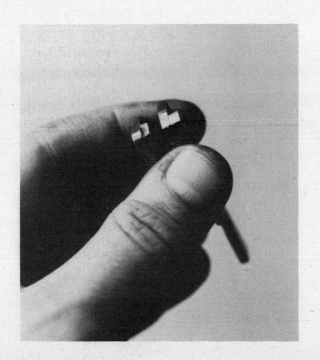

6. Finished, the Smith & Wesson-altered connector (on the right) is ready to install in the Noble shotgun. If good quality drill rod is used, no heat treatment is necessary.

Keeping the Carbine Going

Chambered for the equivalent of a high-powered pistol cartridge, the M-1 Carbine is one of those guns which has produced two widely-divergent schools of thought: Those shooters who like it say it's one of the neatest, handiest little guns ever made; those who sneer at it say it's useless for any practical purpose, especially in sporting use. Well, there's one non-military area where you'll get no argument: law enforcement. Many ex-army Carbines, and those of current manufacture by Plainfield (Iver Johnson) and Universal are in use by county and city police forces today. Personally, I think the Carbine has certain sporting applications, too. One fact is indisputable: There are a lot of them out there, and that's why I'm including the gun here.

1. The short-stroke gas piston of the Carbine is retained by a three-lug nut (two lugs in some commercial versions), and free movement of the piston is essential. If the bolt is failing to make full travel when the gun is fired, check this first. As with all gas-operated systems, be sure that there is no heavy build-up of gas scale on the piston or inside its mount on the barrel. Check to see that there are no burrs on the piston or on the inside of the nut (a slightly bent or burred nut lug can cause binding). Never use oil or grease in the vicinity of the gas piston or its housing.

2. When cleaning scale from the gas system, remember to see that the port is clear. An angled access hole in the housing allows a tool to reach the port. In most carbines, a number 46 drill (.0810″) or a number 45 (.0820″) will come closest to matching the original port size.

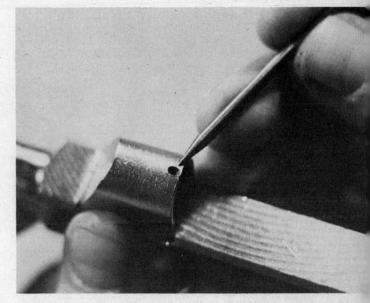

3. Never use a powered drill to turn the drill bit in the port. If the bit should catch and break off, you would have an interesting problem. Also, there is the chance of the tip going too far, and damaging the rifling. A pin vise or a tap wrench, turned by hand, is the best way. Some Carbines with a sensitivity to varying loads may benefit from a slight enlargement of the gas port size. It's not advisable, though, to go further than one drill size (#44 / .0860″) in enlargement.

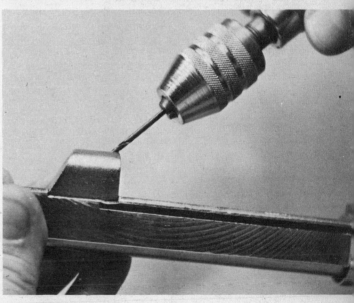

4. The Carbine has a "double-feed" magazine. That is, its double-column of cartridges feeds alternately from the left and right side of the feed lips. On most guns, the feed ramp in the receiver has the shape of a flat-bottomed "U". Carbine owners tend to have a number of spare magazines, and there is enough variation in their dimensions and feed surfaces that the standard ramp will occasionally cause a problem.

5. To be sure the ramp will function properly with almost any magazine, its rear side edges are slanted outward, with care taken not to alter the upper or front portion of the ramp. After shaping with a rotary stone and power tool, the ramp is polished and its rear edges are rounded.

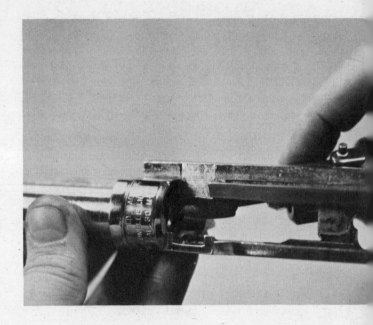

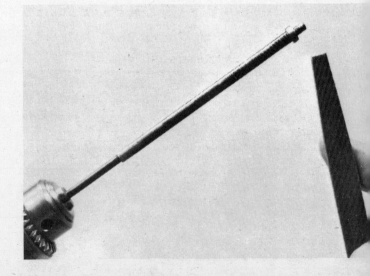

6. Here is the altered feed ramp, after shaping, ready to be polished. During shaping, care must be taken when working near the top of the ramp sides, to avoid damage to the bolt rails just above.

7. There is one small Carbine ailment that causes no operational problem, but makes disassembly and reassembly difficult: The collar at the front of the recoil spring guide may peen at its edges after long use, and this will result in insufficient clearance when the guide and spring are removed or replaced. It's a simple matter to chuck the guide in a drill and touch its edge with a file, and this will cure the problem.

Savage/Stevens 87-Series Rifles

It was difficult to pick a sub-title designation for this rifle, because one that listed all of its model variations would take nearly a third of a page. I won't try to list every one, but slight variations of this basic design were made as the Savage Model 6, Model 7, and Models 60 and 90. In the Stevens and Springfield line, the models were the familiar 87, 88, 85, 57, 388, 187, and 850. All of these were also made in several sub-models, with suffix letters from A through N. Among these models and sub-models, the main variations were in the feed system and the safety location.

Over the years, the two versions that I've seen the most have been the Model 87 and Model 187 in the Stevens line. These are the guns covered here, but their firing mechanism is so similar to all of the others that much of the information can be used on those as well. One characteristic that is constant is the unusual disconnector system used in this design. When the gun is fired, the bolt opens and ejects the fired case, and remains in the open position until the trigger is released. Only then does it run forward to chamber the next round. On some versions, the bolt handle can be pushed in to lock the bolt in forward position, allowing the gun to be used as a manually-operated repeater, rather than a semi-auto.

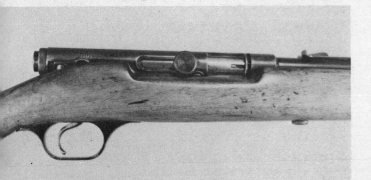

1. This is a typical Model 87A, with tubular-magazine feed. Some versions of the basic design were made with a detachable box magazine. But these were produced in lesser quantities.

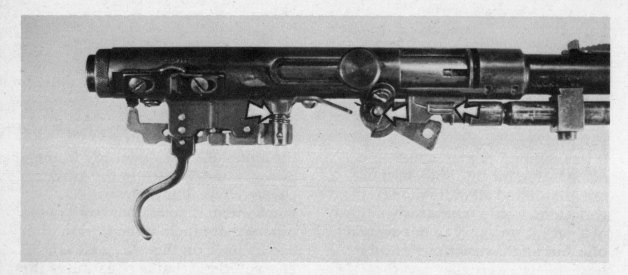

2. Here is the 87A out of its stock, showing the firing and feed mechanisms. The left arrow indicates the disconnector and its spring, the center arrow the lifter spring, and the arrow at the right points to the cartridge guide spring. The external disconnector spring also powers the trigger return, and its internal spring allows its depression by the recoiling bolt. Weakness of either of these can cause "double-firing" and jamming.

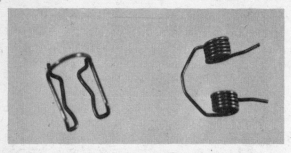

3. The cartridge guide spring is at the left, and the other one powers the cartridge lifter. Fortunately, in case of weakness or breakage, both can be made in the shop without great difficulty. Unfortunately, both can be easily installed backwards, and they often are.

4. The two bolt-contact lobes at the rear of the cartridge lifter and the small hump at its upper front are essential to proper feeding. When they become worn, as on the lower one shown, it's time for a replacement. It should be pointed out that the design of this part was changed at least once during the years of production, so be sure that the shape matches the one being replaced. The two shown are from the Model 87A.

5. The ejector (arrow) is an integral part of the cartridge feed housing. If it breaks off, replacement of the entire housing is the only remedy, as this part is made of formed sheet steel, and there is no feasible way to add steel to it by welding. Unfortunately, this early 87-type feed housing is not easily found.

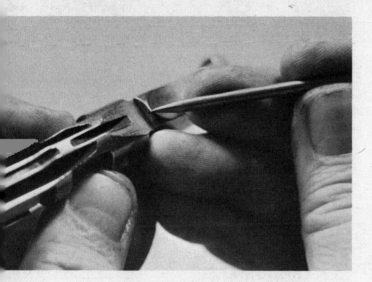

6. The bolt is usually quite hard, but extreme wear may require recutting of the disconnector step (shown), and/or the beak of the disconnector, to restore positive engagement.

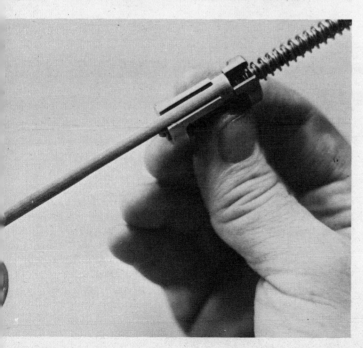

7. Early versions of these guns had a firing pin and hammer, or striker, like the ones shown here. The firing pin occasionally fractured at the attaching "T", at the rear. The later firing pin, more easily obtained, will work in the early guns, but only if the striker is also replaced. If both parts of the broken firing pin are present, the crosspiece can be rejoined with silver solder or weld, and this repair will last for some time.

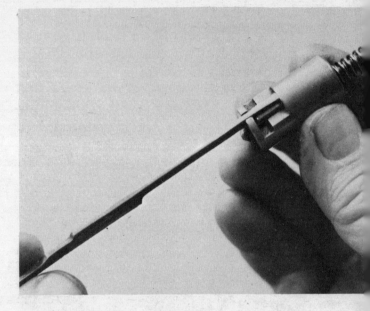

8. Here is the later firing pin and striker assembly. These tend to break at the same location, at the attachment tip in the rear. Of thinner stock, they do not sustain repair as well. However, they are generally available from most parts sources.

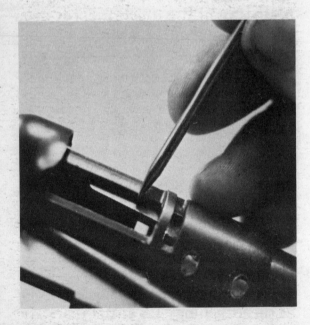

9. Just above the chamber, there is a sloping block powered by a small coil spring in the roof of the receiver, and this serves as an upper cartridge guide. The guide block seldom breaks, but the spring occasionally will weaken or be deformed during amateur disassembly. The little spring can be replaced with any small

coil of suitable tension, but installation is quite a job. It requires driving out the two crosspins that retain the barrel and removing the barrel from the receiver. Then, when reassembling, the spring must be kept depressed as the barrel is moved back, or it will be ruined.

A final note on the 87/187-series guns: Late extractors are the "saddle" type, fitting onto the bolt like a pencil-clip. These are still readily obtainable. Older guns will have separate extractors, right and left, with separate plungers and coil springs. Since these have become difficult to find, it is worth noting that the bevel-ended left extractor can be recut, if necessary, to a beak shape, and used on the right side. Note also that the left extractor, as originally installed, has a lighter spring than the one on the right.

Barrel Cutting

There are many reasons for shortening barrels. Sometimes it's made necessary by damage, as when a shotgun barrel is split or bulged near the muzzle. Or, in any gun, there may be a bend or other deformation in some forward location, so that taking off a few inches would still leave the total at a legal and usable length. Speaking of that factor, let's put it in here for reference: Rifles must be over 16″ and for shotguns the magic number is 18″. The proper legal measurement is taken by inserting a rod down the bore, with the breech closed, and measuring the length of the rod at the muzzle. Whenever I'm asked to cut a gun back to the minimum, I always make them a ¼″ over the limit, just to be safe.

When a gun has a barrel rib, or when there are elaborate front sights to be re-installed, cutting off the barrel can get fairly complicated and difficult. Double barrel shotguns are particularly tricky, as the exposed space between the barrels must be filled with solder, without loosening the original solder that holds barrels, top rib, and under-rib together. Here, though, we will look at a good method of cutting off a simple round barrel. In the example shown, the gun was a military rifle being sporterized for hunting.

1. First, determine the original length, by the rod-down-the-bore method, and decide the length you want the barrel to be. Then, measure back from the muzzle, and use a knife-edge file to mark the barrel at that point. Allow about ¹⁄₁₆″ (toward the muzzle) when you mark the point, to compensate for the width of the saw blade, and the finishing adjustment. I usually mark the point three times, at equidistant locations around the barrel, measuring separately for each one.

2. Using the file marks as a reference, wrap the barrel with glass-fiber tape, keeping the marks just visible at the forward edge of the tape. Take care to keep the tape absolutely even in relation to the marks. About four layers of tape should be sufficient. The tape not only serves as a cutting guide, it also protects the finish at the new muzzle. If the gun is not to be refinished after cutting, this is important.

3. Before using the saw, deepen one of the marks with a knife-edge file. This will give the saw a starting groove, and make it less likely to jump out before the slot is sufficiently deep to hold it.

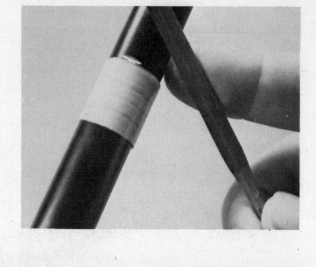

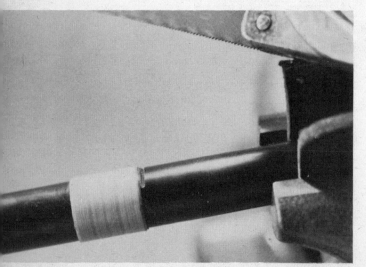

4. Even though it will slow the work, use a fine-toothed saw. It will make a smoother cut, and lessen the amount of smoothing that must be done with a file after cutting. Make the initial cut shallow—*don't* cut through into the bore. Hold the barrel in a leather-padded vise.

5. When a perceptible slot has been made, loosen the vise and turn the barrel a small amount. Using the initial slot as a guide (and the edge of the tape, of course), saw at a new angle. Keep turning the barrel as each cut is made, until the slot completely encircles it, and is of a uniform depth that almost reaches the bore. Then, go ahead and saw through.

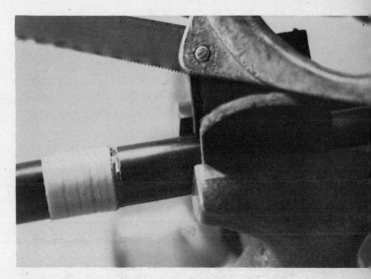

6. When the cut is completed, *don't* remove the tape. It can now serve as a guide for perfect levelling of the muzzle. At this point, before filing the muzzle, insert a ball of cotton into the bore, pushing it down about a ½". This will keep steel filings from falling down the bore and getting into the action, and will obviate the necessity of a complete cleaning after the work is done. When filing the muzzle, rotate it frequently, just as during the cutting, and level all of the edge to the tape.

7. The crowning and finishing operation is described elsewhere in this book, so I won't repeat it here. The finished muzzle is shown. It can now be cold-blued, or, as some prefer, left bright.

Renewing Worn Revolver Actions

The Webley was a random choice here, as both of the things shown can be applied to any double action revolver having a similar mechanism. Except for occasional breakage of its flat V-type springs that power the hammer and barrel latch, the Webley is practically indestructible. The discontinuance this year (1982) of the 38-cal. Mark IV is cause for lament, as this was one of the finest revolver designs ever made.

1. In military service, many of the older guns received long, hard use, and some wear of the sear extension on the trigger and the sear step on the hammer is inevitable. When this is severe, it can allow the rear extension of the trigger to slip off when the hammer is drawn fully back. It would be possible, of course, to add steel weld to the mating surfaces and recut them to shape, but this would require re-hardening afterward. A quick and simple cure for this problem is to drill a small angled hole in the top of the frame at the rear of the hammer slot, and drive a small tapered pin into the hole. The pin is then cut off at a point that will cause it to stop the hammer at the precise location of full-cock engagement. This prevents it from travelling far enough for the trigger slip-off to occur. The pin is not obtrusive, and otherwise has no effect on the operation of the gun.

2. Another location where extreme wear can cause a problem is the rebound lobe, at the lower rear of the hammer. The symptom here is that when the trigger is released, the hammer does not move fully back to its rebound position, and the firing pin will protrude slightly at the breech face, a very unhealthy condition. To correct this, the rear face of the lobe is marked with a punch at the location indicated, and a small blind hole is drilled at that point.

3. A small "insert pad" with a tapered shaft is made, to be driven into the hole in the rebound lobe. Shown here is the insert after shaping, and the drilled lobe. Depending on the size of the "pad" portion, one or more of the edges may have to be cut straight during installation.

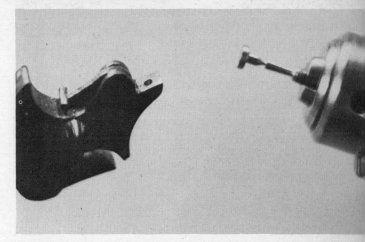

4. The insert pad has been installed here, but the rebound fitting has not yet been made. If the tapering of the shaft has been done properly, just driving it into place will retain the insert.

5. When fitting the pad to the rebound system, install the hammer and rebound lever in the gun frequently, filing the pad until the lever acting on it tips the hammer to its proper rebound position. With the lever pressed down, and the trigger forward, the firing pin should be well inside its aperture in the breech face. On the pad shown here, this adjustment has been done.

6. With the hammer re-installed, and all other parts in place, the rebound is now at the correct position. This will vary in different guns, and must be determined in each separate case.

Solving Solid-Frame Revolver Problems

The solid-frame revolver shown is a "U.S." brand, made by Iver Johnson in the 1875-1910 period. It is a cheaper counterpart of an almost identical but better finished gun also made by Iver Johnson, but under their own name. A slightly different version was made until

1947. The basic design is typical of several guns by other makers, having a removable base pin that allows the cylinder to be taken out of the frame. The cylinder base pin is held in place by a spring latch on the front of the frame, just below the pin. When the spring that powers this latch is weak or broken, the cylinder base pin is frequently lost. Since replacement parts for these older revolvers are often difficult to find, the cylinder base pin will usually have to be made in the shop.

1. Select a piece of rod stock that is slightly larger in diameter than the center hole in the cylinder, and cut it to length as shown. Allow about ¼″ at the rear for the reduced tip that enters the breech face, and a sufficient length at the front for a grasping knob.

2. With a drill and file, reduce the diameter of the rod stock until it will pass through the center hole in the cylinder, fitting snugly but allowing the cylinder to turn freely. It is not necessary to reduce the entire length of the rod, just the portion which will enter the frame and cylinder. After this is done, reduce the rear tip to a diameter that will allow entry in the center hole in the breech face. If you have no outside calipers to check the diameter of the tip, try it frequently in the gun during the reduction filing. Bevel the end of the rear tip and the shoulder of the pin at the reduced point.

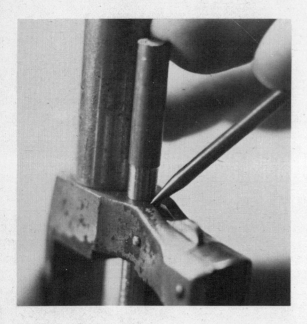

3. Location of the pin retaining groove is not as difficult as it might seem. With the pin held firmly in place, use a very sharp pointed tool (an icepick point is ideal) to either scribe or indent the pin at the front of the pin latch. From this mark, the retaining groove will be cut just to its rear.

4. Determine the dimensions of the retaining lug on top of the latch, and select a file or saw that will match its width. With the pin in a drill/lathe, I usually make the initial cut with a disc in the Dremel tool, but it can be done just as well with a file. Then, with file or saw, cut a groove with square edges, just touching your previous mark on the pin. Make the groove only as deep as the height of the lug on the latch.

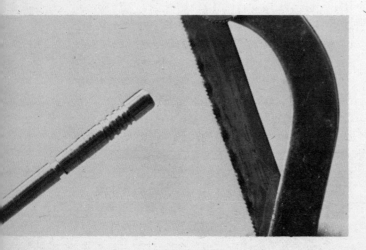

5. Bevel the end of the knob at the front, and with a file or a disc in the Dremel cut a row of grooves in the pin for grasping serrations. After these grooves are started, I usually finish them with a saw blade. Resting the turning pin on a grooved piece of steel in a vise will help to keep the grooves uniform in depth.

6. Here is the finished cylinder base pin, installed in the gun. It can now be finished or left bright, depending on the finish of the gun. Although it requires no heat-treatment, I usually finish base pins by the torch-and-oil method (described elsewhere in this book), and this does impart some surface-hardness.

to keep the cylinder from turning when it is not being rotated by the cylinder hand, since these guns have no standing latch.

7. A common ailment of the solid-frame revolver is cylinder end-play, a thing which frequently occurs after long years of use. Both the center extension at the front of the cylinder and the ratchet at the rear will wear, and this will allow some front-to-rear movement. Fortunately, in the basic design of the gun, there is a built-in way to correct this. It involves a change in the cylinder arbor tension plug, shown here, a plunger powered by a vertical coil spring which bears on the front extension of the cylinder. The original purpose of this device is

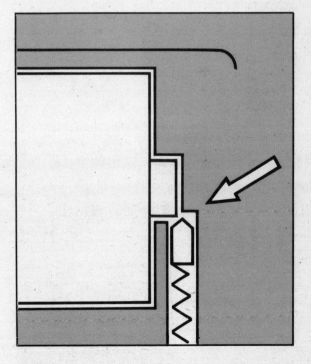

8. A simple cure for end-play is to replace the arbor tension plug with a plunger having a sharply coned

upper end. By making the plunger slightly longer to increase the compression, the same spring can usually be used. The slope of the cone will bear on the front edge of the cylinder extension, rather than its side, camming the cylinder toward the rear. The cylinder/barrel gap will be slightly increased, but not enough to matter.

9. The main reason for loss of the base pin is weakness or breakage of the spring that powers the base pin latch. The original spring was a flat V-type, very small and narrow. The one shown here is not an original, but a clock-spring replacement. It was far too weak, and on firing this gun (it's a 38), the base pin would come out during recoil. Unfortunately, the narrow space of the latch slot will not allow a doubled round-wire replacement spring. Fortunately, there is another method.

10. It's not difficult to convert the cylinder base pin latch to a coil spring system. The first step is to use a cone-point cutter in the Dremel tool to start a channel at the center of the latch slot. With the cone cutter, you can carefully center the channel. If a drill bit were used first, it would drift to one side, and give you an off-center spring channel.

11. With a ⅛" drill bit in either the Dremel tool or a power drill, extend the channel to the back wall of the latch slot. The slimness of the Dremel will allow a more level channel, but this is not an essential point. *Be very careful to stop drilling when the tip of the bit makes a bright spot on the back wall.* Do the drilling in several brief passes, checking the depth frequently.

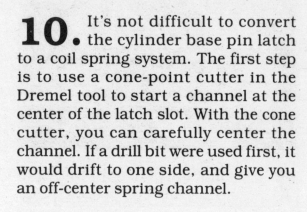

12. Select an old ⁷⁄₆₄″ bit that has a dull point but still has sharp side flutes, and cut its tip off square. Use this tool in the Dremel to open the channel to this diameter, and to square its inside end with the back wall. *Again, when the bit makes a bright mark on the rear wall, stop.*

13. Select a small coil spring of the proper diameter, and cut it off to about the depth of the channel. Reduce its outermost coil to prevent binding, especially if it is nearly the diameter of the channel. Insert the spring in the channel, install the latch, and try the base pin engagement. If the tension is too light, go to a slightly heavier spring.

14. Here is the coil spring system installed, and the base pin in place. The only external indication of the change will be the small semi-circular cuts visible at the edges of the latch slot on each side.

Chamber Sleeves

We had some difficulty in deciding whether this was really a "Repair Tip" or a "Custom Alteration," but since it does restore an otherwise unusable gun to shooting condition, perhaps it belongs here. The two guns covered are the Mannlicher Model 1901/05 and the French Model 1935A, but the principle can be applied to any gun having a similar obsolete-cartridge problem.

1. The Mannlicher Model 1901/05 pistol (above left) was originally chambered for a unique 7.63mm cartridge, similar to the standard 32 ACP round, but longer. The French Model 1935A pistol (above right) also uses an odd 7.65mm round, with the same relation to the 32 ACP, but the case is not quite as long as the 7.63mm Mannlicher. In all three of the cartridges mentioned, the bullet diameter is virtually the same, around .308".

2. Since the principal difference between these rounds was length, I decided to try "sleeving" the chambers of the two guns to allow use of the regular 32 ACP round. Noting that the 30 M-1 Carbine case has essentially the same diameter at its mouth, I located a few World War II *steel* Carbine cases, and cut two "rings" from the case ends at the mouth. The rings were of different widths to match the chamber depth of the guns to the 32 ACP case.

3. The chamber ring, or sleeve, for the French 1935A is shown with a regular 32 ACP round. The ring was then expanded slightly on one side with a tapered drift punch, and an empty 32 ACP case was used to push it into the chambers. No other anchoring was necessary, or at least hasn't been necessary so far. If it were ever necessary, it would be relatively easy to silver-solder them in place.

Springs

Spring Winding

Spring winding can be done beautifully on a lathe, or, in an emergency, somewhat crudely with an altered pair of Vise-Grips. The most practical way, and the easiest, is with a manual spring-winder. The one I use, shown in the photos, is an antique, made many years ago by the Hjorth Lathe & Tool Company of Woburn, Massachusetts. For a number of years, Brownells offered an excellent winder, but the maker went out of business a while back, and they're now trying to find another. In the meantime, the Brookstone Co. offers a winder of good quality for about $12. It operates on exactly the same principle as my old Hjorth.

There is a limit to the size of spring wire that can be used in these small hand-winders. I have used wire of up to .051″ diameter in my winder, but beyond this, I think it would be difficult. Fortunately, most of the hand-wound springs that will be needed will be smaller ones. The beginner at spring-winding should not be discouraged if his initial efforts produce something that resembles a badly deformed worm. It takes a little practice, and a smooth job depends most on keeping the tool level, and keeping the tension constant and even.

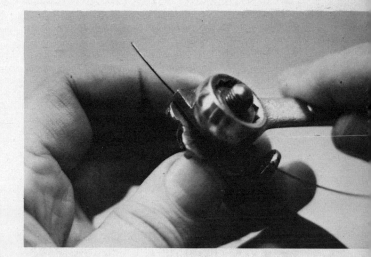

1. Loosen the nut on the spring winder, lift the plate and pressure tab, and turn the plate to the step that will produce the right coil spacing. Push the plate back down onto its lock stud. Cut a piece of spring wire of the right diameter and length for the job, and insert the wire through the loop on the handle and the hole in the center of the post, leaving about 2″ protruding from the winder. Tighten the nut firmly, trapping the wire between the pressure tab and the step plate. Use round-nosed pliers to bend a loop at the free end of the wire. This is done to prevent injury, as the end will whip around as the winding is done. It will also serve as a stop when the wire reaches the end.

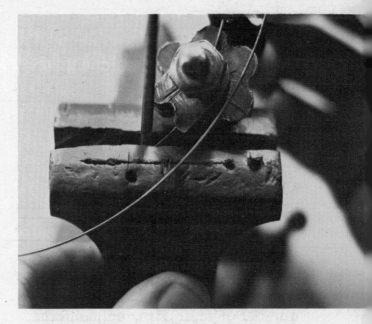

2. Select a rod of the diameter needed to make the outside diameter of the spring come out right, and keep in mind that after winding, the spring will "jump" slightly to a larger diameter. This varies with the diameter of wire used, so no constant figure can be given. For this, you'll just have to experiment. Insert both the vertical rod and the spring end into a vise, and clamp them tightly. It's best to use a rod that is not too hard, so the spring wire will indent it at the contact point as the vise is tightened. Be sure it is gripped firmly. If it comes loose during winding, the spring will probably be ruined.

3. Turn the winder around the rod, keeping it level, and keeping the pressure firm and constant. If a long spring is being wound, it may be necessary to tighten the nut on the winder about midway in the operation. When this is done, take care that the pressure and tension are maintained, and be sure the end of the tool stays snug against the rod. Keep turning until the wire runs out. The finished spring can be cut to the proper length, and extra pieces are always useful.

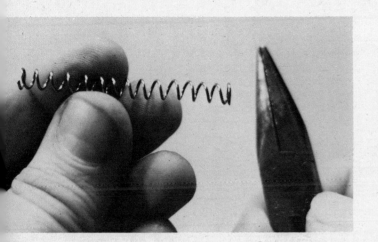

4. When the winding is completed, slowly rotate the tool in the opposite direction until the tension is reduced, and with the spring still attached, push the spring down on the rod to compress it. This will "set" the coils, so you won't be deceived about the length when cutting it. Clip off the ends of the wire at the first coil on each end of the spring, and use sharp-nosed pliers to bend the ends down to touch the next coil. The finished spring is shown.

5. Here is a close view of the "steps" on the plate of the winder. These control the spacing of the coils, with the thickness of the selected step corresponding to the measurement between each coil of the spring. The very thin steps are used only when making springs of tiny size and wire diameter.

6. Here is the spring winder from Brookstone, mentioned earlier. It is entirely satin chromed, and seems to be of excellent quality. Note that in design and operation it is identical to my old winder.

7. In showing the Brookstone winder, I will also show here a different method of anchoring the starting end of the spring wire. As you can see, it's simply a cross-drilled hole in the winding shaft, and the end of the wire is inserted through it at the start. This method has two disadvantages, though: It's difficult to cut the wire close to the shaft (you have to, to get it off!), and, it will not work on very small springs, as cross-drilling the shaft would make it too weak to take the pressure of winding.

As mentioned at the start, winding springs takes practice and experimentation. At times, I have even found it necessary to turn a winding rod to exact diameter for a special job.

"Helper" Springs

There may be times when a quick repair must be made of a weak recoil spring, striker spring, or some other spring operating on a guide rod. Perhaps you have no other coil springs on hand of the proper size, and no spring wire of the right diameter to wind one. In that case, look through your "junk box" and find a short length of coil spring that is as close as possible in diameter of spring and wire to the weak original, and determine whether there would be room in the normal compression of the spring for installation of a "helper" spring.

1. When you have determined how much space is available, cut your spring scrap to the proper length, and level the end curls by turning them down until the free end rests against the next curl, as shown. At the same time, turn the end curls

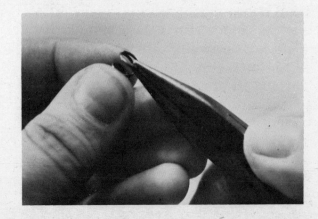

slightly inward, toward the center, to prevent the one contacting the original from "riding over."

2. Install the "helper" spring on the guide, behind the weak

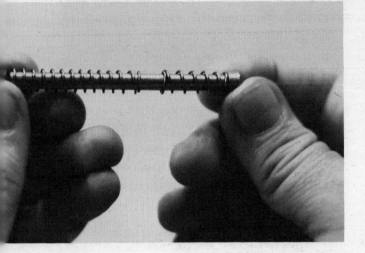

original, and check to be sure that at their point of contact, one cannot enter the other. Try the assembled springs in the gun, to be sure that the added spring does not keep the parts from full travel. Make this check by hand, not by test firing.

It's always best to replace a weak spring, either with the original type or with one wound in the shop. For a "quick repair," though, the method described above works. I did this on the recoil spring of a 22-cal. Beretta Model 948 once, then forgot about it. Three years later, I noticed it and wound a new replacement, but not because it became necessary. The gun was still working!

Simple Torsion Loop Springs

Quite often, in shops which have a resident "Parts Replacer" rather than a gunsmith, simple repair jobs can be held up for a month or two while an order is placed to one of the factories for the simplest of all gun parts to make: A torsion loop spring. Modern guns use this type of spring with great frequency, and while the shape and length of the round-wire arms will vary widely, the basic one or two-turn loop is the same. With a pair of round-nosed pliers and a

piece of spring wire of suitable diameter, making a spring of this type takes about one minute.

1. With the spring wire gripped firmly in the round-nosed pliers, bring one end of the wire across the other to begin making the loop. With small-diameter wire, this can be done by hand. In heavier wire, another pair of pliers can be used. According to the manner in which the spring bears on the parts in the gun, note beforehand whether to bring the wire end over or under the other extension.

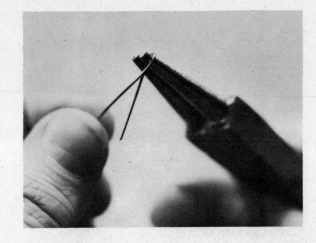

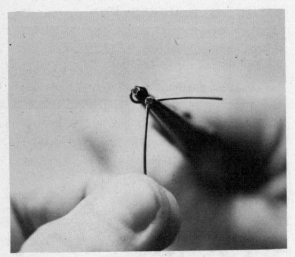

2. After the first bend, change the position of the pliers as shown, and close the pliers to form the loop. The angle of the spring arms can be adjusted at this point. If the spring has a double or triple loop, just repeat the operation to form the additional loops, but do it on alternate sides, to keep the loop diameter constant. This is important, to allow for passage of the mounting pin.

3. When the loops are finished and the angle of the arms is set, the ends of the spring arms can be shaped as needed for proper contact with the parts. One word of caution: When spring wire is cut, the cutter leaves a chisel-point which is very sharp. Handle spring wire with extreme care to avoid injury.

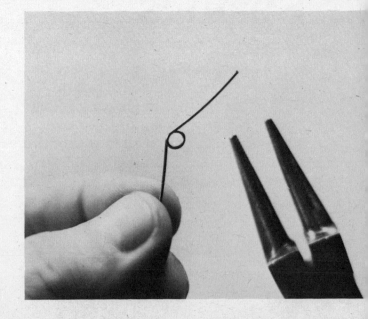

Broken Spring Repairs— Round for Flat

1. The Colt Model M, popularly known as the Pocket Auto, was a good and dependable John M. Browning design. Its weak points were two blade-type springs, both in very important positions. A light inner spring has three arms at the top, two resting on the sear, and the center arm powering the disconnector. The lower end of the same spring tensions the magazine catch. To the rear of this, a heavy V-blade powers the hammer and the grip safety. Breakage of either of these springs is a real problem, as parts for the Model M have become increasingly difficult to find, and making these springs, especially the heavy one, can be quite tedious.

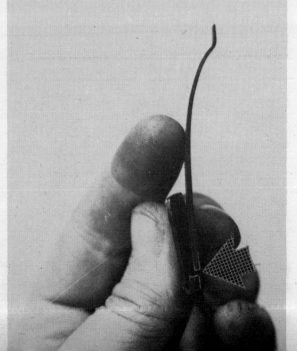

2. The hammer and grip safety spring will usually snap at the point shown, at the base of the longer arm.

3. A replacement spring is made of heavy (.071") round wire. Note that its curve is more pronounced than the shape of the original, since the round wire doesn't exert as much tension as the original leaf. The extra curve compensates in this manner.

4. The broken short arm of the original spring is used as a base for the round-wire replacement.

5. The replacement spring, just before installation. Note that the tips of the short arms are bent outward, to bear in the original spring lobe recesses in the frame, and to keep the spring from moving upward as it is flexed.

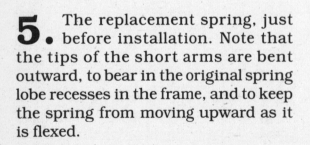

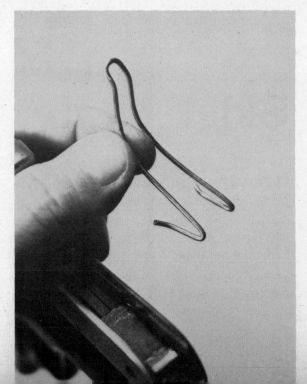

6. The new spring in the gun, just before installation of the grip safety and the hammer.

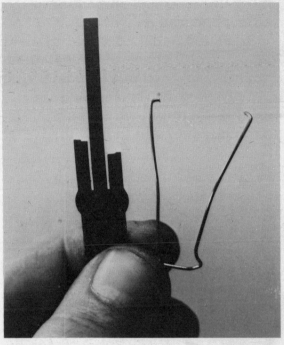

7. When the outer arms of the combination spring that powers the sear, disconnector, and magazine catch are broken, as on the one shown, an auxiliary round wire spring can be made of lighter stock, and used in conjunction with the broken original. Note the turned-in upper tips, bearing on the sear, and the lobes at the lower end, which keep the spring in place.

Sidelock Springs

On many old sidelock double-barreled shotguns, the internal hammer and sear are powered by a single combination flat spring which is looped around a small screw or stud at the rear of the lock. These springs have never been commercially reproduced, and finding replacements for those that break can be a real problem. I frequently make replacements from round spring wire, as shown in the photo. Because of the short hammer arc, heavy spring wire must be used, usually .065″ in diameter or larger. At the rear, a full coil of the spring encircles the original retaining screw, and the short lower arm rests on the upper surface of the sear. The longer upper arm is curved upward at the front, and its front tip must be rounded and polished, as it must slip freely down the back of the hammer. Using this method is a lot easier than making a new flat spring, and the new torsion round-wire type is practically immune to breakage.

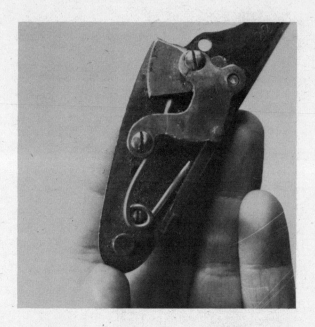

Winchester 90/06 Springs

1. In an earlier time, one of the best-known repeating 22-cal. rifles in the world was the slide-action Winchester Model 1890. In 1906, the design was very slightly altered to allow the gun to be used with Short, Long, and Long Rifle rounds interchangeably. Except for the little lever in the carrier that accomplished this, the gun was mechanically the same as the earlier version. As with many of the older designs, blade-type springs were used in several critical areas. The two that most often break are the hammer spring and the carrier lever spring. Up until about five years ago, parts for the Model 90 and Model 06 could usually be found among the used-parts dealers. Now, with many of these old Winchesters disappearing

into collections, fewer of them are sold as "parts guns," and replacements are becoming hard to find.

2. When the hammer spring is broken, it presents an interesting problem for round-wire replacement, as the hammer connection to the spring is via a stirrup, and the rear of the original spring is threaded for a retaining screw which enters from the outside, through the lower receiver tang. At the stirrup connection, this is solved by making a curl at the forward end of the wire spring, with a vertical tip which locks behind the cross-piece of the stirrup. The other arm of the doubled spring is simply bent across to fit below the stirrup, acting as a support. At the rear, a screw of smaller diameter is inserted through the loop of the spring, and a nut installed on the inside to hold the spring in place. The nut will require a small clearance cut in the stock recess.

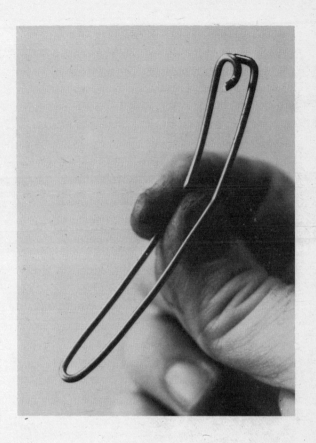

3. Here is a closer view of the forward end of the spring, showing the shape of the stirrup contact arms. The diameter of the spring wire used here was .063″, but there is some leeway in this measurement—it can be a bit heavier or lighter.

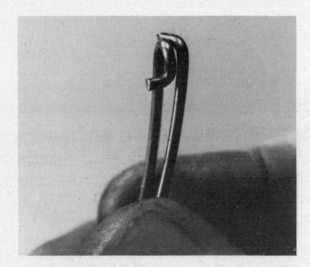

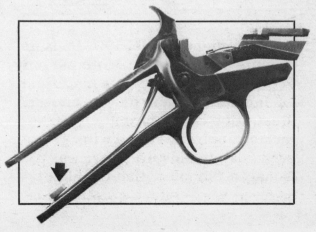

4. The finished spring is shown in place in the gun. Note the retaining nut at the rear (arrow), the screw tip trimmed flush with the nut.

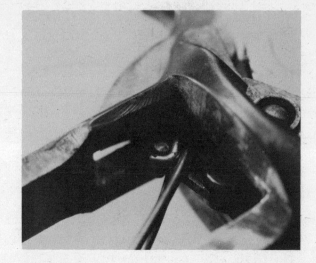

5. A close view of the engagement of the replacement spring with the hammer stirrup. The "curl" encircles the stirrup lever, and the turned-up tip locks it in place, bearing on the cross-piece.

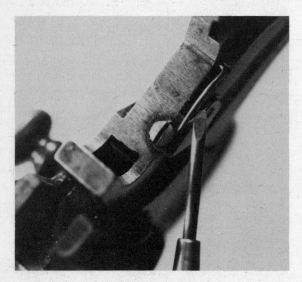

6. The other spring which frequently weakens or breaks, the carrier lever spring, is replaced even more easily with round wire of smaller diameter (about .035″ is right). A curl is made to accept the retaining screw, and the forward arm curved downward, somewhat more acutely than the flat original. The tip is turned inward and trimmed to clear the side of the carrier.

Flat Springs—Another Fix

The Mannlicher Model 1901/05 is an obscure pistol that is of interest only to collectors and firearms historians. I'm including it here only as another illustration of flat spring replacement with round wire. The particular gun involved here was a damaged "shooter" that could not be restored to collector status (the barrel had been cut off!). If the gun had been in perfect condition, I would have taken several days to make replacements that were exactly like the original springs. All I wanted to do in this case was to sleeve the chamber to 32 Auto and shoot the pistol. So, I reshaped and crowned the crudely cut off barrel, and installed a Luger front sight in the top rib. Steel weld was added to the broken disconnector, and recut to original shape. This left only two

problems: the mainspring, and the combination spring that powered the trigger, disconnector, and sear. Both were missing.

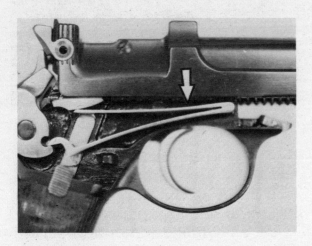

1. Here is an unaltered original pistol, the arrow indicating the mainspring. At its forward end, it is mounted by a lateral post which enters a recess in the frame. Its lower arm is the hammer spring, while the upper extension supplies tension to the slide locking block. The "beak" on the hammer spring arm also cams the slide locking block out of engagement when the hammer is depressed beyond full-cock position. Duplicating this spring, exactly as the original, is a lengthy and tedious operation.

2. Using .075″ round spring wire, the problem was solved this way: A round post was made to fit the original mounting recess (right arrow), and the head of the post was cross-drilled for passage of the spring. After the spring was shaped, it was found that it did not always give reliable ignition, so a tension block with grooves for the spring was made and added (left arrow), and small pins on each side of it kept it in place in the center of the spring. Note that the replacement round-wire spring has a more pronounced curve than the flat original. This is generally necessary with round wire springs, and length-allowance must be made for it.

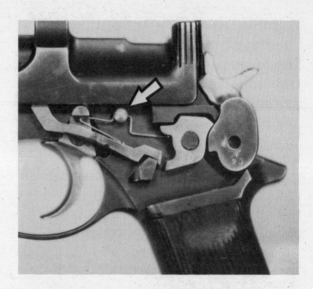

3. On the unaltered original gun, the arrow indicates the combination spring that powers the trigger, disconnector, and sear (von Mannlicher was a genius!). This spring is mounted in the same manner as the mainspring, by a post at upper center. This spring would be even more difficult to reproduce than the mainspring. Also, it was found that a round-wire replacement in the same shape as the original did not give the proper tension to all of the parts.

4. Again, a post was made (arrow) and cross-drilled for the .031" round-wire spring. As you can see, the shape of the spring was entirely changed. This is sometimes necessary when changing from flat springs to round wire, as their tension properties are not the same. On the gun shown, both of the replacement springs function perfectly, and I've been shooting the gun for several years.

Replacement Hammer Springs

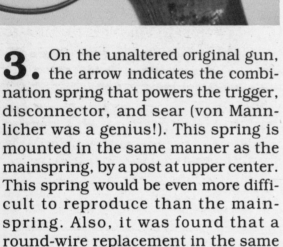

Most of the old top-break revolvers, the Iver Johnson, Harrington & Richardson, and others of the 1880-1900 period, have flat-type hammer springs. When these break, replacements are available from Wolff, but at times the smaller shops will not want to order a set of these just to repair one gun. Fortunately, there is an alternative. For years, I've been making replacement hammer springs for these guns out of round spring wire, the usual diameter being about .051″. The wire is bent in a long, narrow "U" shape, the rounded end being at the top to contact the spring recess in the hammer. It may be necessary to grind a slightly sharper point at the top, bevelling the upper and lower surfaces to fit the tip into the recess. The free lower ends are cut to length last, to give the spring the proper arc and tension. The replacement round-wire spring is not made in exactly the same shape as the original flat spring, but is straighter, with the flexing of installation giving it the right curve to clear the grip screw. In installation, the free ends are lifted into their recess at the bottom of the grip frame one at a time.

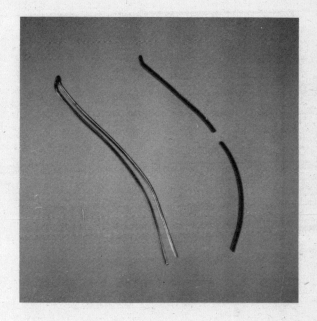

Off-Brand Revolver Springs

1. The average Spanish revolvers, such as the one shown, by Garate, Anitua y Compania, have an obvious external resemblance to earlier Smith & Wesson guns. Inside, though, the mainspring arrangement is closer to the Colt design.

2. Though the V-type flat spring is similar to the one used in Colt revolvers, the Spanish guns usually do not have a separate rebound lever. Instead, the lower arm of the spring has an integral vertical extension which engages a recess on the inside of the cylinder hand, supplying tension to both the hand and the trigger. This extension is the part that frequently breaks off. Because of the wide dimensional variations among numerous makers, and a low survival rate, replacement springs are almost impossible to find among the used-parts dealers. Since Spanish revolvers have an often undeserved reputation

for poor quality, and since making one of these terrible springs will take most of a day, some good guns are frequently relegated to the junk box.

3. To restore these guns to shooting order, the three spring functions are separated. First, a cut is made in the frame to a small cross-

drilled hole (arrow, lower left), to allow installation of a standard Smith & Wesson Model 10 hammer spring. Some fitting will likely be required at the engagement of the spring hooks with the hammer stirrup (arrow, upper left). The trigger is then drilled vertically to make a recess for a coil spring and plunger (right arrow), bearing on the inside of the frame.

4. This leaves only the cylinder hand to be powered, and for this we go back to the early Smith & Wesson design. The sideplate is drilled at the upper rear of the hand recess for a small spring and plunger (arrow), and the conversion is complete.

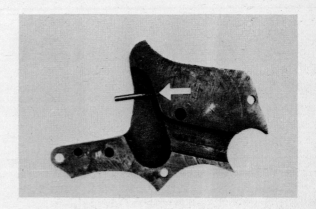

From Blade to Coil

Sometimes, changing from a blade spring to a helical coil can be as simple as fitting the replacement spring into an existing recess, as in this cartridge stop from an early Savage Model 99 rifle.

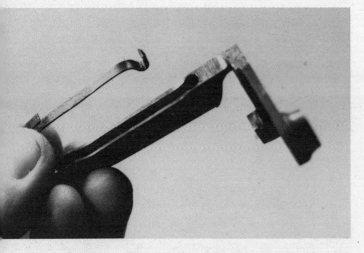

1. The original cartridge stop spring was a flat type, and the one shown is broken. Note that the anchoring recess at the end of the spring slot is a round hole.

2. Without any alteration of the cartridge stop, a round-wire helical coil spring is fitted into the anchoring recess. It worked perfectly.

It should be noted that it's not always this simple. In most cases, a recess for the coil spring will have to be drilled in the part, locating it in a position where it will give the proper tension, and where it will have a good bearing surface inside the receiver. On the early Savage Model 99 rifle, though, this is a quick repair.

The Mauser and the Bobby-Pin

It may be hard to believe, but I can remember my very first repair job, back in 1947. It involved a Mauser pocket automatic with a missing sear/safety spring. Since this was a 32 caliber, it should properly be called a Model 1914. The first gun of this pattern appeared in 25 ACP chambering, in 1910, and later both calibers were very slightly re-designed to become the Model 1934. Internally, all of these guns are identical, so the repair described could be applied to any of them. I'm including this repair mainly to show how ordinary household items can sometimes be used for repair purposes.

Just as a safety pin with its point and clasp cut off can sometimes be used to replace a torsion-loop spring, a lady's bobby-pin can be used as a replacement for some blade-type springs. In this particular case, the spring can actually be made much easier in this manner than with proper flat spring stock. There is one stipulation—the bobby-pin used must be of the flat, rather than rounded, type.

1. In the basic Mauser design, the combination spring that powers the sear and the safety bar is looped around a fixed stud in a recess on the frame. An original is shown here. Breakage is not unusual, as this flat spring receives full compression each time the safety is applied.

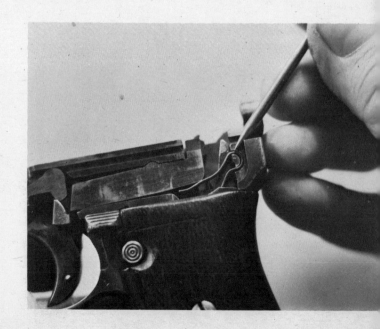

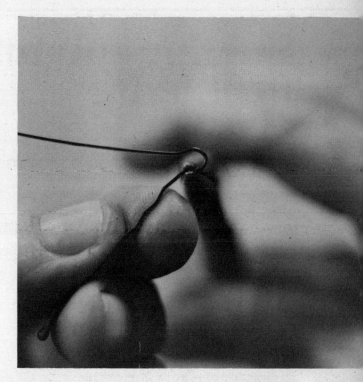

2. A flat-type bobby-pin is easily cold-shaped, as shown, to the contour of an original type. After shaping, the ends are cut to the proper length. The bobby-pin is of slightly lighter spring stock, but the difference is not enough to prevent proper functioning. Also, some compensation can be accomplished by giving the new spring a "wider" shape.

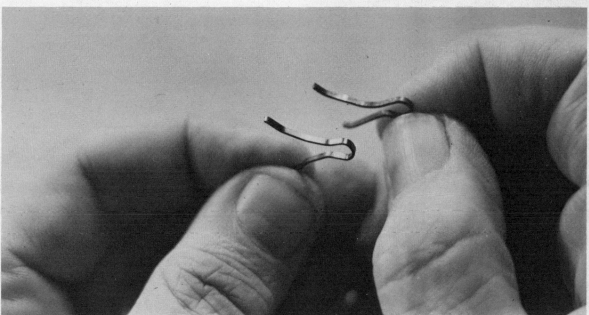

3. Here are the original Mauser spring, on the right, and the bobby-pin replacement. I kept the gun I first repaired this way for a number of years, and it was fired with some frequency. When it was finally traded, it was still working perfectly. As far as I know, it still is. So, when a spring of this general type needs replacing, remember the lowly bobby-pin.

Solving the Impossible Problem

The revolver shown here is an obscure little Belgian piece, made by an unknown maker. It is chambered for the 32 ACP cartridge, not unusual for guns of this type. Quite a few of them were also made in 25 ACP. It is included here only because the method of repair may have some application on more practical pieces, or in mechanical restoration for collectors. When I first obtained this gun, it was in perfect condition, except for the absence of the original V-type spring which powered the hammer, cylinder hand, and trigger.

My first idea was to adapt a Smith & Wesson flat hammer spring, and to make a round-wire spring for the cylinder hand and trigger. However, the thinness of the frame at the bottom of the grip would not allow slotting for the lower end of the hammer spring, and the shape of the grip did not lend itself to the

usual mounting of a round-wire hand and trigger spring. There seemed to be no way to anchor either spring in the position they would have to be for functioning.

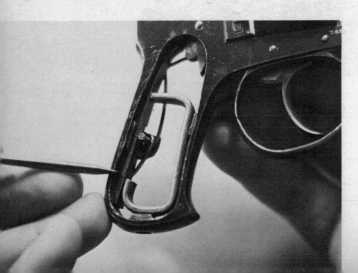

1. The problem was solved in this way: The upper two-thirds of a standard Smith & Wesson blade spring was used for the hammer spring, and by chance its stirrup hooks exactly fit the stirrup-lever on the hammer. A piece of bar stock was shaped to bear on the spring at two points—at its lower end, and about 1″

from the top. The straight vertical front section of this "retainer" was held against the inside of the grip front-strap by the tension of the spring. This arrangement not only retained the spring and supplied tension, it also cleared the center of the grip frame for passage of the grip screw. Installation of the grip panels would keep the "retainer" from shifting to the side.

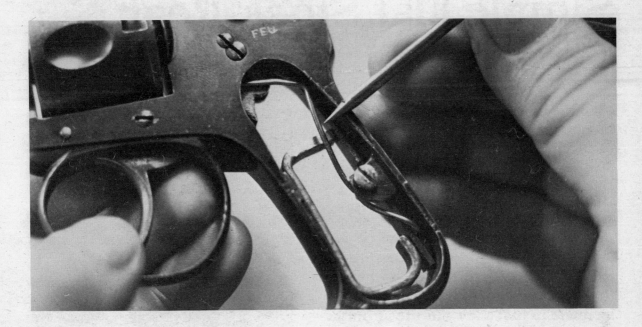

2. The original V-spring had a post on its left side at the apex of the "V," and this mounted the spring via a hole in a projecting plate, located midway down the grip frame on the left side. The hole was threaded and a screw installed, to serve as a mounting post for a single-loop, round-wire, torsion spring of .043" diameter wire. The shorter lower arm of the spring was shaped to hook behind the hammer spring, and its long upper arm was extended upward to bear against the inside rear of the frame, then angled forward to contact the shelf in the cylinder hand. From the elbow in contact with the frame, the spring had two slight downward bends, one visible in the photo, the other just inside the frame, giving it exactly the right contact angle with the hand shelf. This combination worked perfectly, and has been working during occasional firing for the past 8 or 9 years. There is one drawback to this method of spring replacement: The original V-spring worked against a lobe at the bottom of the hammer to rebound it when the trigger was released, and this function was now absent. When loading, it is now necessary to position the protruding firing pin point between two of the cartridges for safe carrying. The seemingly impossible problem, though, did have a solution.

Sights

Simple Flat Stock Rear Sights

When a dovetail-mounted rear sight is missing or broken, there are plenty of good modern replacements available. On some of the older guns, though, such as the little "boy's rifles" of earlier times, the modern ones just don't look right. Also, there may be times when replacements are not readily available, and a sight is needed immediately. In either of these cases, a good usable sight can be made in just a few minutes from flat steel stock. These aren't pretty, and are adjustable only for windage, but they are functional. Here are the steps for making a simple open rear sight.

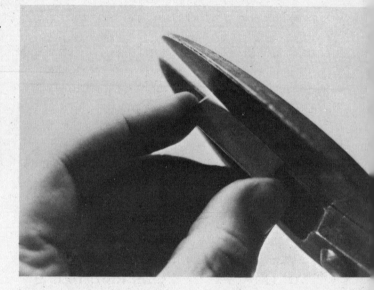

1. The sheet steel used in these illustrations was of .035″ thickness, but this can be varied. Decide on the width wanted for the sight (to fill or slightly overhang the dovetail slot), and cut a strip this width and about 1½″ long.

2. Using a vise and hammer, fold the strip at the center, over to a right angle.

3. Judging from the height of the front sight, determine the height of the new rear, and make the second fold to give this measurement from the fold to the center bend. Then, complete the center fold, bringing the longer extension of the strip down tight, and hammering it together.

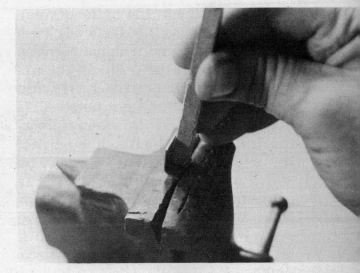

4. Make the final fold, leaving an upright doubled portion with single flanges at the bottom. Grip the doubled portion in a vise as this is done, to keep the flanges even.

5. Trim the flanges to a total size that is slightly larger than the dovetail cut, and file them to fit, keeping the edge angles straight so the upright doubled portion will stay straight across the barrel.

6. When the fitting to the dovetail is complete, file the sides level, and slightly round the upper corners. Make a mark at the center of the upright, and with a cutting disc and Dremel tool, cut the sight notch. This can also be done with a very narrow file, but be sure the notch is neither too wide nor too deep. Check the width of the notch by slipping the sight into place and viewing the front sight through it. You should be able to see a little light between the front sight blade and both sides of the notch.

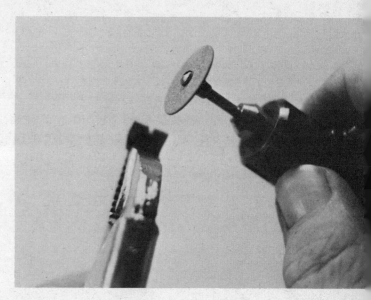

7. The finished sight can be colored by the torch-and-oil method or with cold chemical blue. If too much was taken off the lower edges during fitting, a stake mark in each of the flanges will hold it in place. Fire the gun at a target before staking, though, in case lateral adjustment is necessary.

Sight Installation on Uncut Slide

For those who are making up a Government Model pistol from commercial parts, one of the slides offered by Essex may be a surprise. Because many different rear sights are used in making up guns of this type, the factory leaves the rear of the slide uncut for *any* sight. The front sight slot is cut, though, and the rectangular opening is provided for its mounting post. A heavy raised rib with deep lengthwise grooves runs the full length of the slide top, and this makes cutting a level cross-dovetail much easier. For the gun shown here, the choice of the shooter was between two fixed combat-style rear sights: the MMC, and the Millett. Both have a white inlay, and both are excellent sights.

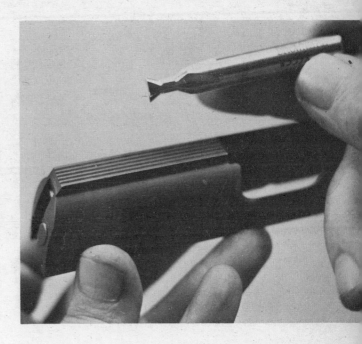

1. Here is the uncut Essex slide. The tool shown is from Brownells, and if you have access to a cross-milling rig, it will cut the sight dovetail accurately and easily. While this is unquestionably the best way, it is not the only way. With care, a good job can be done with files.

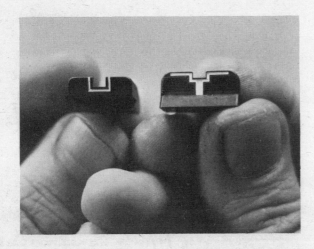

2. The two rear sights being considered for this job were the MMC (left), and the Millett. Because of the width of the top rib on the Essex slide, the MMC was chosen.

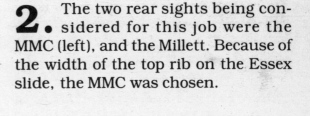

3. The first step is to select the position of the sight, and to scribe a small mark on top at that location.

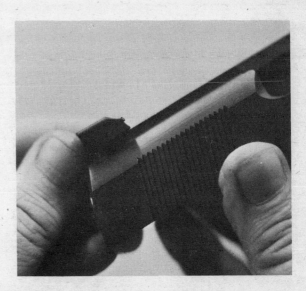

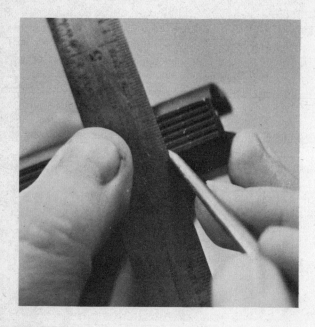

4. Using the initial mark as a guide, two heavier marks are scribed across the top of the rib, the distance between them corresponding to the narrowest portion of the dovetail block on the sight.

5. I prefer to make the starting cross-cuts with a disc in the Dremel tool, but this requires a steady hand and long experience with the tool. It's easy to make a crooked cut, or to go too deep. A safer way is to use a file or hacksaw. Take care to keep the cuts straight across, and keep the depth to about ¹/₁₆″ or less.

6. Select a medium to coarse file that has an edge width slightly less than the distance between the cuts, and make a square cut downward, keeping the floor of the cut level across the rib. Take care that the front and rear walls of the cut are kept straight across, and make the depth of the cut slightly less than the vertical height of the dovetail lug on the sight.

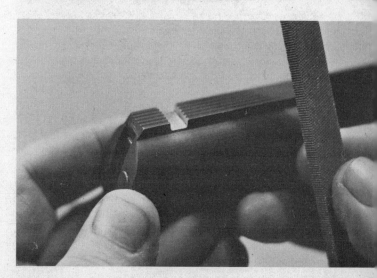

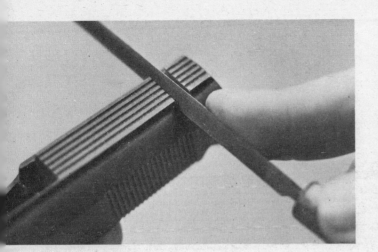

7. While the dovetailing can be done with a regular triangular file, a better job can be done with the special one available from Brownells, having teeth on only one face. During this phase of the job, there should be frequent comparisons with the dovetail lug on the sight. Be careful that the floor of the cut is not taken down too far. Dull the sharp upper edges of the cut with two or three file strokes when fitting.

8. The dovetail is almost finished here, and the special uniface file from Brownells is shown.

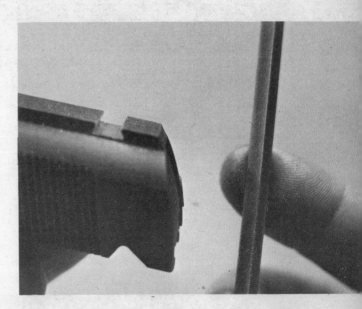

9. The sight is shown installed. If the dovetail is a little loose in final fitting, it can be tightened by light staking of the rear edge of the dovetail cut, before the sight is driven into place. Use a nylon drift and a small hammer to move the sight into the dovetail.

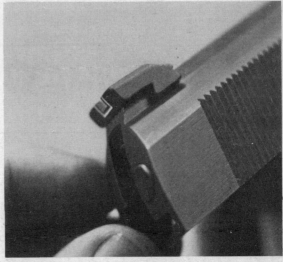

10. As noted earlier, the front sight slot and aperture are already made in the slide. The vertical underpost on the sight may have to be tapered slightly to enter the aperture. It is then driven gently into place, using a nylon drift and a hammer.

11. There are several ways to rivet the end of the post inside the slide, but the best way is to use this staking tool, available from MMC. For use on the Essex slide, a small alteration of the edges indicated by the scribe was necessary. With the tool in place, holding the sight, one tap of the hammer on the plunger of the tool instantly clinches the sight in place.

Make Your Own Sight Inserts

It was Smith & Wesson, I think, that first offered factory-installed front sight inserts. In low-light situations, this little block of reddish-orange plastic really improved the visibility of the front sight. In the years since their introduction, many other substances and colors have been tried, and more than one kit has been marketed to allow both gunsmiths and careful amateurs a way of adding front sight inserts to other guns. A few years ago, I developed my own method, using regular hardware-store items. I was later amused to note that one of the commercial kits used a very similar method. No, they didn't steal the idea from me—they just happened to think of the same thing.

The general purpose of front sight inserts is, of course, to make the sight more visible in poor light, and for this the colors used are mostly light ones—bright red, orange, and so on. Fluorescent colors are also used, such as the "hot pink" plastic insert offered by SSK.

Luminous versions for shooting in fully darkened situations have also become available. I have also installed black inserts on guns which had integral stainless steel front sights. Actually, any color is possible, and I have seen inserts made of metal as well, in silver, gold and aluminum. The plastic insert blocks present several problems. They are difficult to properly fit, and unless they are glued in place, they will almost inevitably work loose, especially in the larger calibers. They are also subject to breakage if they're struck in just the right way.

My own method is with Devcon 5-minute epoxy, the kind that comes in an applicator that resembles two medical hypos joined together. For a coloring agent, I use Testor's model enamel, which is available in an almost infinite array of colors, including silver, gold, and fluorescents. To contain the stuff

while it hardens in the sight, I've made little "fences" out of sheet aluminum, in varying dimensions to fit different sights. An opened paper clip makes an excellent applicator, and this completes the list of necessary equipment, except for the tools to cut the dovetail recess in the blade.

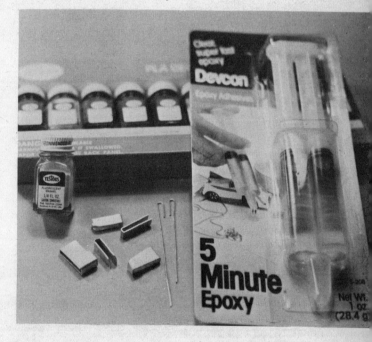

1. Here are the necessary ingredients and equipment for a liquid front sight insert. It should be noted that the Testor's model enamel combines perfectly with the epoxy shown, without affecting its adhesion or curing time.

2. I usually make the initial slanted cuts in the front sight blade with a cutting disc in the Dremel tool, but the entire job can be done with a triangular file. The one shown is a special type available from Brownells, having two blank sides, and it is the best for this purpose. After the dovetail is shaped, I use a tiny Grobet triangular file to sharpen the internal corners. Before beginning the cut, use the tiny file to "mark" two places on the rear face of the blade, to lay out the length of the cut. The finished insert should just fill the rear sight notch, when viewed at normal arm extension.

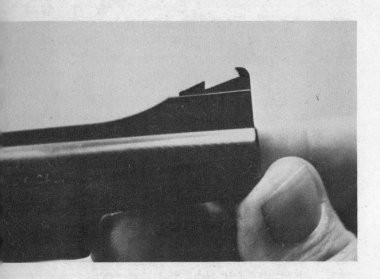

3. The depth of the dovetail can be varied, and need not be as deep as the one shown. Be sure the side and top edges are sharp, with no edge extrusions from the filing, as this will interfere with the fit of the pouring fence.

4. Use a center punch to mark the exact center of the floor of the recess, and drill a shallow hole at that location. This is to stabilize the insert against lateral movement. Here, on the sight of a Ruger Security-Six, a 1/16″ drill was used, and the hole depth was about 1/8″. The drill size can be varied, of course, according to the width of the blade.

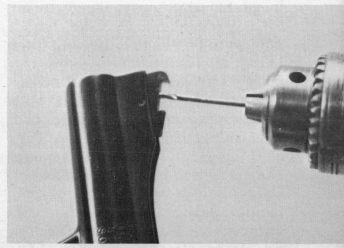

5. The sheet aluminum fence is squeezed to insure a tight fit, and slipped onto the sight blade. Since I now have a number of these little fences, I've scribed the make and model of each gun they're used for on the outside of each of them, to save selection time. After the fence is on the sight, the gun is clamped by its trigger guard in a leather-padded vise, the barrel tilted slightly downward.

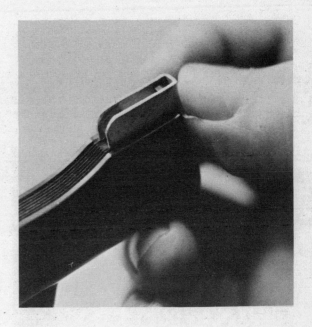

6. When squeezing out the epoxy resin and hardener, control the pressure on each wing of the plunger, to insure that equal portions are dispensed. For the average sight insert, a pool about the size of a nickel should be adequate. With one of two opened paper clips, mix the epoxy thoroughly for about 15 seconds.

7. Dip the other paper clip in the Testor's enamel, and add 4 or 5 drops of the enamel to the epoxy. Mix it well, until the color is uniform, but do it gently, to avoid bubbles. Note that when the manufacturer says "five minute epoxy," he's not kidding. If you delay too long, it will begin to "set."

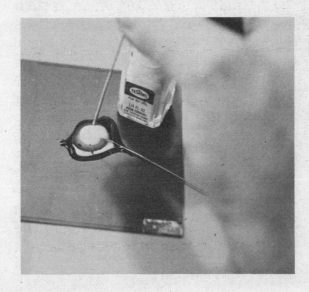

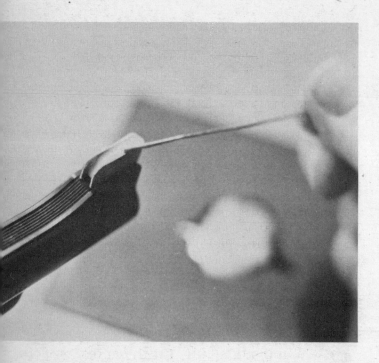

8. Dipping the original paper clip in the colored epoxy, transfer it as quickly as possible to the sight, filling the fence to its top. At some point during this operation, insert the tip of the paper clip into the stabilizing hole in the recess, to be sure that the epoxy flows into it. Though the epoxy will, indeed, begin to harden within 5 minutes, it's best to allow it to set for at least 2 or 3 hours. I usually leave it overnight, just to be certain that there are no soft spots.

9. After the epoxy has "cured," the sides of the fence are gently sprung away from the sight blade, and the fence is then slid off toward the front. A sharp knife or an industrial single-edged razor blade is then used to trim away most of the excess epoxy. A rocking motion of the blade will do it best. Extreme pressure should be avoided. When the insert is trimmed to within 1/16″ of the top of the sight blade, the final shaping is done with a medium file. I reserve for this a file that has never been used on metal, as any tiny metal flakes in the file grooves can be transferred and imbedded into the epoxy. When the sides and top conform to the shape of the sight blade, the bright spots and scratches made by the file on the steel are treated with cold chemical blue. This will not harm the epoxy.

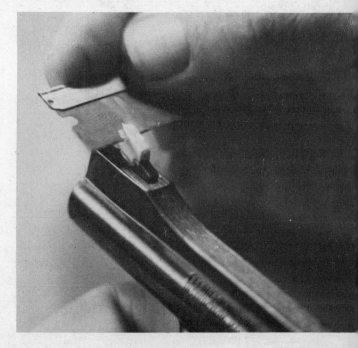

10. Here is the finished sight. After application of the cold blue, I usually drag a vertical razor blade over the top surface and the upper edges, to smooth the surface and brighten the color.

11. In this side view of the finished sight, note the very small bubble that developed near the front edge of the cut on the side. If this were a customer's gun, I'd re-pour the insert. Since it's mine, and the bubble doesn't affect the top surface and the eye-picture, I'll just use it as is.

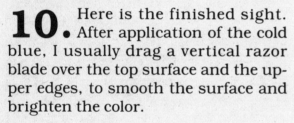

The insert shown is bright yellow, a color that I usually recommend. Sights made by this method are remarkably durable. The finished epoxy is not really hard, and has a slight resilience. I'm still using several guns on which the front sights were done this way about 10 years ago. My 22-cal. Star Model FM is one of these, and its insert is not of the usual design, so perhaps it should be described here. The rear face of the Star sight was not large enough for the regular dovetail cut, so a simple V-cut was made instead. A hole was drilled in the lower arm of the "V," and a tiny tapered steel pin driven into the hole. When the epoxy was poured in, the pin anchored it in the V-cut. This, along with the adhesive qualities of the epoxy, is enough to keep it in place. Variations of this method can be used on any sight that is too small to allow a dovetail. I have even used it on the small original sights of the U.S. Government Model Colt auto.

White Dot Applications

As I may have mentioned elsewhere, the range where I shoot is located in a hollow with hills on three sides, and in late afternoon the light can quickly become dim. This situation has made me particularly appreciative of sights designed for low-light use. For practical shooting, such as late evening or night use by law enforcement officers, the advantage of high-visibility sights will be obvious. A touch of white or yellow enamel on front and rear sights will temporarily give good eye pick-up in poor light, but it will quickly wear off in the holster. For some guns, white-outline rear sights are available, and, of course, there are the excellent replacement sights for many popular guns by Millett, MMC, and others. On revolvers which have front sights large enough to allow the installation, a light insert will help the picture. These are covered elsewhere in this section.

On some fixed-sight guns, the alternatives mentioned above may not be practical, because of sight size, or shape, or the fact that no special replacements are made for them. For these I have frequently used a variation of the well-known Stavenhagen-pattern sights, as found on several fine European automatic pistols. As used on the Walther and the SIG/Sauer pistols, these consist of a recessed white dot in the rear face of the front sight, and a white square below the notch of the rear sight. You just set the dot on top of the square, and you're on target. It occurred to me that two dots would work as well as a dot-and-square, and I have applied this system to quite a few guns. It's not difficult.

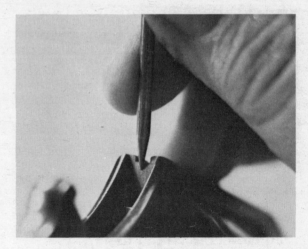

1. The revolver shown here is a Charter 44 Bulldog, but the system can be applied to almost any fixed-sight gun, adjusting the size of the dots to the available space. The first step is to use a hard, sharp-pointed tool to find and mark a point below the exact center of the rear sight notch. In marking the point, keep in mind the proposed diameter of the dot, and leave a small space at the top, between the dot and the notch.

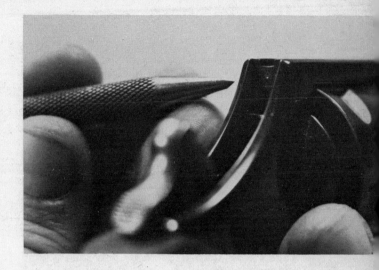

2. After the point is lightly marked, use a punch to make an indentation at that point, and take care that the location is still well-centered. Also, be sure that the indentation is adequate to keep a drill tip in place.

3. A regular drill can be used, but I find the Dremel is easier to handle, especially since it has a speed control. In this case, I used a #44 drill bit to turn the mark into a neat, very shallow circular hole. It would be advisable to use a new drill bit, or one that is very sharp. Also, take care to avoid drifting off-center. Centrifugal force will tend to cause drift, and you must hold the tool tightly to compensate for this.

4. After the shallow hole is drilled, use a fine file to remove any burred-up edges around the hole. Cold blue is then used to cover the bright marks.

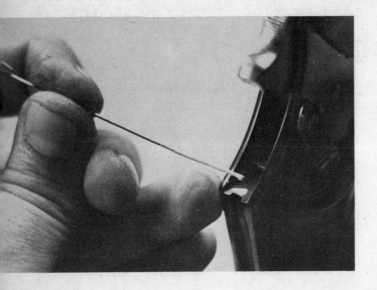

5. With an opened paper clip dipped in white Testor's model enamel, a drop is applied to the hole, just enough to fill it. Wipe off any excess, even with the surface.

6. Allowed to dry overnight, the finished dot is recessed and protected from rubbing off. It should be noted that some solvents and oils will attack the enamel, so these solutions should be kept away from the dot. An occasional twirl with a dry Q-tip will keep it bright.

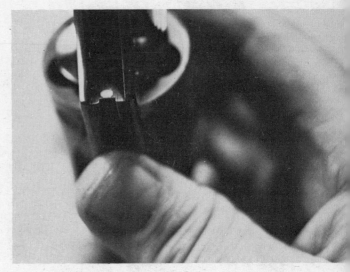

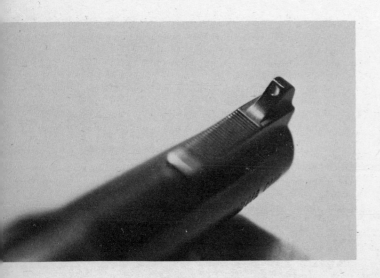

7. The companion white dot on the front sight was done in exactly the same way, except that a slightly smaller drill, a #50, was used. I have exactly the same arrangement on my own Charter Bulldog, and even though the enamel is not a luminous type, it's surprising how well it shows up in low light.

MMC Adjustable Sight on GM Colt

Aside from the fact that the adjustable sights made by MMC (Miniature Machine Company) are beautiful little pieces of machinery, there are two reasons why they are so popular with owners of the Colt Government Model and its variants:

The MMC sight is low profile, and it can be used with the original front sight. In addition to this, it is not difficult to install. The adjustable leaf is available in different notch-widths, and a white-outline version is also offered.

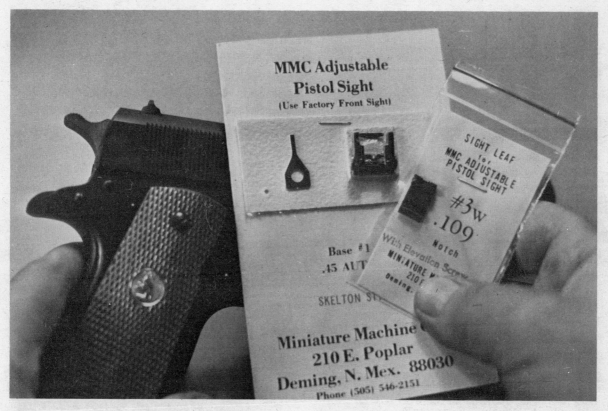

1. As noted above, the sight base and the leaf are separate units, so you can choose a leaf that exactly suits your purposes. A wide notch would be chosen, for example, in combat-shooting applications.

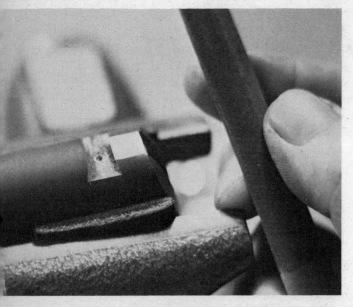

2. The MMC sight does require one little piece of gunsmithing work during installation: For clearance at the rear, and to give the elevation screw an even surface for unvarying increments, a flat must be filed at the back of the rear sight slot. The width of the hammer recess in the slide can be used as a guide. When the sides of the flat align with the recess, it's perfect. Take care that the flat is absolutely level. Don't allow the file stroke to "drop off" toward the side.

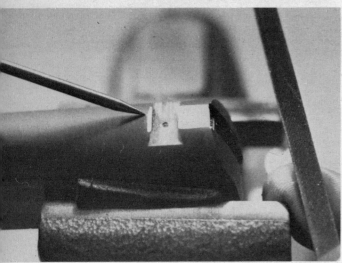

3. For clearance at the front, a small "shelf" must be filed at the edge of the sight slot. This must be very slightly wider and deeper than the flat at the rear. Check frequently, while filing, by inserting the sight base to check the clearance. On this narrow shelf, you'll find it is a bit more difficult to keep the cut level and straight, so proceed with care.

4. The sight base should slip easily into place on most guns. If not, it may be necessary to do some very light filing on the floor of the slot. A staking notch is provided on the inside rear of the sight base. Center the base, and use a punch and small hammer to stake the edge into the notch. Be sure it is clenched securely.

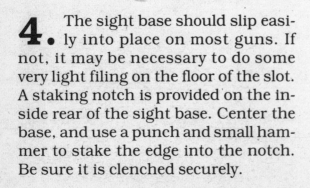

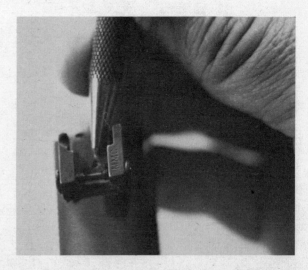

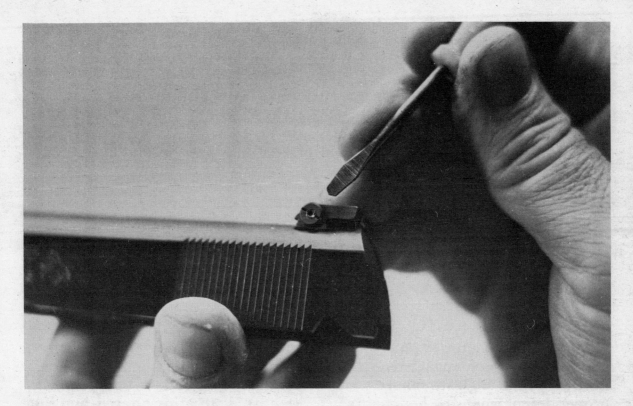

5. The sight leaf, its spring, and the windage screw and nut are assembled according to the instructions that are furnished with each sight (and those are very clear). The final operation is the staking of the windage nut on the left side. This will require that a simple tool be made from a small screwdriver, its tip cut as shown, into a shallow "V" shape. Be sure that the right side of the sight (not the slide!) is solidly supported on a block of hard wood while the tip of the windage screw is staked into the slots on the nut.

6. The completed installation is solidly mounted and is fully adjustable for windage and elevation. It will now be necessary to fire the pistol from a sandbag rest at a selected distance, to set the sight. This should be done with one consistent load, the one which will be used most. Radically different loads will require a different sight setting, due to varying bullet weights, powder charges, etc.

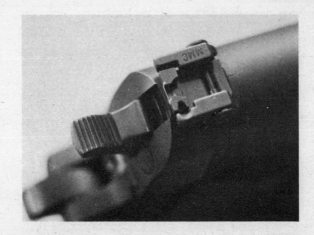

Custom Alterations

Recutting Sears and Sear Steps on Hammers

As made by the factories, many sear and hammer notch engagements have a definite angle, to insure proper detent when the hammer is cocked. In some cases, this arrangement is designed with product liability in mind. Unless the gun is a target-type, no manufacturer is going to send out a piece with a very light trigger pull, one that might lend itself to accidental firing. Some guns have an engagement so acute that as the sear moves, the hammer must actually be cammed very slightly back before release. Most serious shooters will want this situation altered, and the only way to accomplish this is to recut the sear and the sear step on the hammer. However, some safety hazard is involved. Obviously, as with all the other operations described in this book, you're on your own here. Neither the author, nor the publisher can be responsible for any mishaps that might occur.

1. Shown is a typical angled-detent engagement. In the one illustrated, the arc of the sear and its pivot point are good, and the trigger pull could probably be improved by simply stoning the mating surfaces, without alteration of the angles. When the sear pivot is more forward, though, this engagement would produce the camming effect mentioned above.

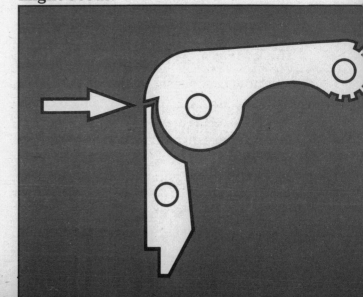

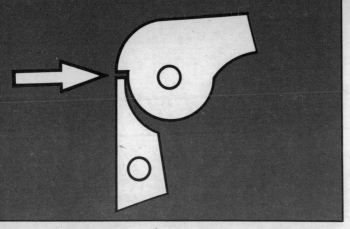

2. When that camming effect is evident, a good pull can be achieved by changing the angle to a straight shelf, as shown here. Since nearly all hammers and sears are fairly hard, a succession of stones will have to be used. I usually make the initial cut with a disc in the Dremel tool, but this requires a very steady hand and experience. I mention it only for those who are adept with a power tool. It's easy with this method to ruin a sear or hammer—stoning by hand is much safer. The important things here are to keep the step and the sear tip absolutely level, and to avoid going too far. Keep in mind that even when done properly, there will be a slight change in the position of the hammer at full cock, because you will have altered the height of the sear and the location of the hammer step. If the gun is an auto pistol, this will mean an increase of "drop" onto the sear from full depression by the slide. This can cause a "bounce out" effect, and may require a slight deepening of the notch when it is levelled. During the operation, frequent testing in the gun is recommended.

A Trigger Job for Auto Pistols

Smoothing the trigger pull in both firing modes of an auto pistol having selective double and single action has many of the same elements of the same job in a double action revolver. However, the engagement of the double action drawbar in an auto does not match, in most cases, the wide contact of a revolver double action system, so there's not as much improvement possible. In most DA autos, polishing the lobe on the hammer at the contact point is all that can be done. For this reason, we will concentrate here on the single action auto pistol. The first example, as you might expect, is the Government Model Colt.

1. As with any other trigger job, it's amazing how much change can be effected in the pull by just carefully polishing the contact points, without changing the angle. Indicated here is the full-cock step on the hammer.

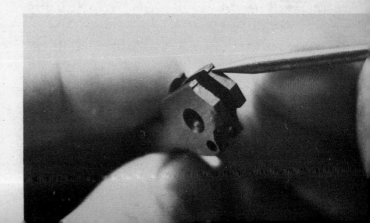

2. The other element to be polished is the top surface of the sear, indicated here. Once again, there is no need to change the angle to achieve a good pull.

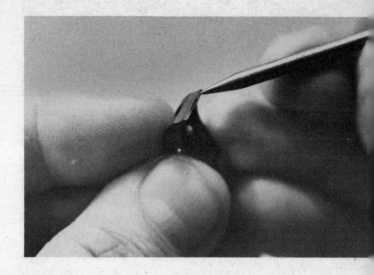

3. The surface hardness of the parts requires that stones be used. Start with a 400 or 600 stone, and for finishing go to a Hard Arkansas. This will impart a mirror polish. Take great care to keep the stone level with the surface as it is moved across, and avoid rounding any edges. If the step is slightly undercut, use a stone with an angled edge, to match the slant. The hammer is shown.

4. The top surface of the sear is done in the same way, with the part gripped firmly in a padded vise. Adjust the angle of the part to make the top surface level, and *keep the stone level as it is moved*. Again, keep the corners sharp, and don't round any edges. Once a bright polish is attained, with no tool marks, stop.

5. During the operation, it's a good idea to frequently check the angle of engagement to be sure it's not being changed. One handy way to do this is to insert the pivot pins in the hammer and sear, and place them in their respective holes on the right side of the frame, as shown. As you can see, this makes it easy to inspect the contact point.

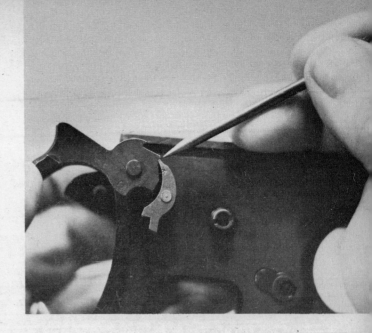

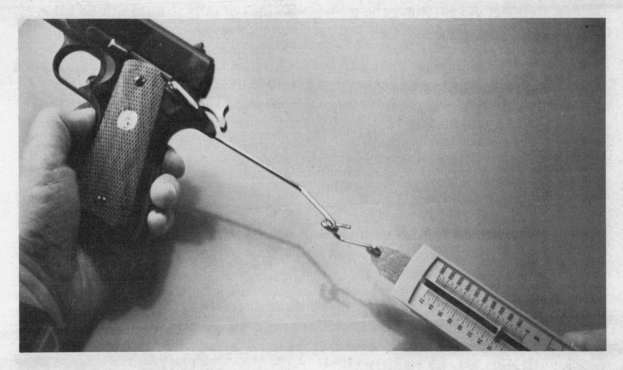

6. After the polishing is completed, a standard trigger pull gauge can be used to check the weight of the trigger pull. This will give you a figure in pounds and ounces, but it won't reveal the quality of the pull. For this, the only way is to actually pull the trigger with the finger. If there are any rough spots, you'll feel them. I've found that I can judge a pull better by actually trying it than with a gauge. Weight of pull is not everything.

If, when the job is finished, the hammer jumps off to the half-cock position when the slide goes forward, you've gone too far, or changed the angle, or rounded the edges. In that case, the original angles will have to be restored, and there's a limit to the number of times this can be done. In extreme cases, the hammer or sear must be replaced.

A Trigger Job for Revolvers

Even among the non-specialist gunsmiths, the "trigger job" has come to be a familiar operation. Sometimes it's an older gun which, from age and wear, has arrived at the point where it will "jump off" if jarred. In other cases, it may be a brand-new piece, with a trigger pull that is either too hard or has "creep." Of course, those who do serious target shooting want the crisp, "breaking-of-a-glass-rod" let-off, and those who engage in combat-style firing want a double action pull that is easy and silky-smooth.

In time (after about 5,000 rounds) any new gun will settle in to a fairly nice pull, as friction polishes the mating surfaces in normal wear. So, in doing a trigger job, the gunsmith simply hurries this situation. With revolvers, in most cases, there is no actual change of the angles where the parts meet, just mirror polishing of the mating surfaces. It should be noted that the weight of pull should not be taken all the way down to the point desired, as no one can get the polishing absolutely level, and there will still be a slight "wearing in" which can further lighten the pull by as much as a half-pound.

We'll begin by illustrating the work to be done on a Ruger Security-Six revolver, but the principles can be applied to others. Later on, we'll cover the pertinent points of both Colt and Smith & Wesson guns.

1. Triggers, hammers, and other internal parts are too hard to work with files, so the tools needed are shown here—a good selection of stones in several different shapes. These range from a medium/fine grade to the very fine India Oilstones and Hard Arkansas stones, the latter used for finishing. Opinion is divided whether to use cutting oil with the stones. I have never used it, but that's a matter of choice. Not shown is very fine emery paper, which I sometimes use for final polishing on flat surfaces. The paper is laid on the workbench,

and the part (the side of a cylinder hand, for example) is moved back and forth across it. This helps to keep the surface being polished quite flat and straight.

2. I usually begin the trigger job by removing the tool marks and polishing the top rear flat of the trigger, the area that contacts the double action lever on the hammer. In all of these operations, care must be taken to keep the stones level, to avoid slanting or rounding any edges that shouldn't be rounded.

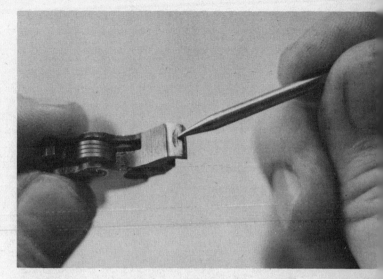

3. When doing the sear surface at the upper rear of the trigger extension, extreme care must be used. Any rounding of edges here will directly affect the single action engagement. Be sure that any sharp edges are still sharp when you finish, and avoid any extensive removal of material. The reach of this extension is critical, and if you go too far, it's time to buy a new trigger.

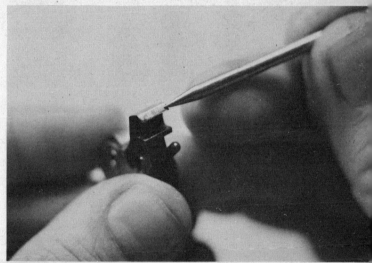

4. Although it's shown still attached here, the double action lever should be removed from the hammer, in most cases, for polishing. Here, if there are square edges at its lower tip, some rounding is acceptable. To ease trigger return, the front of the lever can also be polished.

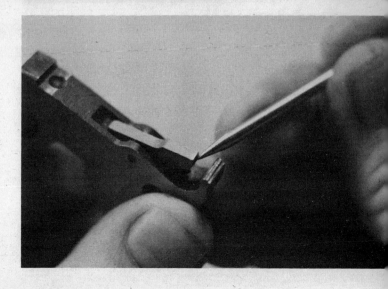

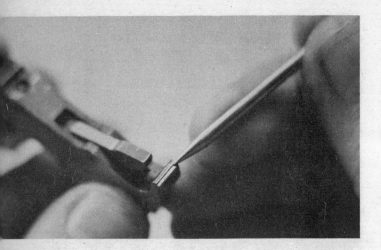

5. Another very critical area is the sear step on the lower front extension of the hammer. In this location, very light polishing should be done, taking care not to alter the depth or angle of the step. As with the sear surface on the trigger, any large mistake here will require a new hammer.

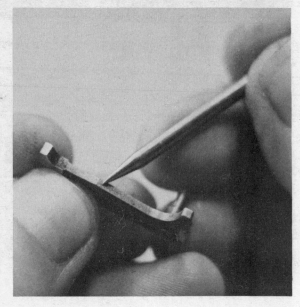

6. In the Ruger revolver, there is a single raised point on the front of the cylinder hand where it touches inside its track in the frame, and this area can be polished. Be sure, though, that the raised portion is not reduced to any great degree—only polished!

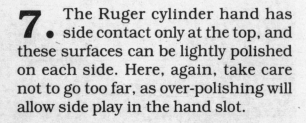

7. The Ruger cylinder hand has side contact only at the top, and these surfaces can be lightly polished on each side. Here, again, take care not to go too far, as over-polishing will allow side play in the hand slot.

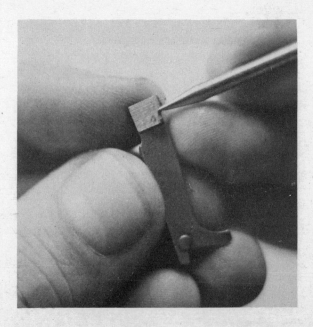

8. If the ratchet is leaving pronounced marks on the breech face as it turns, it can also be polished lightly, but *only* on its rear surface. Don't round any edges.

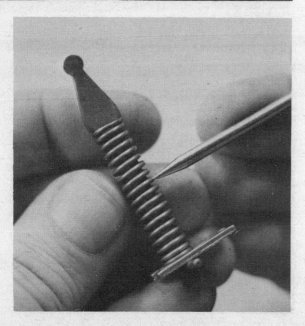

9. An area that is often neglected in action-smoothing operations is the top of the hammer strut, where it contacts its recess at the lower rear of the hammer. On a circular-tipped strut, such as the one used in the Ruger, be careful that its symmetry is not deformed in polishing.

10. Some gunsmiths also lighten the hammer spring and trigger spring, by trimming off a coil or two, and by reshaping the torsion types. There are also kits of replacement springs that accomplish the same purpose. Some of these alterations and kits work well, but I've seen a few cases in which the "lightening" had been over done, and the hammer fall was so soft that there were occasional misfires. In a serious encounter, this could be embarrassing. I'd rather rely on a high polish of all mating surfaces, and leave the original springs intact.

Smith & Wesson___

11. On the Smith & Wesson cylinder hand, the entire side needs to be polished. Take care, though, to just brighten it, as removal of any substantial amount of material will cause side play, and this can affect proper engagement of the hand with the ratchet. The front of the hand can also be polished, where it contacts the slot in the frame.

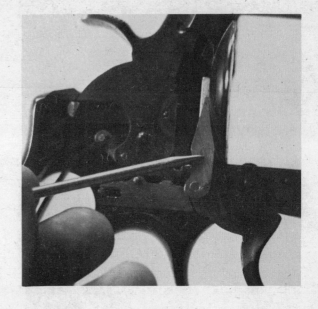

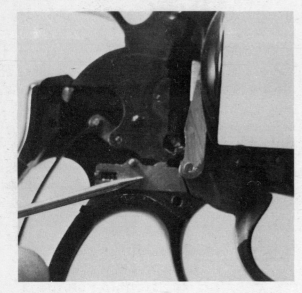

12. Both sides and underside of the rebound slide in the Smith & Wesson are also polished. The same advice about going too far applies here as well.

13. The lug on top of the rebound slide, and its mating lug on the underside of the hammer can be polished, but only if there is roughness there. This engagement is a part of the hammer-block safety system, and too much taken off here can cause big problems.

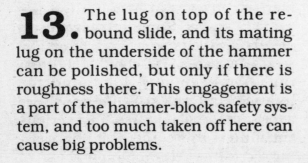

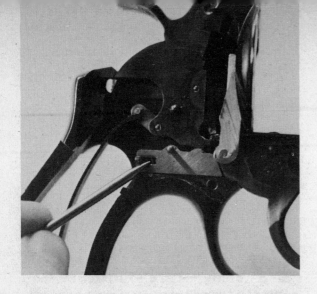

14. Generally, I don't approve of altering springs to lighten trigger pull. However, if desired, the rebound spring can be cut by one or 1½ coils without harm.

15. I have seen the standard Smith & Wesson blade-type hammer spring reshaped into some weird configurations in an effort to lighten its tension, but I definitely do not agree with this practice. It inevitably will make the spring susceptible to future breakage, and if carried to extremes can cause misfires. It is permissible to remove a tiny amount of material from the tip of the hammer spring strain screw, and this will take a little off the tension without adverse effects. The amount that can be removed varies with each gun, but generally I think the maximum should be no more than .035″ on guns that have seen some use.

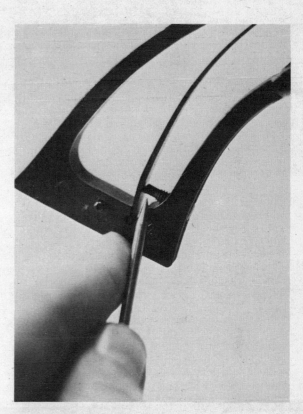

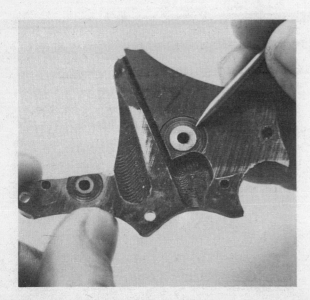

16. The pivot rings on the sideplate at the hammer and trigger post location can be lightly polished, if necessary. There is very little projection above the main surface here, and too much polishing will produce side play.

Colt_____

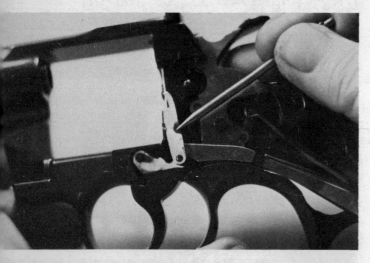

17. As on the Smith & Wesson, the entire side of the Colt cylinder hand, and its front surface, can be lightly polished. Be sure not to remove any significant amount of metal.

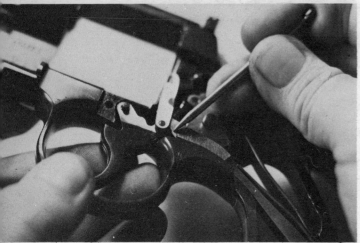

18. The forward underside of the rebound lever can be polished on the Colt, at the point of engagement with its shelf in the cylinder hand. Extreme care must be taken to avoid altering the angle of this surface, and its slant into the hand shelf.

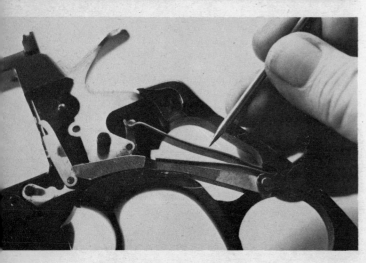

19. The Colt mainspring is also sometimes reshaped to lessen its tension. This is even less desirable than when done to a Smith & Wesson, as this is not only the hammer spring, but it also powers the trigger and cylinder hand. Altering the spring will eventually cause not only misfires, but also incomplete trigger return. It's best to rely on a high polish of the mating parts, and leave the springs alone.

A Trigger Job for the Browning HP

Because part of its trigger/sear linkage is in the slide, it has been said that a decent trigger pull is impossible to achieve in the Browning Hi-Power. A little more work, yes . . . but not impossible. The first step, described elsewhere in this section, is to remove the magazine safety system from the trigger. Just deleting the friction of this part against the front of the magazine will have a surprising effect on the pull. On some late guns, which have the sear pad as standard equipment, this may be all that is necessary to produce a nice pull, especially if the gun is already well broken-in. Otherwise, a careful polishing of the usual parts is always beneficial.

1. Since the angle of engagement of the hammer and sear in the HP is on top of the frame, rather than below as in most other guns, the Browning is less tolerant of changes in the shape of the full-cock step on the hammer. In polishing, care must be taken not to alter the angle of the step.

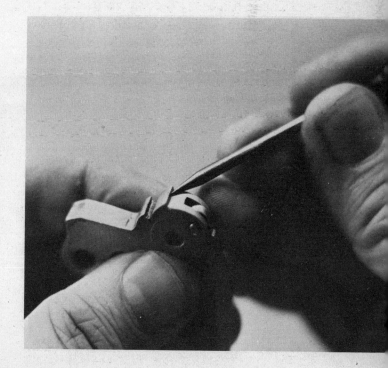

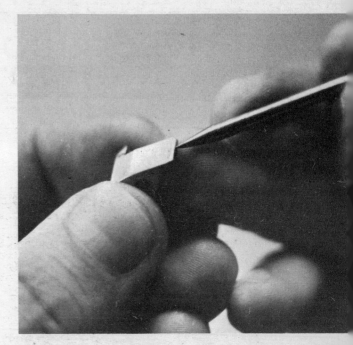

2. Again, unlike other guns, the contact tip of the sear need not be absolutely flat. In some cases, a good pull can be enhanced by a slight bevelling of the edges, reducing the contact area.

3. Just stoning the notch, with care to preserve its original angle, will produce a good pull. In some advanced alterations, the depth of the step is also slightly reduced, to shorten the distance the sear tip must travel for release. It's easy to go too far with this, though, and cause the hammer to "jump off" to half-cock as the slide closes. If this alteration is desired, it's best to leave it to a pistolsmith, one who specializes in the HP.

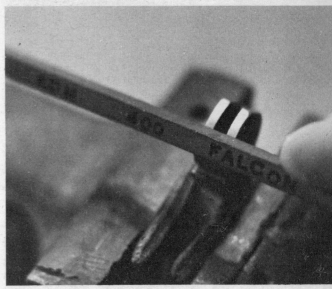

4. When stoning the sear tip, its shape makes it necessary to use a spacer block in the vise, as shown. As mentioned earlier, the edges can be slightly bevelled. I have examined one HP in which the sear tip was actually rounded, and it had a superb pull.

However, the contact face must be kept exactly straight, in relation to the step on the hammer. As with the hammer notch, use a 400 or 600 stone for the initial work, and do the final polish with a Hard Arkansas stone.

5. Commercial Hi-Powers made in the 1960s have a little "pad" on the right front corner of the sear, at the point contacted by the sear lever in the slide. This takes most of the slack out of the trigger pull. A similar pad can be added to the earlier sears, if necessary, but it's easier to just install a late-type sear, as they are interchangeable. The sear shown is an early war-time sear without the pad. The tool indicates the position of the pad on late-type sears.

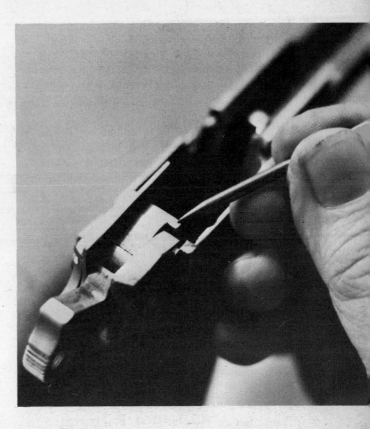

Magazine Safety Removal

For the uninitiated who might be reading this, perhaps it would be well to define "magazine safety." The term is applied to any device which blocks the firing mechanism of an automatic pistol when the magazine is taken out. The purpose, of course, is to protect those of limited experience, who might not realize, after removing the magazine, that there could be a round left in the chamber. I have, on occasion, referred to the magazine safety as an "abomination," but on further reflection I've come to believe that it does have some merit when included in the design of very small pocket pistols. Today's product liability jungle is also a consideration—any added safety device that might keep an inept person from injuring himself or others could discourage litigation. And, the small pocket automatics are often used by those who are not "gun people," and are relatively inexperienced with firearms.

For the rest of us, and on larger pistols, the magazine safety can be anything from a minor nuisance to a major detriment. One scenario that occurs to me is a situation in which the magazine is lost under survival circumstances, but the person still has a box of cartridges or some loose ammo. If there is no magazine safety, he still has a usable single-shot pistol. If there is a magazine safety device, and if its removal is not a simple in-the-field operation, then he has an interestingly-shaped and very expensive boat anchor.

On some pistols, there is an interdependence of the magazine safety with other parts, and removal will require a slight internal redesign by a gunsmith. In most of these cases, future restoration of the magazine safety is not possible without replacement of parts. Examples of this are the Mauser HSc and the Heckler & Koch HK4. Fortunately, on most of the large and medium-frame pistols of recent manufacture, removal of the magazine safety is a relatively simple operation, and simple reinstallation of the part (and sometimes its spring) will restore operation, if it's ever wanted.

Before we look at some examples of removable magazine safety systems, a word of caution: If you make this alteration on a pistol you own, be sure that *you* don't forget it's no longer there, and don't fail to point it out to anyone you allow to handle the pistol. For future trade or resale of the gun, note on a card to be kept with it that the magazine safety has been cancelled. This simple precaution may keep someone from being injured, and keep you out of a lawsuit. Another point to consider is that *any* alteration of the original factory mechanism of the gun will usually void any warranty. This point would apply to almost any custom alteration, other than replacement of grips, so keep it in mind.

1. One of the most frequently-removed magazine safety systems is the one in the Browning Hi-Power, mostly because it also affects the trigger pull. The magazine safety consists of a plunger (right arrow) at the rear of the trigger which bears on the front of the magazine. The friction at this point adds a fraction of an ounce to the pull. With the trigger removed from the gun, and the trigger lever taken off, drifting out the small cross-pin in the trigger (left arrow) will allow

the magazine safety and its spring to be removed toward the rear. The pin is then replaced to fill the hole, and the parts can be saved for future replacement, if desired.

2. Considering its size, it might be best to leave the Astra Cub with its magazine safety intact. The 22-caliber version, though, is used by some in survival kits and in that case removal would make sense. This is one of the easiest of all to take out, and doesn't even require that the grips be taken off. With the magazine out of the gun, drift out the small cross-pin (arrow) behind the lower end of the trigger, and the magazine safety and its spring will fall out of the lower opening of the magazine well. The pin is then replaced to fill the hole, and the parts can be saved.

3. On the Star Model FM 22 shown, and on the larger centerfires, such as the BM and BKM, removal of the magazine safety is particularly easy. After the grip panels are taken off, the post of the magazine safety is pushed toward the right side, and the magazine safety can then be lifted off.

4. The Beretta Model 84 and its counterpart, the 380-cal. Browning BDA, have a magazine safety that is simply a round-wire torsion-type spring, located under the right grip panel. While removal is not difficult, it does require several precise moves. This operation is detailed for the Model 84 in the *Gun Digest Book of Firearms Assembly/Disassembly, Part I, Automatic Pistols.* The procedure is the same for the BDA, except that the upper grip screw escutcheon must also be removed.

5. The Mauser HSc, in both its original and post-war versions, has a magazine safety that is not routinely removable. A single part performs two functions. Its rear portion is the slide hold-open latch, and a hook on the front blocks movement of the trigger when the magazine is removed. To deactivate the magazine safety the forward hook portion could be sliced off, but this would not be a reversible job unless an entire new part were later installed.

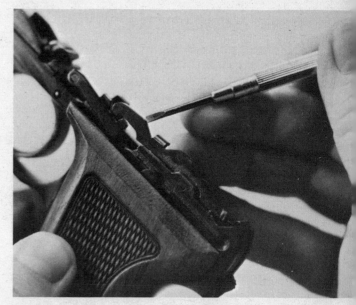

6. The Heckler & Koch Model HK4 is mechanically similar to the Mauser HSc, and has a magazine safety system that is almost identical. The remarks on the HSc also apply here— deactivation is a one-way street if you don't have a replacement safety/hold-open on hand.

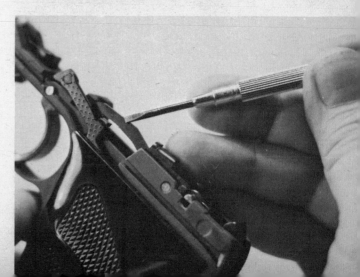

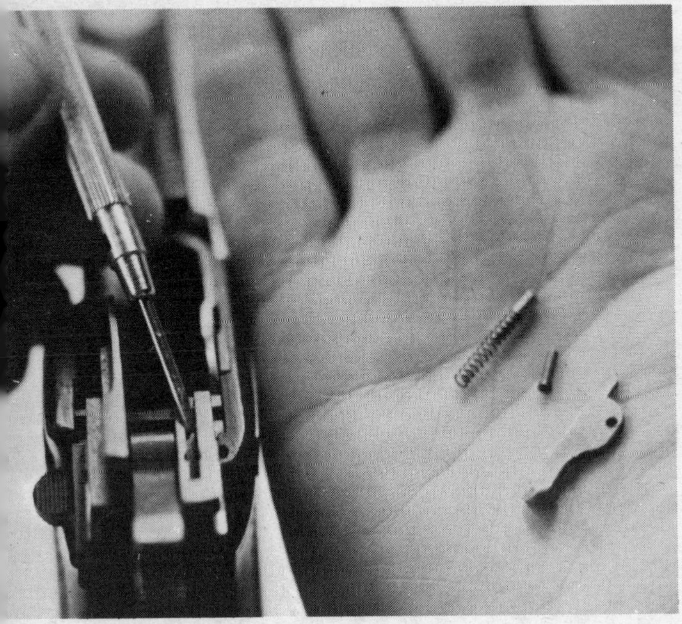

7. As originally made, the magazine safety of the French MAB PA-15 was a particular nuisance, as it acted directly on the sear. If the magazine was taken out before the hammer was cocked, the slide could not be opened, as the sear would bind on the hammer. The gun shown is the early model. Taking out the pivot pin toward the right allows the magazine safety and its spring and plunger to be removed upward. On the current guns, the removal procedure is the same, but the magazine safety system has been redesigned. It now bears on the trigger bar, and simply depresses it out of engagement with the sear. With the magazine out and the hammer down, the slide can still be opened.

8. The magazine safety on the little Bauer 25 ACP performs only that function, but its spring also powers the magazine catch. If the magazine safety is removed, a separate spring must be made for the magazine catch. As most readers already know, the Bauer is essentially a stainless steel American version of the old Browning "Baby" 25, so this data will also apply to that one.

9. In his new stainless double action 25, Larry Seecamp cleverly designed the magazine safety with an interdependence on other parts that makes its removal virtually impossible. To cancel its operation, you would have to make an entire new part, shaped differently, and non-pivoting. As mentioned earlier, on a small pocket pistol of this type, perhaps it's just as well that the magazine safety be left functioning.

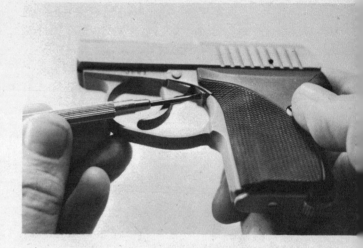

Cancelling an Auto Pistol's Grip Safety

I consider all grip safety mechanisms to be abominations, no matter how efficient or how well-contoured they may be. But, that's just my personal opinion. In all cases, they are unnecessary additions, and they never fail to make the pistol feel uncomfortable in the hand. The one on the Government Model Colt is a good example . . . or, perhaps, a bad example? There are those who say, "Yes, but if the gun is dropped, the grip safety will prevent it from firing!" In a magazine article a few years ago, one of the "Great Names" in firearms writing repeated this, but even when intoned by a "Gun Guru," it's still not true. The grip safety on the old warhorse directly blocks the *trigger* movement, and that's all. Judging from the number of grip safety systems I've blocked out of operation on the GM Colt, quite a few shooters share my feelings about this. The method I've always used is to install a small blocking stud in the top of the mainspring housing, as described here.

1. On the left side of the top surface of the mainspring hous-

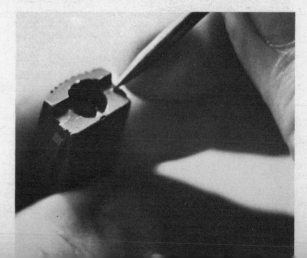

ing, just slightly away from the step at upper rear, use a center punch to indent an index mark, as shown. Center it between the mainspring well and the outside edge of the housing.

2. With the housing gripped firmly in a padded vise, its top surface level, drill a ¹⁄₁₆″ hole about ¼″ deep, straight down in relation to the top of the housing. Use extreme care to see that the drill is not tilted in any direction to insure that the hole will not come through into the spring well or on the outside.

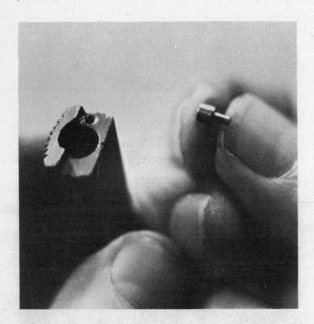

3. From a nail or a piece of rod stock, turn a stepped pin with a tail ³⁄₁₆″ long and about .065″ in diameter, tapered, for a snug fit in the hole. The head of the pin should be the size of a #28 or #29 drill bit—.136″ to .140″ in diameter—and about ⅛″ in height.

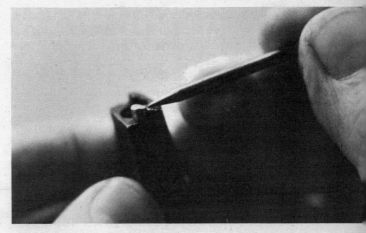

4. Before the cancelling stud is driven into place on top of the housing, one side will have to be filed at a slant, to mate with outer shelf on top. This will depend on how close the hole was drilled to the shelf. After the stud is in place, its top is filed to conform with the slant of the shelf top. If the hole is in exactly the right place, and the dimensions are as outlined above, no further fitting will be required.

stud will hold the grip safety in, as shown. There are no external or visible alterations, and if some subsequent owner should want the grip safety to work again, simple removal of the stud will restore it.

5. With the grip safety held in the depressed position, the housing is moved up into place, and the

Speaking of subsequent owners, or anyone else who might be handling or shooting the gun, you should be sure that they are told about the cancellation of the grip safety.

Cancelling the AMT Back-Up's Grip Safety

I like the little stainless-steel 380 Back-Up pistol, and have carried mine often. I found this grip safety, though, to be even more objectionable than most designs. It is hinged at the top, and protrudes at the lower rear. The grip angle is rather straight, and depressing the grip safety requires a conscious change in the normal holding position of the gun, a change that tends to tip the muzzle downward. In rapid-fire practice on combat-style targets, the point-of-impact was always low.

Since the Back-Up is an internal hammer gun, I never use either of the safety systems, anyway, as I load

the chamber only just before firing. So, I decided to cancel the grip safety. This proved to be very easy.

1. The unaltered Back-Up is shown, with the internal ham-

mer cocked and the grip safety protruding. The grip safety blocks the sear, and it must be fully depressed before firing is possible.

2. A vertical hole is drilled in the grip frame, just to the rear of the magazine catch. The grip safety is then depressed, even with the frame, and a sharp-pointed rod is inserted and tapped with a hammer to mark the underside of the grip safety piece. A matching hole is then drilled in the lower end of the grip safety. The most difficult part of this operation is getting the holes centered properly, as there is very little room on the bottom of the grip safety. Maximum size of the hole in the grip safety piece should be about .065". The hole in the frame is threaded to about half its depth, and a headless screw is made, with a long unthreaded section that will extend upward to enter the hole in the grip safety.

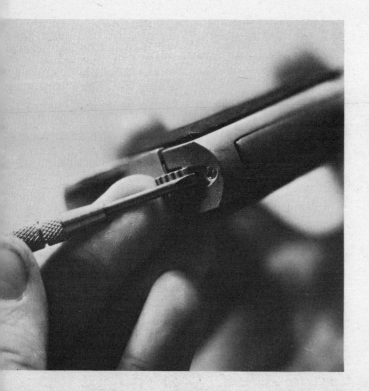

3. When the screw is installed, the grip safety is effectively cancelled. I can't imagine why anyone would want the grip safety activated again, but if so, just taking out the screw will restore it to operation. As always, when any modification is done to the safety systems of any gun, be sure anyone who handles it knows of the alteration.

Chamber Throating

Most automatic pistols are designed to work properly only with loads having full-jacketed bullets, but many of today's shooters insist on using the "funny stuff"—hollow point, soft point, and so on. A few guns, such as the Walther PPK/S, will digest almost anything with infallible precision. For most guns, though, the use of "non-standard" rounds will require an operation that is popularly called "throating." This involves rounding and smoothing all sharp edges at the chamber mouth, and altering the feed ramp on the frame. In some cases, the slide latch is also modified.

While these things are possible for the very knowledgeable amateur, it's an operation that should not be attempted by the beginner. The parts involved are major ones, and if mistakes are made, the replacement costs can be considerable. The tools used are the Dremel (or another power tool), rotary stones, rotary polishing heads (abrasive-impregnated rubber), and a split-end rod with fine emery paper. The watchwords for this procedure are care and caution. Work slowly and patiently. Wear safety glasses, of course.

1. A medium to fine rotary stone with a semi-coned shape is used to round all sharp angles at the chamber entrance. This includes the side edges, up to about the half-way mark, and the roll-over at the lower edge of the chamber. When doing this, remember that going too far will leave the head of the cartridge case unsupported. I've seen incidents of this carried too far, with the result that the case blew out at the bottom, damaging the gun and the shooter's hand. All that's needed is to gently round off the edges on the bottom half of the chamber mouth.

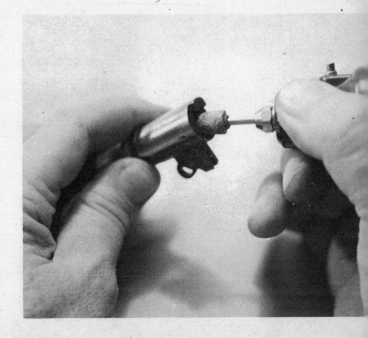

2. When the barrel of the gun is not routinely removable, a different stone must be used, one with a ball shape. This is a more difficult operation, as the stone will tend to "crawl" in the direction of its rotation (see the Tool Use Section), and reverse pressure must be applied to compensate for the pull. When final polishing of the fixed-barrel type is done, a polishing head with a rounded tip must be used, and the same advice applies.

3. After the reshaping is finished, the rotary stone is exchanged for a conical head of rubber impregnated with a fine abrasive. All of the surfaces that were ground with the stone must be polished bright. This fine-grit polishing head will also remove steel, although more slowly, so take care not to apply it with too much enthusiasm. When the surfaces are bright, stop.

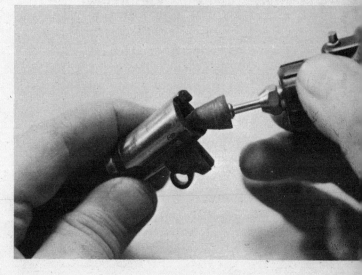

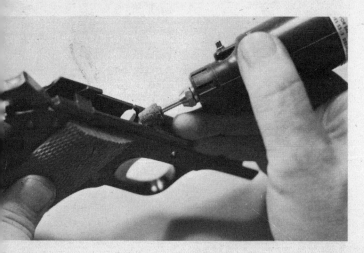

4. When part of the feed ramp is also on the frame, it, too, should be altered. From the sides of the magazine well to the ramp should be a continuous curve, with no "step" or narrowing. The top of the ramp should exactly meet the lower rear edge of the entry slope on the barrel chamber, without a step or gap. To pre-determine the frame ramp angle, I usually put the barrel in place, insert the slide latch to retain it, and move it back to its rearmost position. A line is then scribed on top of the frame at the lower edge of the rear face of the barrel as a reference point. The frame ramp is then shaped with the same rotary stone.

5. Just as with the barrel, the polishing head is then used to put the finishing touches on the frame ramp. In regard to both the rotary stone and the polisher, note that frames of alloy will cut away much more rapidly then those of steel. If the frame is alloy, as on the Star BKM shown, adjust the pressure and duration of cutting and polishing accordingly. It's easy to go too far too fast here, so be careful. A new frame is expensive!

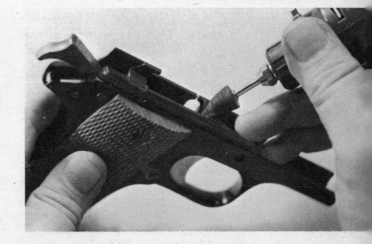

6. In many cases, the inner projection of the slide latch should also be worked over, especially if its rear surface has an edge that might become an obstruction for flat-nosed bullets. Depending on the latch, this modification can be either a flat slope or a dished-out shape. The flat cut is shown here, with the polishing head giving it a final brightening.

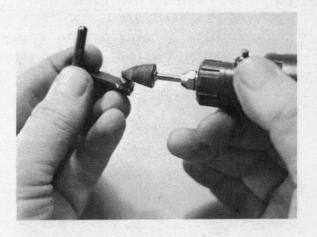

7. The finished barrel should show no sharp angles at the lower edge and sides of the chamber. Some pistolsmiths also round the top edge of the chamber slightly, but this is a matter of choice and individual requirements. With a split-end rod and fine emery paper, I usually make a few passes into the chamber at the finish.

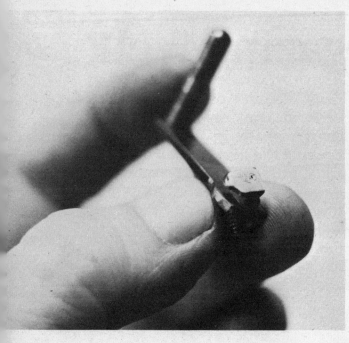

8. Because of its internal cross-pin, this slide latch was given a flat slope. It is shown here after the final polishing.

9. On this black anodized alloy frame, the reshaped and polished feed ramp is very visible.

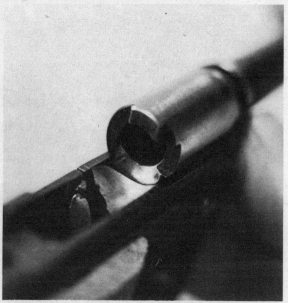

10. The finished assembly. During the entire operation, it's a good idea to frequently assemble the parts in this manner, to check the matching of the ramps. A shadow in the photo magnifies the gap between the chamber and frame ramps. Actually, it is very small.

As an afterword, I will note the method I use to check all throating jobs: Locking the slide open, I load one *empty* case in the magazine, insert it, and trip the slide latch. If it will feed this properly, it will feed *any* loaded round.

Bevelling a Magazine Well

One of the elementary custom jobs performed on automatic pistols in combat competition use is bevelling of the magazine entry. Since most factory magazine openings are made with rather square edges, almost any change in this area will make magazine replacement quicker and easier. A few manufacturers, like Detonics and Safari Arms, have the magazine entry bevelled as a standard feature. On most other guns, it's not a difficult operation to perform. The only part that might give an amateur some trouble is keeping the bevels straight and of equal proportion. I have made the initial cuts with discs and stones in the Dremel tool, but for those who lack experience with hand power tools, this is risky. The best way is to use a group of files, in varying grades and shapes.

1. Here is a typical square-edged magazine entry, the one shown on a Government Model frame by Essex.

2. Two layers of heavy tape are applied to the front and rear of the opening to protect those surfaces from the file. A medium double-cut

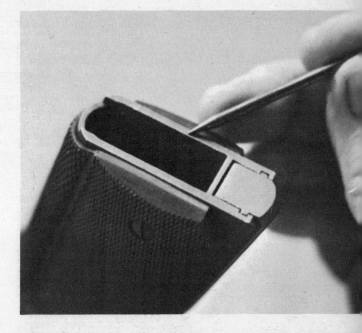

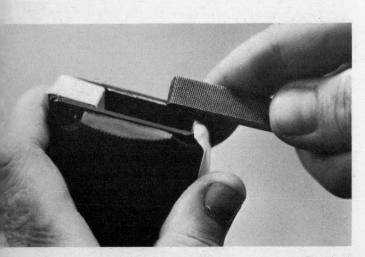

file with a safe edge is then used, lengthwise, to cut the bevel on each side. With a lengthwise stroke, it is easier to keep the bevel even and aligned with the edges.

3. After the bevel is made, a finer file is used to complete it and smooth its edges. Any necessary small adjustments to match the two sides can be made at this time.

4. A medium double-cut quarter-round file is used to shape the front curve of the entry. Here, a bevel is not done—the edge is rounded. A twisting motion added to the inward stroke will help to keep the shaping equal from side to side. Avoid bringing the front to a sharp edge—leave a small flat space at the rim.

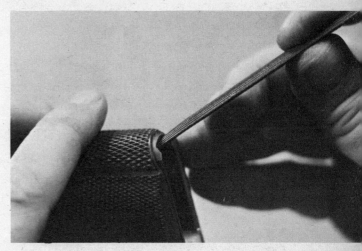

5. With a fine file, the shaping and smoothing is completed.

6. At the rear, the bevel should match the width and angle of the side planes. Since this is a straight inward cut, across the edge, a finer file can be used from the start. Leave a small flat at the rear, next to the mainspring housing.

7. After the rear bevel is done, use a fine small file to fair the corners into the side bevels, a sort of "picture-frame" effect. This is the point which requires the greatest care, as it's easy to spoil the symmetry of the side bevels while mating the corner.

8. If very fine files have been used for finishing, further polishing will not be necessary, but fine emery paper or cloth can be used, if needed. Cold chemical blue can then be applied. If the frame was not disassembled (as this one wasn't), take care that the blue doesn't run inside the frame at the rear.

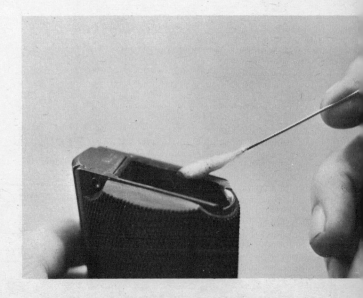

9. Here is the finished alteration of the magazine entry. I prefer a moderate bevel, as shown here, but it is possible to bring it all the way to the outer edges, and extend it further into the magazine well, if desired.

Slimming and Trimming Handguns

I may or may not be the first to use the term "reduction" to describe the process of making a gun smaller for purposes of concealed carrying, but it is an appropriate descriptive word. In the larger calibers, this operation is an extensive (and expensive!) alteration, and as perfected by Devel, ASP, and others it involves shortening the barrel, slide, magazine, and grip frame in automatics. In revolvers, reduction is often no more than cutting off the barrel, resetting the front sight, and replacing the original grips with a pair that are as slim and unobtrusive as possible.

Small to medium-frame automatic pistols can be reduced quite a bit by just rounding any

sharp corners, taking off sights, and bobbing some projections, such as hammer spurs and safety levers. In the case of hammer spurs, though, the operation should be approached with some caution. In many cases, the weight of the hammer is a major factor in reliable ignition, and taking off too much will result in a light blow and a misfire.

It's sometimes amazing how much smaller a gun will feel and appear by just taking off the high spots and thinning the grips. When alterations are made to guns of conventional steel, refinishing is mandatory. With stainless steel, though, it's only necessary that the degree of finish be matched—high polish, matte, and so on. For my own personal use, I performed several alterations, including "reduction," on a 25 ACP Bauer stainless steel pistol, and the results are shown here.

1. On the Bauer, the front and rear sights and their raised rib are really unnecessary, so all of this was neatly removed by filing. The grips, which on this gun were the early walnut type, were thinned to about half their original thickness. The button at the end of the safety lever was trimmed by at least half its thickness. On this particular gun, I use the safety only as a takedown aid, as I carry the gun with the chamber empty. The back edge of the magazine catch, which is very sharp on the Bauer pistols as they come from the factory, was rounded, along with all of the other sharp edges, especially at the front of the slide and frame. The rear underside of the safety lever and the same area on the trigger bar were also rounded at the point where they touch the web of the hand. Unrelated to reduction, the magazine safety and

its spring were also removed, and a separate spring was made to power the magazine catch. The gun was also throated, and the extractor altered slightly to increase the inward reach of its beak.

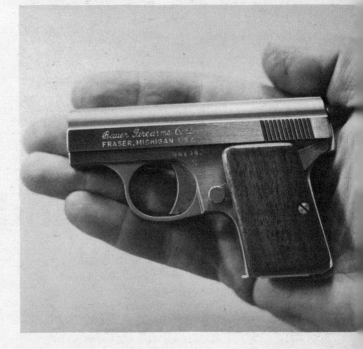

2. When thinning the grips, it was also necessary to recut the slot

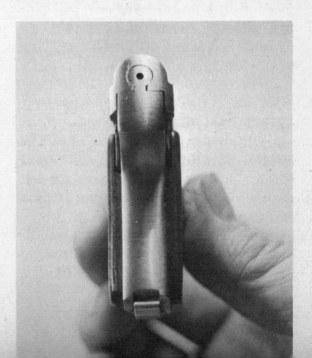

in the grip screw to deepen it, and the head of the screw and its nut were both thinned along with the grips. Most of the Bauer pistols I've seen in recent times have been supplied with grips of imitation pearl, and I'm not sure how suitable these would be for thinning. If the walnut grips are not still available from the factory, it might be necessary to make your own set of thin wood grips.

3. When removing the sights and sight rib, the last file strokes (if not all of them) should be done lengthwise, taking care to keep the surface level with the top of the slide. When this is completed, the edges at the front and rear should be rounded over. As noted earlier, one of the beauties of stainless steel is that it requires no finishing when the work is completed. If the filing is done carefully,

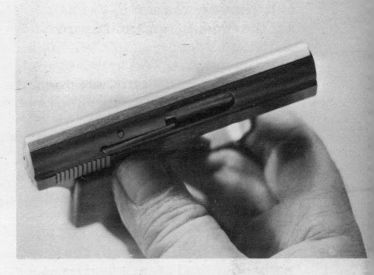

altered areas will exactly match the rest of the finish on the gun. Even if they don't, a bit of emery cloth wrapped around a flat file will polish up any rough surfaces. By varying the grit of the emery cloth, you can get different finishes, from matte to near mirror-like gloss.

Cartridge Conversion—the Astra 400

In earlier times, when the long-nosed Astra Model 400 came on the U.S. market as surplus, quite a lot of misinformation was published about it. This gun, it was said, would work with almost any 9mm cartridge that the shooter wanted to feed it. Unfortunately, this was occasionally true. In 9mm Luger, for example, some European cartridges with slightly larger case-head dimensions would "wedge" in the rear of the deep chamber, and would actually fire and function. Sometimes. Then, running out of the European stuff, the shooter would use the more straight-cased U.S. ammunition and these dropped all the way in. If the Astra firing pin managed to reach them, the violent setback from that position often broke the extractor.

The gun was actually chambered for the 9mm Bergmann-Bayard cartridge, of course, called in Spain the "9mm Largo," or, in translation, "9mm Long." The gun was intended to be used with no other round. As the surplus stocks of 9mm Bergmann-Bayard ammo ran out, many shooters correctly noted that in dimensions and power, the old 38 Auto (38 ACP) cartridge was very close. In some guns, in fact, it would work perfectly. Some Model 400 pistols, though, especially the very early ones, had breech face recesses that were *exactly* the diameter of the Bergman-Bayard rim—.392″. In these, when the 38 Auto was tried, the slide would not quite close on it. The rim of the 38 Auto, as made today, has a diameter of .405″.

Some of these guns, such as those with Guardia Civil or Navy markings, are valuable collector pieces, and shouldn't be altered. For the large quantity that are just shooters, though, I designed a tool for opening the breech face just .013″, and it would be easy for the small-shop gunsmith to duplicate it. The tool has to have a long shank, at least 6¼ inches overall, as it must reach in from the front of the long slide to the breech face. It must be made of rod stock that is slightly larger than .405″, obviously. The tip is turned down to exactly .405″, and mine has four cutting points, but they are sharp at the *sides only*. The end is neutral, to prevent deepening of the recess. After it was shaped, the end was heated and oil-hardened. A T-handle was made by cross-drilling the other end and inserting a large nail.

1. Here is the familiar Astra Model 400, also called the Modelo 1921, after the year of its adoption by the Spanish military services.

2. Comparing the 9mm Berg-mann-Bayard (left) and the 38 Auto, the difference in rim diameter can almost be seen with the eye. The working end of the breech face tool is shown at the right.

3. Before the tool can be used, the extractor must be taken out. Thanks to the ingenious L-pins used in the design of the Astra, this is easy. In the recess in the right under-edge of the slide, use a small screwdriver to lift out the forward L-pin. (The other one retains the firing pin, and it need not be removed.)

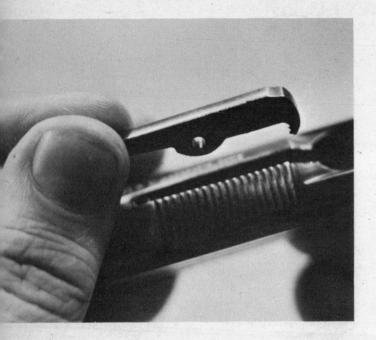

4. After the pin is taken out, remove the extractor. If its coil spring is left in its well at the rear, take care that it doesn't fall out and become lost.

5. The tool is inserted from the front of the slide, and carefully centered on the breech face recess. With firm but moderate rearward pressure, the tool is then turned until its end has bottomed in the recess. The diameter of the recess is now .405", and 38 Auto ammunition can be used.

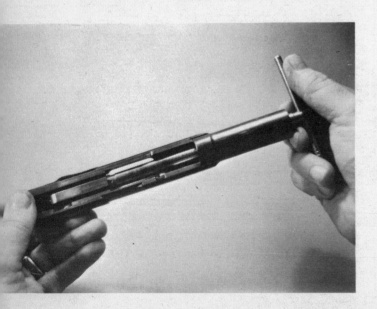

As always, when writing about this gun, I'll add this warning: The 38 Super cartridge has the same dimensions as the 38 Auto, and it's easy for the unknowing shooter, and sometimes even for gun shop clerks, to confuse them. **Never Use 38 Super In The Astra 400 Pistol!** It's not even considered safe in the early Colt pistols, and they are locked-breech guns. The Astra 400 is a blow-back action, and the use of 38 Super rounds may create some interesting problems for your local hospital, with you as the subject.

Conversion Tables

The tables below will allow you to convert weights and measures into the desired equivalent. Simply find the weight or measure you're working with in the left-hand column and multiply it by the number in the far right-hand column. The correct designation for the resulting figure will be found in the center column.

Conversion Factors

TO CONVERT	INTO	MULTIPLY BY
A		
Abcoulomb	Statcoulombs	2.998×10^{10}
Acre	Sq. chain (Gunters)	10
Acre	Rods	160
Acre	Square links (Gunters)	1×10^5
Acre	Hectare or sq. hectometer	.4047
acres	sq feet	43,560.0
acres	sq meters	4,047.
acres	sq miles	1.562×10^{-3}
acres	sq yards	4,840.
acre-feet	cu feet	43,560.0
acre-feet	gallons	3.259×10^5
amperes/sq cm	amps/sq in.	6.452
amperes/sq cm	amps/sq meter	10^4
amperes/sq in.	amps/sq cm	0.1550
amperes/sq in.	amps/sq meter	1,550.0
amperes/sq meter	amps/sq cm	10^{-4}
amperes/sq meter	amps/sq in.	6.452×10^{-4}
ampere-hours	coulombs	3,600.0
ampere-hours	faradays	0.03731
ampere-turns	gilberts	1.257
ampere-turns/cm	amp-turns/in.	2.540
ampere-turns/cm	amp-turns/meter	100.0
ampere-turns/cm	gilberts/cm	1.257
ampere-turns/in.	amp-turns/cm	0.3937
ampere-turns/in.	amp-turns/meter	39.37
ampere-turns/in.	gilberts/cm	0.4950
ampere-turns/meter	amp/turns/cm	0.01
ampere-turns/meter	amp-turns/in.	0.0254
ampere-turns/meter	gilberts/cm	0.01257
Angstrom unit	Inch	3937×10^{-9}
Angstrom unit	Meter	1×10^{-10}
Angstrom unit	Micron or (Mu)	1×10^{-4}
Are	Acre (US)	.02471
Ares	sq. yards	119.60
ares	acres	0.02471
ares	sq meters	100.0
Astronomical Unit	Kilometers	1.495×10^3
Atmospheres	Ton/sq. inch	.007348
atmospheres	cms of mercury	76.0
atmospheres	ft of water (at 4°C)	33.90
atmospheres	in. of mercury (at 0°C)	29.92
atmospheres	kgs/sq cm	1.0333
atmospheres	kgs/sq meter	10,332.
atmospheres	pounds/sq. in.	14.70
atmospheres	tons/sq ft	1.058

Conversion Factors

TO CONVERT	INTO	MULTIPLY BY
B		
Barrels (U.S., dry)	cu. inches	7056.
Barrels (U.S., dry)	quarts (dry)	105.0
Barrels (U.S., liquid)	gallons	31.5
barrels (oil)	gallons (oil)	42.0
bars	atmospheres	0.9869
bars	dynes/sq cm	10^6
bars	kgs/sq meter	1.020×10^4
bars	pounds/sq ft	2,089.
bars	pounds/sq in.	14.50
Baryl	Dyne/sq. cm.	1.000
Bolt (US Cloth)	Meters	36.576
Btu	Liter-Atmosphere	10.409
Btu	ergs	1.0550×10^{10}
Btu	foot-lbs	778.3
Btu	gram-calories	252.0
Btu	horsepower-hrs	3.931×10^{-4}
Btu	joules	1,054.8
Btu	kilogram-calories	0.2520
Btu	kilogram-meters	107.5
Btu	kilowatt-hrs	2.928×10^{-4}
Btu/hr	foot-pounds/sec	0.2162
Btu/hr	gram-cal/sec	0.0700
Btu/hr	horsepower-hrs	3.929×10^{-4}
Btu/hr	watts	0.2931
Btu/min	foot-lbs/sec	12.96
Btu/min	horsepower	0.02356
Btu/min	kilowatts	0.01757
Btu/min	watts	17.57
Btu/sq ft/min	watts/sq in.	0.1221
Bucket (Br. dry)	Cubic Cm.	1.818×10^4
bushels	cu ft	1.2445
bushels	cu in.	2,150.4
bushels	cu meters	0.03524
bushels	liters	35.24
bushels	pecks	4.0
bushels	pints (dry)	64.0
bushels	quarts (dry)	32.0
C		
Calories, gram (mean)	Btu (mean)	3.9685×10^{-3}
Candle/sq. cm	Lamberts	3.142
Candle/sq. inch	Lamberts	.4870
centares (centiares)	sq meters	1.0
Celsius	fahrenheit	(C°x9/5) + 32

Conversion Factors

TO CONVERT	INTO	MULTIPLY BY
centigrams	grams	0.01
Centiliter	Ounce fluid (US)	.3382
Centiliter	Cubic inch	.6103
Centiliter	drams	2.705
centiliters	liters	0.01
centimeters	feet	3.281×10^{-2}
centimeters	inches	0.3937
centimeters	kilometers	10^{-5}
centimeters	meters	0.01
centimeters	miles	6.214×10^{-6}
centimeters	millimeters	10.0
centimeters	mils	393.7
centimeters	yards	1.094×10^{-2}
centimeter-dynes	cm-grams	1.020×10^{-3}
centimeter-dynes	meter-kgs	1.020×10^{-8}
centimeter-dynes	pound-feet	7.376×10^{-8}
centimeter-grams	cm-dynes	980.7
centimeter-grams	meter-kgs	10^{-5}
centimeter-grams	pound-feet	7.233×10^{-5}
centimeters of mercury	atmospheres	0.01316
centimeters of mercury	feet of water	0.4461
centimeters of mercury	kgs/sq meter	136.0
centimeters of mercury	pounds/sq ft	27.85
centimeters of mercury	pounds/sq in.	0.1934
centimeters/sec	feet/min	1.1969
centimeters/sec	feet/sec	0.03281
centimeters/sec	kilometers/hr	0.036
centimeters-sec	knots	0.1943
centimeters/sec	meters/min	0.6
centimeters/sec	miles/hr	0.02237
centimeters/sec	miles/min	3.728×10^{-4}
centimeters/sec/sec	feet/sec/sec	0.03281
centimeters/sec/sec	kms/hr/sec	0.036
centimeters/sec/sec	meters/sec/sec	0.01
centimeters/sec/sec	miles/hr/sec	0.02237
Chain	Inches	792.00
Chain	meters	20.12
Chain (surveyors' or Gunter's)	yards	22.00
circular mils	sq cms	5.067×10^{-6}
circular mils	sq mils	0.7854
Circumference	Radians	6.283
circular mils	sq inches	7.854×10^{-7}
Cords	cord feet	8
Cord feet	cu. feet	16
Coulomb	Statcoulombs	2.998×10^{9}
coulombs	faradays	1.036×10^{-5}
coulombs/sq cm	coulombs/sq in.	64.52
coulombs/sq cm	coulombs/sq meter	10^{4}
coulombs/sq in.	coulombs/sq cm	0.1550
coulombs/sq in.	coulombs/sq meter	1,550.
coulombs/sq meter	coulombs/sq cm	10^{-4}
coulombs/sq meter	coulombs/sq in.	6.452×10^{-4}
cubic centimeters	cu feet	3.531×10^{-5}
cubic centimeters	cu inches	0.06102
cubic centimeters	cu meters	10^{-6}
cubic centimeters	cu yards	1.308×10^{-6}
cubic centimeters	gallons (U.S. liq.)	2.642×10^{-4}
cubic centimeters	liters	0.001

Conversion Factors

TO CONVERT	INTO	MULTIPLY BY
cubic centimeters	pints (U.S. liq.)	2.113×10^{-3}
cubic centimeters	quarts (U.S. liq.)	1.057×10^{-3}
cubic feet	bushels (dry)	0.8036
cubic feet	cu cms	28,320.0
cubic feet	cu inches	1,728.0
cubic feet	cu meters	0.02832
cubic feet	cu yards	0.03704
cubic feet	gallons (U.S. liq.)	7.48052
cubic feet	liters	28.32
cubic feet	pints (U.S. liq.)	59.84
cubic feet	quarts (U.S. liq.)	29.92
cubic feet/min	cu cms/sec	472.0
cubic feet/min	gallons/sec	0.1247
cubic feet/min	liters/sec	0.4720
cubic feet/min	pounds of water/min.	62.43
cubic feet/sec	million gals/day	0.646317
cubic feet/sec	gallons/min	448.831
cubic inches	cu cms	16.39
cubic inches	cu feet	5.787×10^{-4}
cubic inches	cu meters	1.639×10^{-5}
cubic inches	cu yards	2.143×10^{-5}
cubic inches	gallons	4.329×10^{-3}
cubic inches	liters	0.01639
cubic inches	mil-feet	1.061×10^{5}
cubic inches	pints (U.S. liq.)	0.03463
cubic inches	quarts (U.S. liq.)	0.01732
cubic meters	bushels (dry)	28.38
cubic meters	cu cms	10^{6}
cubic meters	cu feet	35.31
cubic meters	cu inches	61,023.0
cubic meters	cu yards	1.308
cubic meters	gallons (U.S. liq.)	264.2
cubic meters	liters	1,000.0
cubic meters	pints (U.S. liq.)	2,113.0
cubic meters	quarts (U.S. liq.)	1,057.
cubic yards	cu cms	7.646×10^{5}
cubic yards	cu feet	27.0
cubic yards	cu inches	46,656.0
cubic yards	cu meters	0.7646
cubic yards	gallons (U.S. liq.)	202.0
cubic yards	liters	764.6
cubic yards	pints (U.S. liq.)	1,615.9
cubic yards	quarts (U.S. liq.)	807.9
cubic yards/min	cubic ft/sec	0.45
cubic yards/min	gallons/sec	3.367
cubic yards/min	liters/sec	12.74

D

TO CONVERT	INTO	MULTIPLY BY
Dalton	Gram	1.650×10^{-24}
days	seconds	86,400.0
decigrams	grams	0.1
deciliters	liters	0.1
decimeters	meters	0.1
degrees (angle)	quadrants	0.01111
degrees (angle)	radians	0.01745
degrees (angle)	seconds	3,600.0
degrees/sec	radians/sec	0.01745
degrees/sec	revolutions/min	0.1667
degrees/sec	revolutions/sec	2.778×10^{-3}
dekagrams	grams	10.0
dekaliters	liters	10.0
dekameters	meters	10.0
Drams (apothecaries' or troy)	ounces (avoirdupois)	0.1371429

Conversion Factors

TO CONVERT	INTO	MULTIPLY BY
Drams (apothecaries' or troy)	ounces (troy)	0.125
Drams (U.S., fluid or apoth.)	cubic cm.	3.6967
drams	grams	1.7718
drams	grains	27.3437
drams	ounces	0.0625
Dyne/cm	Erg/sq. millimeter	.01
Dyne/sq. cm.	Atmospheres	9.869×10^{-7}
Dyne/sq. cm.	Inch of Mercury at 0°C	2.953×10^{-5}
Dyne/sq. cm.	Inch of Water at 4°C	4.015×10^{-4}
dynes	grame	1.020×10^{-3}
dynes	joules/cm	10^{-7}
dynes	joules/meter (newtons)	10^{-5}
dynes	kilograms	1.020×10^{-6}
dynes	poundals	7.233×10^{-5}
dynes	pounds	2.248×10^{-6}
dynes/sq cm	bars	10^{-6}

E

TO CONVERT	INTO	MULTIPLY BY
Ell	Cm.	114.30
Ell	Inches	45
Em, Pica	Inch	.167
Em, Pica	Cm.	.4233
Erg/sec	Dyne — cm/sec	1.000
ergs	Btu	9.480×10^{-11}
ergs	dyne-centimeters	1.0
ergs	foot-pounds	7.367×10^{-8}
ergs	gram-calories	0.2389×10^{-7}
ergs	gram-cms	1.020×10^{-3}
ergs	horsepower-hrs	3.7250×10^{-14}
ergs	joules	10^{-7}
ergs	kg-calories	2.389×10^{-11}
ergs	kg-meters	1.020×10^{-8}
ergs	kilowatt-hrs	0.2778×10^{-13}
ergs	watt-hours	0.2778×10^{-10}
ergs/sec	Btu/min	$5,688 \times 10^{-9}$
ergs/sec	ft-lbs/min	4.427×10^{-6}
ergs/sec	ft-lbs/sec	7.3756×10^{-8}
ergs/sec	horsepower	1.341×10^{-10}
ergs/sec	kg-calories/min	1.433×10^{-9}
ergs/sec	kilowatts	10^{-10}

F

TO CONVERT	INTO	MULTIPLY BY
farads	microfarads	10^{6}
Faraday/sec	Ampere (absolute)	9.6500×10^{4}
faradays	ampere-hours	26.80
faradays	coulombs	9.649×10^{4}
Fathom	Meter	1.828804
fathoms	feet	6.0
feet	centimeters	30.48
feet	kilometers	3.048×10^{-4}
feet	meters	0.3048
feet	miles (naut.)	1.645×10^{-4}
feet	miles (stat.)	1.894×10^{-4}
feet	millimeters	304.8
feet	mils	1.2×10^{4}
feet of water	atmospheres	0.02950
feet of water	in. of mercury	0.8826
feet of water	kgs/sq cm	0.03048
feet of water	kgs/sq meter	304.8
feet of water	pounds/sq ft	62.43
feet of water	pounds/sq in.	0.4335
feet/min	cms/sec	0.5080
feet/min	feet/sec	0.01667

Conversion Factors

TO CONVERT	INTO	MULTIPLY BY
feet/min	kms/hr	0.01829
feet/min	meters/min	0.3048
feet/min	miles/hr	0.01136
feet/sec	cms/sec	30.48
feet/sec	kms/hr	1.097
feet/sec	knots	0.5921
feet/sec	meters/min	18.29
feet/sec	miles/hr	0.6818
feet/sec	miles/min	0.01136
feet/sec/sec	cms/sec/sec	30.48
feet/sec/sec	kms/hr/sec	1.097
feet/sec/sec	meters/sec/sec	0.3048
feet/sec/sec	miles/hr/sec	0.6818
feet/100 feet	per cent grade	1.0
Foot — candle	Lumen/sq. meter	10.764
foot-pounds	Btu	1.286×10^{-3}
foot-pounds	ergs	1.356×10^{7}
foot-pounds	gram-calories	0.3238
foot-pounds	hp-hrs	5.050×10^{-7}
foot-pounds	joules	1.356
foot-pounds	kg-calories	3.24×10^{-4}
foot-pounds	kg-meters	0.1383
foot-pounds	kilowatt-hrs	3.766×10^{-7}
foot-pounds/min	Btu/min	1.286×10^{-3}
foot-pounds/min	foot-pounds/sec	0.01667
foot-pounds/min	horsepower	3.030×10^{-5}
foot-pounds/min	kg-calories/min	3.24×10^{-4}
foot-pounds/min	kilowatts	2.260×10^{-5}
foot-pounds/sec	Btu/hr	4.6263
foot-pounds/sec	Btu/min	0.07717
foot-pounds/sec	horsepower	1.818×10^{-3}
foot-pounds/sec	kg-calories/min	0.01945
foot-pounds/sec	kilowatts	1.356×10^{-3}
Furlongs	miles (U.S.)	0.125
furlongs	rods	40.0
furlongs	feet	660.0

G

TO CONVERT	INTO	MULTIPLY BY
gallons	cu cms	3,785.0
gallons	cu feet	0.1337
gallons	cu inches	231.0
gallons	cu meters	3.785×10^{-3}
gallons	cu yards	4.951×10^{-3}
gallons	liters	3.785
gallons (liq. Br. Imp.)	gallons (U.S. liq.)	1.20095
gallons (U.S.)	gallons (Imp.)	0.83267
gallons of water	pounds of water	8.3453
gallons/min	cu ft/sec	2.228×10^{-3}
gallons/min	liters/sec	0.06308
gallons/min	cu ft/hr	8.0208
gausses	lines/sw in.	6.452
gausses	webers/sq cm	10^{-8}
gausses	webers/sq in	6.452×10^{-8}
gausses	webers/sq meter	10^{-4}
gilberts	ampere-turns	0.7958
gilberts/cm	amp-turns/cm	0.7958
gilberts/cm	amp-turns/in	2.021
gilberts/cm	amp-turns/meter	79.58
Gills (British)	cubic cm.	142.07
gills	liters	0.1183
gills	pints (liq.)	0.25
Grade	Radian	.01571
Grains	drams (avoirdupois)	0.03657143

Conversion Factors

TO CONVERT	INTO	MULTIPLY BY
grains (troy)	grains (avdp)	1.0
grains (troy)	grams	0.06480
grains (troy)	ounces (avdp)	2.0833×10^{-3}
grains (troy)	pennyweight (troy)	0.04167
grains/U.S. gal	parts/million	17.118
grains/U.S. gal	pounds/million gal	142.86
grains/Imp. gal	parts/million	14.286
grams	dynes	980.7
grams	grains	15.43
grams	joules/cm	9.807×10^{-5}
grams	joules/meter (newtons)	9.807×10^{-3}
grams	kilograms	0.001
grams	milligrams	1,000.
grams	ounces (avdp)	0.03527
grams	ounces (troy)	0.03215
grams	poundals	0.07093
grams	pounds	2.205×10^{-3}
grams/cm	pounds/inch	5.600×10^{-3}
grams/cu cm	pounds/cu ft	62.43
grams/cu cm	pounds/cu in	0.03613
grams/cu cm	pounds/mil-foot	3.405×10^{-7}
grams/liter	grains/gal	58.417
grams/liter	pounds/1,000 gal	8.345
grams/liter	pounds/cu ft	0.062427
grams/liter	parts/million	1,000.0
grams/sq cm	pounds/sq ft	2.0481
gram-calories	Btu	3.9683×10^{-3}
gram-calories	ergs	4.1868×10^{7}
gram-calories	foot-pounds	3.0880
gram-calories	horsepower-hrs	1.5596×10^{-6}
gram-calories	kilowatt-hrs	1.1630×10^{-6}
gram-calories	watt-hrs	1.1630×10^{-3}
gram-calories/sec	Btu/hr	14.286
gram-centimeters	Btu	9.297×10^{-8}
gram-centimeters	ergs	980.7
gram-centimeters	joules	9.807×10^{-5}
gram-centimeters	kg-cal	2.343×10^{-8}
gram-centimeters	kg-meters	10^{-5}

H

TO CONVERT	INTO	MULTIPLY BY
Hand	Cm.	10.16
hectares	acres	2.471
hectares	sq feet	1.076×10^{5}
hectograms	grams	100.0
hectoliters	liters	100.0
hectometers	meters	100.0
hectowatts	watts	100.0
henries	millihenries	1,000.0
Hogsheads (British)	cubic feet	10.114
Hogsheads (U.S.)	cubic ft.	8.42184
Hogsheads (U.S.)	gallons (U.S.)	63
horsepower	Btu/min	42.44
horsepower	foot-lbs/min	33,000.
horsepower	foot-lbs/sec	550.0
horsepower (metric) (542.5 ft lb/sec)	horsepower (550 ft lb/sec)	0.9863
horsepower (550 ft lb/sec)	horsepower (metric) (542.5 ft lb/sec)	1.014
horepower	kg-calories/min	10.68
horsepower.	kilowatts	0.7457
horsepower	watts	745.7
horsepower (boiler)	Btu/hr	33,479
horsepower (boiler)	kilowatts	9.803
horsepower-hrs	Btu	2,547.

Conversion Factors

TO CONVERT	INTO	MULTIPLY BY
horsepower-hrs	ergs	2.6845×10^{13}
horsepower-hrs	foot-lbs	1.98×10^{6}
horsepower-hrs	gram-calories	641,190.
horsepower-hrs	joules	2.684×10^{6}
horsepower-hrs	kg-calories	641.1
horsepower-hrs	kg-meters	2.737×10^{5}
horsepower-hrs	kilowatt-hrs	0.7457
hours	days	4.167×10^{-2}
hours	weeks	5.952×10^{-3}
Hundredweights (long)	pounds	112
Hundredweights (long)	tons (long)	0.05
Hundredweights (short)	ounces (avoirdupois)	1600
Hundredweights (short)	pounds	100
Hundredweights (short)	tons (metric)	0.0453592
Hundredweights (short)	tons (long)	0.0446429

I

TO CONVERT	INTO	MULTIPLY BY
inches	centimeters	2.540
inches	meters	2.540×10^{-2}
inches	miles	1.578×10^{-5}
inches	millimeters	25.40
inches	mils	1,000.0
inches	yards	2.778×10^{-2}
inches of mercury	atmospheres	0.03342
inches of mercury	feet of water	1.133
inches of mercury	kgs/sq cm	0.03453
inches of mercury	kgs/sq meter	345.3
inches of mercury	pounds/sq ft	70.73
inches of mercury	pounds/sq in.	0.4912
inches of water (at 4° C)	atmospheres	2.458×10^{-3}
inches of water (at 4° C)	inches of mercury	0.07355
inches of water (at 4 ° C)	kgs/sq cm	2.540×10^{-3}
inches of water (at 4° C)	ounces/sq in.	0.5781
inches of water (at 4° C)	pounds/sq ft	5.204
inches of water (at 4° C)	pounds/sq in.	0.03613
International Ampere	Ampere (absolute)	.9998
International Volt	Volts (absolute)	1.0003
International volt	Joules (absolute)	1.593×10^{-19}
International volt	Joules	9.654×10^{4}

J

TO CONVERT	INTO	MULTIPLY BY
joules	Btu	9.480×10^{-4}
joules	ergs	10^{7}
joules	foot-pounds	0.7376
joules	kg-calories	2.389×10^{-4}
joules	kg-meters	0.1020
joules	watt-hrs	2.778×10^{-4}
joules/cm	grams	1.020×10^{4}
joules/cm	dynes	10^{7}
joules/cm	joules/meter (newtons)	100.0
joules/cm	poundals	723.3

TO CONVERT	INTO	MULTIPLY BY
joules/cm	pounds	22.48

K

TO CONVERT	INTO	MULTIPLY BY
kelvin	celsius	$C° + 273.16$
kilograms	dynes	980,665.
kilograms	grams	1,000.0
kilograms	joules/cm	0.09807
kilograms	joules/meter (newtons)	9.807
kilograms	poundals	70.93
kilograms	pounds	2.205
kilograms	tons (long)	9.842×10^{-4}
kilograms	tons (short)	1.102×10^{-3}
kilograms/cu meter	grams/cu cm	0.001
kilograms/cu meter	pounds/cu ft	0.06243
kilograms/cu meter	pounds/cu in.	3.613×10^{-5}
kilograms/cu meter	pounds/mil-foot	3.405×10^{-10}
kilogams/meter	pounds/ft	0.6720
Kilogram/sq. cm.	Dynes	980,665
kilograms/sq cm	atmospheres	0.9678
kilograms/sq cm	feet of water	32.81
kilograms/sq cm	inches of mercury	28.96
kilograms/sq cm	pounds/sq ft	2,048.
kilograms/sq cm	pounds/sq in.	14.22
kilograms/sq meter	atmospheres	9.678×10^{-5}
kilograms/sq meter	bars	98.07×10^{-6}
kilograms/sq meter	feet of water	3.281×10^{-3}
kilograms/sq meter	inches of mercury	2.896×10^{-3}
kilograms/sq meter	pounds/sq ft	0.2048
kilograms/sq meter	pounds/sq in.	1.422×10^{-3}
kilograms/sq mm	kgs/sq meter	10^6
kilogram-calories	Btu	3.968
kilogram-calories	foot-pounds	3,088.
kilogram-calories	hp-hrs	1.560×10^{-3}
kilogram-calories	joules	4,186.
kilogram-calories	kg-meters	426.9
kilogram-calories	kilojoules	4.186
kilogram-calories	kilowatt-hrs	1.163×10^{-3}
kilogram meters	Btu	9.294×10^{-3}
kilogram meters	ergs	9.804×10^7
kilogram meters	foot-pounds	7.233
kilogram meters	joules	9.804
kilogram meters	kg-calories	2.342×10^{-3}
kilogram meters	kilowatt-hrs	2.723×10^{-6}
kilolines	maxwells	1,000.0
kiloliters	liters	1,000.0
kilometers	centimeters	10^5
kilometers	feet	3,281.
kilometers	inches	3.937×10^4
kilometers	meters	1,000.0
kilometers	miles	0.6214
kilometers	millimeters	10^6
kilometers	yards	1,094.
kilometers/hr	cms/sec	27.78
kilometers/hr	feet/min	54.68
kilometers/hr	feet/sec	0.9113
kilometers/hr	knots	0.5396
kilometers/hr	meters/min	16.67
kilometers/hr	miles/hr	0.6214
kilometers/hr/sec	cms/sec/sec	27.78
kilometers/hr/sec	ft/sec/sec	0.9113
kilometers/hr/sec	meters/sec/sec	0.2778
kilometers/hr/sec	miles/hr/sec	0.6214
kilowatts	Btu/min.	56.92
kilowatts	foot-lbs/min	4.426×10^4
kilowatts	foot-lbs/sec	737.6
kilowatts	horsepower	1.341
kilowatts	kg-calories/min	14.34
kilowatts	watts	1,000.0
kilowatt-hrs	Btu	3,413.
kilowatt-hrs	ergs	3.600×10^{13}
kilowatt-hrs	foot-lbs	2.655×10^6
kilowatt-hrs	gram-calories	859,850.
kilowatt-hrs	horsepower-hrs	1.341
kilowatt-hrs	joules	3.6×10^6
kilowatt-hrs	kg-calories	860.5
kilowatt-hrs	kg-meters	3.671×10^5
kilowatt-hrs	pounds of water evaporated from and at 212° F.	3.53
kilowatt-hrs	pounds of water raised from 62° to 212° F.	22.75
knots	feet/hr	6,080.
knots	kilometers/hr	1.8532
knots	nautical miles/hr	1.0
knots	statute miles/hr	1.151
knots	yards/hr	2,027.
knots	feet/sec	1.689

L

TO CONVERT	INTO	MULTIPLY BY
league	miles (approx.)	3.0
Light year	Miles	5.9×10^{12}
Light year	Kilometers	9.46091×10^{12}
lines/sq cm	gausses	1.0
lines/sq in.	gausses	0.1550
lines/sq in.	webers/sq cm	1.550×10^{-9}
lines/sq in.	webers/sq in.	10^{-8}
lines/sq in.	webers/sq meter	1.550×10^{-5}
links (engineer's)	inches	12.0
links (surveyor's)	inches	7.92
liters	bushels (U.S. dry)	0.02838
liters	cu cm	1,000.0
liters	cu feet	0.03531
liters	cu inches	61.02
liters	cu meters	0.001
liters	cu yards	1.308×10^{-3}
liters	gallons (U.S. liq.)	0.2642
liters	pints (U.S. liq.)	2.113
liters	quarts (U.S. liq.)	1.057
liters/min	cu ft/sec	5.886×10^{-4}
liters/min	gals/sec	4.403×10^{-3}
lumens/sq ft	foot-candles	1.0
Lumen	Spherical candle power	.07958
Lumen	Watt	.001496
Lumen/sq. ft.	Lumen/sq. meter	10.76
lux	foot-candles	0.0929

M

TO CONVERT	INTO	MULTIPLY BY
maxwells	kilolines	0.001
maxwells	webers	10^{-8}
megalines	maxwells	10^6
megohms	microhms	10^{12}
megohms	ohms	10^6
meters	centimeters	100.0
meters	feet	3.281
meters	inches	39.37

Conversion Factors

TO CONVERT	INTO	MULTIPLY BY
meters	kilometers	0.001
meters	miles (naut.)	5.396×10^{-4}
meters	miles (stat.)	6.214×10^{-4}
meters	millimeters	1,000.0
meters	yards	1.094
meters	varas	1.179
meters/min	cms/sec	1.667
meters/min	feet/min	3.281
meters/min	feet/sec	0.05468
meters/min	kms/hr	0.06
meters/min	knots	0.03238
meters/min	miles/hr	0.03728
meters/sec	feet/min	196.8
meters/sec	feet/sec	3.281
meters/sec	kilometers/hr	3.6
meters/sec	kilometers/min	0.06
meters/sec	miles/hr	2.237
meters/sec	miles/min	0.03728
meters/sec/sec	cms/sec/sec	100.0
meters/sec/sec	ft/sec/sec	3.281
meters/sec/sec	kms/hr/sec	3.6
meters/sec/sec	miles/hr/sec	2.237
meter-kilograms	cm-dynes	9.807×10^{7}
meter-kilograms	cm-grams	10^{5}
meter-kilograms	pound-feet	7.233
microfarad	farads	10^{-6}
micrograms	grams	10^{-6}
microhms	megohms	10^{-12}
microhms	ohms	10^{-6}
microliters	liters	10^{-6}
Microns	meters	1×10^{-6}
miles (naut.)	feet	6,080.27
miles (naut.)	kilometers	1.853
miles (naut.)	meters	1,853.
miles (naut.)	miles (statute)	1.1516
miles (naut.)	yards	2,027.
miles (statute)	centimeters	1.609×10^{5}
miles (statute)	feet	5,280.
miles (statute)	inches	6.336×10^{4}
miles (statute)	kilometers	1.609
miles (statute)	meters	1,609.
miles (statute)	miles (naut.)	0.8684
miles (statute)	yards	1,760.
miles/hr	cms/sec	44.70
miles/hr	feet/min	88.
miles/hr	feet/sec	1.467
miles/hr	kms/hr	1.609
miles/hr	kms/min	0.02682
miles/hr	knots	0.8684
miles/hr	meters/min	26.82
miles/hr	miles/min	0.1667
miles/hr/sec	cms/sec/sec	44.70
miles/hr/sec	feet/sec/sec	1.467
miles/hr/sec	kms/hr/sec	1.609
miles/hr/sec	meters/sec/sec	0.4470
miles/min	cms/sec	2,682.
miles/min	feet/sec	88.
miles/min	kms/hr	1.609
miles/min	knots/min	0.8684
miles/min	miles/hr	60.0
mil-feet	cu inches	9.425×10^{-6}
milliers	kilograms	1,000.
Millimicrons	meters	1×10^{-9}
Milligrams	grains	0.01543236

Conversion Factors

TO CONVERT	INTO	MULTIPLY BY
milligrams	grams	0.001
milligrams/liter	parts/million	1.0
millihenries	henries	0.001
milliliters	liters	0.001
millimeters	centimeters	0.1
millimeters	feet	3.281×10^{-3}
millimeters	inches	0.03937
millimeters	kilometers	10^{-6}
millimeters	meters	0.001
millimeters	miles	6.214×10^{-7}
millimeters	mils	39.37
millimeters	yards	1.094×10^{-3}
million gals/day	cu ft/sec	1.54723
mils	centimeters	2.540×10^{-3}
mils	feet	8.333×10^{-5}
mils	inches	0.001
mils	kilometers	2.540×10^{-8}
mils	yards	2.778×10^{-5}
miner's inches	cu ft/min	1.5
Minims (British)	cubic cm.	0.059192
Minims (U.S., fluid)	cubic cm.	0.061612
minutes (angles)	degrees	0.01667
minutes (angles)	quadrants	1.852×10^{-4}
minutes (angles)	radians	2.909×10^{-4}
minutes (angles)	seconds	60.0
myriagrams	kilograms	10.0
myriameters	kilometers	10.0
myriawatts	kilowatts	10.0

N

TO CONVERT	INTO	MULTIPLY BY
nepers	decibels	8.686
Newton	Dynes	1×10^{5}

O

TO CONVERT	INTO	MULTIPLY BY
OHM (International)	OHM (absolute)	1.0005
ohms	megohms	10^{-6}
ohms	microhms	10^{6}
ounces	drams	16.0
ounces	grains	437.5
ounces	grams	28.349527
ounces	pounds	0.0625
ounces	ounces (troy)	0.9115
ounces	tons (long)	2.790×10^{-5}
ounces	tons (metric)	2.835×10^{-5}
ounces (fluid)	cu inches	1.805
ounces (fluid)	liters	0.02957
ounces (troy)	grains	480.0
ounces (troy)	grams	31.103481
ounces (troy)	ounces (avdp.)	1.09714
ounces (troy)	pennyweights (troy)	20.0
ounces (troy)	pounds (troy)	0.08333
Ounce/sq. inch	Dynes/sq. cm.	4309
ounces/sq in.	pounds/sq in.	0.0625

P

TO CONVERT	INTO	MULTIPLY BY
Parsec	Miles	19×10^{12}
Parsec	Kilometers	3.084×10^{13}
parts/million	grains/U.S. gal	0.0584
parts/million	grains/Imp. gal	0.07016
parts/million	pounds/million gal	8.345
Pecks (British)	cubic inches	554.6
Pecks (British)	liters	9.091901
Pecks (U.S.)	bushels	0.25
Pecks (U.S.)	cubic inches	537.605

Conversion Factors

TO CONVERT	INTO	MULTIPLY BY
Pecks (U.S.)	liters	8.809582
Pecks (U.S.)	quarts (dry)	8
pennyweights (troy)	grains	24.0
pennyweights (troy)	ounces (troy)	0.05
pennyweights (troy)	grams	1.55517
pennyweights (troy)	pounds (troy)	4.1667×10^{-3}
pints (dry)	cu inches	33.60
pints (liq.)	cu cms.	473.2
pints (liq.)	cu feet	0.01671
pints (liq.)	cu inches	28.87
pints (liq.)	cu meters	4.732×10^{-4}
pints (liq.)	cu yards	6.189×10^{-4}
pints (liq.)	gallons	0.125
pints (liq.)	liters	0.4732
pints (liq.)	quarts (liq.)	0.5
Planck's quantum	Erg — second	6.624×10^{-27}
Poise	Gram/cm. sec.	1.00
Pounds (avoirdupois)	ounces (troy)	14.5833
poundals	dynes	13,826.
poundals	grams	14.10
poundals	joules/cm	1.383×10^{-3}
poundals	joules/meter (newtons)	0.1383
poundals	kilograms	0.01410
poundals	pounds	0.03108
pounds	drams	256.
pounds	dynes	44.4823×10^{4}
pounds	grains	7,000.
pounds	grams	453.5924
pounds	joules/cm	0.04448
pounds	joules/meter (newtons)	4.448
pounds	kilograms	0.4536
pounds	ounces	16.0
pounds	ounces (troy)	14.5833
pounds	poundals	32.17
pounds	pounds (troy)	1.21528
pounds	tons (short)	0.0005
pounds (troy)	grains	5,760.
pounds (troy)	grams	373.24177
pounds (troy)	ounces (avdp.)	13.1657
pounds (troy)	ounces (troy)	12.0
pounds (troy)	pennyweights (troy)	240.0
pounds (troy)	pounds (avdp.)	0.822857
pounds (troy)	tons (long)	3.6735×10^{-4}
pounds (troy)	tons (metric)	3.7324×10^{-4}
pounds (troy)	tons (short)	4.1143×10^{-4}
pounds of water	cu feet	0.01602
pounds of water	cu inches	27.68
pounds of water	gallons	0.1198
pounds of water/min	cu ft/sec	2.670×10^{-4}
pound-feet	cm-dynes	1.356×10^{7}
pound-feet	cm-grams	13,825.
pound-feet	meter-kgs	0.1383
pounds/cu ft	grams/cu cm	0.01602
pounds/cu ft	kgs/cu meter	16.02
pounds/cu ft	pounds/cu in.	5.787×10^{-4}
pounds/cu ft	pounds/mil-foot	5.456×10^{-9}
pounds/cu in.	gms/cu cm	27.68
pounds/cu in.	kgs/cu meter	2.768×10^{4}
pounds/cu in.	pounds/cu ft	1,728.
pounds/cu in.	pounds/mil-foot	9.425×10^{-6}
pounds/ft	kgs/meter	1.488
pounds/in.	gms/cm	178.6

Conversion Factors

TO CONVERT	INTO	MULTIPLY BY
pounds/mil-foot	gms/cu cm	2.306×10^{6}
pounds/sq ft	atmospheres	4.725×10^{-4}
pounds/sq ft	feet of water	0.01602
pounds/sq ft	inches of mercury	0.01414
pounds/sq ft	kgs/sq meter	4.882
pounds/sq ft	pounds/sq in.	6.944×10^{-3}
pounds/sq in.	atmospheres	0.06804
pounds/sq in.	feet of water	2.307
pounds/sq in.	inches of mercury	2.036
pounds/sq in.	kgs/sq meter	703.1
pounds/sq in.	pounds/sq ft	144.0
Q		
quadrants (angle)	degrees	90.0
quadrants (angle)	minutes	5,400.0
quadrants (angle)	radians	1.571
quadrants (angle)	seconds	3.24×10^{5}
quarts (dry)	cu inches	67.20
quarts (liq.)	cu cms	946.4
quarts (liq.)	cu feet	0.03342
quarts (liq.)	cu inches	57.75
quarts (liq.)	cu meters	9.464×10^{-4}
quarts (liq.)	cu yards	1.238×10^{-3}
quarts (liq.)	gallons	0.25
quarts (liq.)	liters	0.9463
R		
radians	degrees	57.30
radians	minutes	3,438.
radians	quadrants	0.6366
radians	seconds	2.063×10^{5}
radians/sec	degrees/sec	57.30
radians/sec	revolutions/min	9.549
radians/sec	revolutions/sec	0.1592
radians/sec/sec	revs/min/min	573.0
radians/sec/sec	revs/min/sec	9.549
radians/sec/sec	revs/sec/sec	0.1592
rankin	fahrenheit	$F^\circ + 459.69$
revolutions	degrees	360.0
revolutions	quadrants	4.0
revolutions	radians	6.283
revolutions/min	degrees/sec	6.0
revolutions/min	radians/sec	0.1047
revolutions/min	revs/sec	0.01667
revolutions/min/min	radians/sec/sec	1.745×10^{-3}
revolutions/min/min	revs/min/sec	0.01667
revolutions/min/min	revs/sec/sec	2.778×10^{-4}
revolutions/sec	degrees/sec	360.0
revolutions/sec	radians/sec	6.283
revolutions/sec	revs/min	60.0
revolutions/sec/sec	radians/sec/sec	6.283
revolutions/sec/sec	revs/min/min	3,600.0
revolutions/sec/sec	revs/min/sec	60.0
Rod	Chain (Gunters)	.25
Rod	Meters	5.029
Rods (Surveyors' meas.)	yards	5.5
rods	feet	16.5
S		
Scruples	grains	20
seconds (angle)	degrees	2.778×10^{-4}
seconds (angle)	minutes	0.01667
seconds (angle)	quadrants	3.087×10^{-6}

Conversion Factors

TO CONVERT	INTO	MULTIPLY BY
seconds (angle)	radians	4.848×10^{-6}
Slug	Kilogram	14.59
Slug	Pounds	32.17
Sphere	Steradians	12.57
square centimeters	circular mils	1.973×10^5
square centimeters	sq feet	1.076×10^{-3}
square centimeters	sq inches	0.1550
square centimeters	sq meters	0.0001
square centimeters	sq miles	3.861×10^{-11}
square centimeters	sq millimeters	100.0
square centimeters	sq yards	1.196×10^{-4}
square feet	acres	2.296×10^{-5}
square feet	circular mils	1.833×10^8
square feet	sq cms	929.0
square feet	sq inches	144.0
square feet	sq meters	0.09290
square feet	sq miles	3.587×10^{-8}
square feet	sq millimeters	9.290×10^4
square feet	sq yards	0.1111
square inches	circular mils	1.273×10^6
square inches	sq cms	6.452
square inches	sq feet	6.944×10^{-3}
square inches	sq millimeters	645.2
square inches	sq mils	10^6
square inches	sq yards	7.716×10^{-4}
square kilometers	acres	247.1
square kilometers	sq cms	10^{10}
square kilometers	sq ft	10.76×10^6
square kilometers	sq inches	1.550×10^9
square kilometers	sq meters	10^6
square kilometers	sq miles	0.3861
square kilometers	sq yards	1.196×10^6
square meters	acres	2.471×10^{-4}
square meters	sq cms	10^4
square meters	sq feet	10.76
square meters	sq inches	1,550.
square meters	sq miles	3.861×10^{-7}
square meters	sq millimeters	10^6
square meters	sq yards	1.196
square miles	acres	640.0
square miles	sq feet	27.88×10^6
square miles	sq kms	2.590
square miles	sq meters	2.590×10^6
square miles	sq yards	3.098×10^6
square millimeters	circular mils	1,973.
square millimeters	sq cms	0.01
square millimeters	sq feet	1.076×10^{-5}
square millimeters	sq inches	1.550×10^{-3}
square mils	circular mils	1.273
square mils	sq cms	6.452×10^{-6}
square mils	sq inches	10^{-6}
square yards	acres	2.066×10^{-4}
square yards	sq cms	8,361.
square yards	sq feet	9.0
square yards	sq inches	1,296.
square yards	sq meters	0.8361
square yards	sq miles	3.228×10^{-7}
square yards	sq millimeters	8.361×10^5

T

TO CONVERT	INTO	MULTIPLY BY
temperature ($^\circ$C) + 273	absolute temperature ($^\circ$C)	1.0
temperature ($^\circ$C) + 17.78	temperature ($^\circ$F)	1.8

Conversion Factors

TO CONVERT	INTO	MULTIPLY BY
temperature ($^\circ$F) + 460	absolute temperature ($^\circ$F)	1.0
temperature ($^\circ$F) −32	temperature ($^\circ$C)	5/9
tons (long)	kilograms	1,016.
tons (long)	pounds	2,240.
tons (long)	tons (short)	1.120
tons (metric)	kilograms	1,000.
tons (metric)	pounds	2,205.
tons (short)	kilograms	907.1848
tons (short)	ounces	32,000.
tons (short)	ounces (troy)	29,166.66
tons (short)	pounds	2,000
tons (short)	pounds (troy)	2,430.56
tons (short)	tons (long)	0.89287
tons (short)	tons (metric)	0.9078
tons (short)/sq ft	kgs/sq meter	9,765.
tons (short)/sq ft	pounds/sq in.	2,000.
tons of water/24 hrs	pounds of water/hr	83.333
tons of water/24 hrs	gallons/min	0.16643
tons of water/24 hrs	cu ft/hr	1.3349

V

TO CONVERT	INTO	MULTIPLY BY
Volt/inch	Volt/cm.	.39370
Volt (absolute)	Statvolts	.003336

W

TO CONVERT	INTO	MULTIPLY BY
watts	Btu/hr	3.4129
watts	Btu/min	0.05688
watts	ergs/sec	107.
watts	foot-lbs/min	44.27
watts	foot-lbs/sec	0.7378
watts	horsepower	1.341×10^{-3}
watts	horsepower (metric)	1.360×10^{-3}
watts	kg-calories/min	0.01433
watts	kilowatts	0.001
Watts (Abs.)	B.T.U. (mean)/min.	0.056884
Watts (Abs.)	joules/sec.	1
watt-hours	Btu	3.413
watt-hours	ergs	3.60×10^{10}
watt-hours	foot-pounds	2,656.
watt-hours	gram-calories	859.85
watt-hours	horsepower-hrs	1.341×10^{-3}
watt-hours	kilogram-calories	0.8605
watt-hours	kilogram-meters	367.2
watt-hours	kilowatt-hrs	0.001
Watt (International)	Watt (absolute)	1.0002
webers	maxwells	10^8
webers	kilolines	10^5
webers/sq in.	gausses	1.550×10^7
webers/sq in.	lines/sq in.	10^8
webers/sq in.	webers/sq cm	0.1550
webers/sq in.	webers/sq meter	1,550.
webers/sq meter	gausses	10^4
webers/sq meter	lines/sq in.	6.452×10^4
webers/sq meter	webers/sq cm	10^{-4}
webers/sq meter	webers/sq in.	6.452×10^{-4}

Y

TO CONVERT	INTO	MULTIPLY BY
yards	centimeters	91.44
yards	kilometers	9.144×10^{-4}
yards	meters	0.9144
yards	miles (naut.)	4.934×10^{-4}
yards	miles (stat.)	5.682×10^{-4}
yards	millimeters	914.4

Parts, Tools, Supplies, Etc.

CLEANING & REFINISHING SUPPLIES

A 'n A Co., Box 571, King of Prussia, PA 19406 (Valet shotgun cleaner)
Armite Labs., 1845 Randolph St., Los Angeles, CA 90001/213-587-7744 (pen oiler)
Armoloy Co. of Ft. Worth, 204 E. Daggett St., Ft Worth, TX 76104/817-461-0051
Belltown, Ltd., 33 Belltown Rd., Stamford, CT 06905/203-348-0911 (gun clg. cloth kit)
Birchwood-Casey, 7900 Fuller Rd., Eden Prairie, MN 55344/612-927-7933
Bisonite Co., Inc., P.O. Box 84, Kenmore Station, Buffalo, NY 14217
Blue and Gray Prods., Inc., R.D. #6, Box 348, Wellsboro, PA 16901/717-724-1383
Break-Free, a Div. of San/Bar Corp., 9999 Muirlands Blvd., Irvine, CA 92714/714-855-9911
Jim Brobst, 299 Poplar St., Hamburg, PA 19526/215-562-2103 (J-B Bore Cleaning Compound)
GB Prods. Dept., H & R, Inc., Industrial Rowe, Gardner, MA 01440
Browning Arms, Rt. 4, Box 624-B, Arnold, MO 63010
J.M. Bucheimer Co., P.O. Box 280, Airport Rd., Frederick, MD 21701/301-662-5101
Burnishine Prod. Co., 8140 N. Ridgeway, Skokie, IL 60076 (Stock Glaze)
Call 'N, Inc., 1615 Bartlett Rd., Memphis, TN 38134/901-372-1682 (Gunskin)
Chem-Pak, Inc., Winchester, VA 22601/703-667-1341 (Gun-Savr.protect. & lubricant)
Chopie Mfg. Inc., 700 Copeland Ave., La Crosse, WI 54601/608-784-0926 (Black-Solve)
Clenzoil Co., Box 1226, Sta. C, Canton, OH 44708/216-833-9758
Clover Mfg. Co., 139 Woodward Ave., Norwalk, Ct. 06856/800-243-6492 (Clover compound)
J. Dewey Mfg. Co., 186 Skyview Dr., Southbury, CT 06488/203-264-3064 (one-piece gun clg. rod)
Diah Engineering Co., 5177 Haskell St., La Canada, CA 91011/213-625-2184 (barrel lubricant)
Dri-Slide, Inc.,Industrial Park, 1210 Locust St., Fremont, MI 49412
Forty-Five Ranch Enterpr., 119 S. Main St., Miami, OK 74354/918-542-9307
Gun-All Products, Box 244, Dowagiac, MI 49047
Frank C. Hoppe Div., Penguin Ind., Inc., Airport Industrial Mall, Coatesville, PA 19320/215-384-6000
Jet-Aer Corp., 100 Sixth Ave., Paterson, NJ 07524 (blues & oils)
Kellog's Professional Prods., Inc., P.O. Box 1201, Sandusky, OH 44870
K.W. Kleinendorst, R.D. #1, Box 113B, Hop Bottom, PA 18824/717-289-4687 (rifle clg. cables)
LPS Chemical Prods., Holt Lloyd Corp., 4647 Hugh Howell Rd., Tucker, GA 30048/404-934-7800
LEM Gun Spec., Box 31, College Park, GA 30337/404-761-9054 (Lewis Lead Remover)
Liquid Wrench, Box 10628, Charlotte,.NC 28201 (pen. oil)
Lynx Line Gun Prods. Div., Protective Coatings, Inc., 20626 Fenkell Ave., Detroit, MI 48223/313-255-6032
Marble Arms Co., 420 Industrial Park, Gladstone, MI 49837/906-428-3710
Micro Sight Co., 242 Harbor Blvd., Belmont, CA 94002/415-591-0769 (bedding)
Mirror-Lube, P.O. Box 693, San Juan Capistrano, CA 92675
New Method Mfg. Co., Box 175, Bradford, PA 16701/814-262-6611 (gun blue; Minute Man gun care)
Northern Instruments, Inc., 6680 North Highway 49, Lino Lake, MN 55014 (Stor-Safe rust preventer)
Numrich Arms Co., West Hurley, NY 12491 (44-40 gun blue)
Old World Oil Products, 3827 Queen Ave. No., Minneapolis, MN 55412
Original Mink Oil, Inc., P.O. Box 20191, 10652 N.E. Holman, Portland, OR 97220/503-255-2814
Outers Laboratories, Route 2, Onalaska, WI 54650/608-783-1515 (Gunslick kits)
Radiator Spec. Co., 1400 Independence Blvd., Charlotte, NC 28201 (liquid wrench)
Reardon Prod., 103 W. Market St., Morrison, IL 61270 (Dry-Lube)
Rice Protective Gun Coatings, 235-30th St., West Palm Beach, FL 33407/305-845-2383
Rig Products, P.O. Box 1990, Sparks, NV 89432/703-331-5666
Rusteprufe Labs., Rte. 5, Sparta, WI 54656/608-269-4144
San/Bar Corp., Break-Free Div., 9999 Muirlands Blvd, Irvine, CA 92714/714-855-9911
Saunders Sptg. Gds., 338 Somerset, No. Plainfield, NJ 07060 (Sav-Bore)
Schultea's Gun String 67 Burress, Houston, TX 77022 (pocket-size rifle cleaning kit)

Schwab Industries, Inc., P.O. Box 5705, Santa Monica, CA 90405/213-395-6997 (Rust Guardit)
Service Armament, 689 Bergen Blvd., Ridgefield, NJ 07657 (Parker-Hale)
Silicote Corp., Box 359, Oshkosh, WI 54901 (Silicone cloths)
Silver Dollar Guns, P.O. Box 475, 10 Frances St., Franklin, NH 03235/603-934-3292 (Silicone oil)
Sportsmen's Labs., Inc., Box 732, Anoka, MN 55303 (Gun Life lube)
Taylor & Robbins, Box 164, Rixford, PA 16745 (Throat Saver)
Testing Systems, Inc., 220 Pegasus Ave., Northgale, NJ 07647/201-767-7300 (gun lube)
Texas Platers Supply Co., 2453 W. Five Mile Parkway, Dallas, TX 75233 (plating kit)
Totally Dependable Prods., Inc., (TDP Ind.), P.O. Box 277, Zieglerville, PA 19492/215-287-7851
Treso Inc., 120 N. Pagosa Blvd,. Pagosa Springs, CO 81147/303-264-2295 (mfg. Durango Gun Rod)
C. S. Van Gorden, 120 Tenth Ave., Eau Claire, WI 54701 (Instant Blue)
WD-40 Co., 1061 Cudahy Pl., San Diego, CA 92110
West Coast Secoa, 3915 U S Hwy 98S, Lakeland, FL 33801 (Teflon coatings)
Williams Gun Sight, 7389 Lapeer Rd., Davison, MI 48423 (finish kit)
Winslow Arms Inc., P.O. Box 783, Camden, SC 29020 (refinishing kit)
Wisconsin Platers Supply Co., (See Texas Platers Supply Co.)
Woodstream Corp., P.O. Box 327, Lititz, PA 17543 (Mask)
Zip Aerosol Prods., 21320 Deering Court, Canoga Park, CA 91304

GUNS & GUN PARTS, REPLICA AND ANTIQUE

Antique Gun Parts, Inc., 1118 S. Braddock Ave., Pittsburgh, PA 15218/412-241-1811 (ML)
Armoury Inc., Rte. 202, New Preston, CT 06777
Artistic Arms, Inc., Box 23, Hoagland, IN 46745 (Sharps-Borchardt replica)
Bob's Place, Box 283J, Clinton, IA 52732 (obsolete Winchester parts only)
Dixie Gun Works, Inc., Hwy 51, South, Union City, TN 38261/901-885-0561
Federal Ordnance Inc., 1443 Portrero Ave., So. El Monte, CA 91733/213-350-4161
Fred Goodwin, Goodwin's Gun Shop, Sherman Mills, ME 04776/207-365-4451 (antique guns & parts)
Terry I. Kopp, Highway 13, Lexington, MO 64067/816-259-2636 (restoration & pts. 1890 & 1906 Winch.)
The House of Muskets, Inc., 120 N. Pagosa Blvd., Pagosa Springs, CO 81147/303-264-2295 (ML guns)
Log Cabin Sport Shop, 8010 Lafayette Rd., Lodi, OH 44254/216-948-1082 (ctlg. $30)
Edw. E. Lucas, 32 Garfield Ave., East Brunswick, NJ 08816/201-251-5526 (45/70 Springfield parts)
Lyman Products Corp., Middlefield, CT 06455
Tommy Munsch Gunsmithing, Rt. 2, Box 248, Little Falls, MN 56345/612-632-5835 (parts list $1.50; oth. inq. SASE)
Numrich Arms Co., West Hurley, NY 12491
Replica Models, Inc., 610 Franklin St., Alexandria, VA 22314
S&S Firearms, 88-21 Aubrey Ave., Glendale, NY 11385/212-497-1100
Sarco, Inc., 323 Union St., Stirling, NJ 07980/201-647-3800
C. H. Stoppler, 1426 Walton Ave., New York, NY 10452 (miniature guns)
Upper Missouri Trading Co., 3rd & Harold Sts., Crofton, NB 68730
C. H. Weisz, Box 311, Arlington, VA 22210
W. H. Wescombe, P.O. Box 488, Glencoe, CA 95232 (Rem. R.B. parts)

GUN PARTS, U.S. AND FOREIGN

Badger Shooter's Supply, Box 397, Owen, WI 54460
Behlert Custom Guns, Inc., 725 Lehigh Ave., Union, NJ 07083 (handgun parts)
Philip R. Crouthamel, 513 E. Baltimore, E. Lansdowne, PA 19050/215-623-5685
Charles E. Duffy, Williams Lane, West Hurley, NY 12491
Christian Magazines, P.O. Box 184, Avoca, PA 18641
Federal Ordnance Inc., 1443 Potrero Ave., So. El Monte, CA 91733/213-350-4161
Jack First Distributors Inc., 44633 Sierra Highway, Lancaster, CA 93534/805-945-6981
Gun City, 504 Main, Bismarck, ND 58501/701-223-2304 (magazines, gun parts)
Gun-Tec, P.O. Box 8125, W. Palm Beach, FL 33407 (Win. mag. tubing; Win. 92 conversion parts)
Hunter's Haven, Zero Prince St., Alexandria, VA 22314

Walter H. Lodewick, 2816 N.E. Halsey, Portland, OR 97232/503-284-2554 (Winchester parts)

Marsh Al's, Rte. #3, Box 729, Preston, ID 83263/208-852-2437 (Contender rifle)

Morgan Arms Co., Inc., 1770-C Industrial Rd., Las Vegas, NV 89102 (MK-I kit)

Numrich Arms Co., West Hurley, NY 12491

Pacific Intl. Merch. Corp., 2215 "J" St., Sacramento, CA 95816/916-446-2737 (Vega 45 Colt mag.)

Potomac Arms Corp. (See Hunter's Haven)

Pre-64 Winchester Parts Co., P.O. Box 8125, West Palm Beach, FL 33407 (send stamped env. w. requ. list)

Martin B. Retting, Inc., 11029 Washington Blvd., Culver City, CA 90230/213-837-6111

Sarco, Inc., 323 Union St., Stirling, NJ 07980

Sherwood Intl. Export Corp., 18714 Parthenia St., Northridge, CA 91324

Simms, 2801 J St., Sacramento, CA 95816/916-442-3800

Clifford L. Smires, R.D. 1, Box 100, Columbus, NJ 08022/609-298-3158 (Mauser rifles)

Springfield Sporters Inc., R.D. 1, Penn Run, PA 15765/412-254-2626

Tomark Industries, 12043 S. Paramount Blvd., Downey, CA 90242 (Cherokee gun accessories)

Triple-K Mfg. Co., 568-6th Ave., San Diego, CA 92101 (magazines, gun parts)

GUNSMITH SUPPLIES, TOOLS, SERVICES

Albright Prod. Co., P. O. Box 1144, Portola, CA 96122 (trap buttplates)

Alley Supply Co., Carson Valley Industrial Park, P.O. Box 848, Gardnerville, NV 89410/702-782-3800 (JET line lathes, mills, etc.)

Ametek, Hunter Spring Div., One Spring Ave., Hatfield, PA 19440/215-822-2971 (trigger gauge)

Anderson Mfg. Co., Union Gap Sta., P.O. Box 3120, Yakima, WA 98903/509-453-2349 (tang safe)

Armite Labs., 1845 Randolph St., Los Angeles, CA 90001/213-587-7744 (pen oiler)

B-Square Co., Box 11281, Ft. Worth, TX 76110

Jim Baiar, 490 Halfmoon Rd., Columbia Falls, MT 59912 (hex screws)

Behlert Custom Guns, Inc., 725 Lehigh Ave., Union, NJ 07083

Dennis M. Bellm Gunsmithing, Inc., dba P.O. Ackley Rifle Barrels, 2376 S. Redwood Rd., Salt Lake City, UT 84119/801-974-0697 (rifles only)

Al Biesen, W. 2039 Sinto Ave., Spokane, WA 99201 (grip caps, buttplates)

Billingsley & Brownell, Box 25, Wyarno, WY 82845/307-737-2468 (cust. grip caps, bolt handle, etc.)

Blue Ridge Machine and Tool, 165 Midland Trail, Hurricane, WV 25526/304-562-3538 (machinery, tools, shop suppl.)

Bonanza Sports Mfg. Co., 412 Western Ave., Faribault, MN 55021/507-332-7153

Briganti Custom Gun-Smithing, P.O. Box 56, 475-Route 32, Highland Mills, NY 10930/914-928-9816 (cold rust bluing, hand polishing, metal work)

Brookstone Co., 125 Vose Farm Rd., Peterborough, NH 03458

Bob Brownell's, Main & Third, Montezuma, IA 50171/515-623-5401

Lenard M. Brownell (See Billingsley & Brownell)

W.E. Brownell, 1852 Alessandro Trail, Vista, CA 92083 (checkering tools)

Burgess Vibrocrafters, Inc. (BVI), Rte. 83, Grayslake, IL 60030

M.H. Canjar, 500 E. 45th Denver, CO 80216/303-623-5777 (triggers, etc.)

Chapman Mfg. Co., Rte. 17 at Saw Mill Rd., Durham, CT 06422

Chase Chemical Corp., 3527 Smallman St., Pittsburgh, PA 15201/412-681-6544 (Chubb Multigauge for shotguns)

Chubb (See Chase Chem. Co.)

Chicago Wheel & Mfg. Co., 1101 W. Monroe St., Chicago, IL 60607/312-226-8155 (Handee grinders)

Christy Gun Works, 875-57th St., Sacramento, CA 95819

Classic Arms Corp., P.O. Box 8, Palo Alto, CA 94302/415-321-7243 (floorplates, grip caps)

Clover Mfg. Co., 139 Woodward Ave., Norwalk, CT 06856/800-243 6492 (Clover compound)

Clymer Mfg. Co., Inc., 14241 W. 11 Mile Rd., Oak Park, MI 48237/313-541-5533 (reamers)

Dave Cook, 720 Hancock Ave., Hancock, MI 49930 (metalsmithing only)

Dayton-Traister Co., 9322-900th West, P.O. Box 593, Oak Harbor, WA 98277/206-675-5375 (triggers)

Delta Arms Sporting Goods, Highway 82 West, Indianola, MS 38751/601-887-5566 (Lightwood/England)

Dem-Bart Checkering Tools, Inc., 6807 Hiway #2, Snohomish, WA 98290/206-568-7536

Dremel Mfg. Co., 4915-21st St., Racine, WI 53406 (grinders)

Chas. E. Duffy, Williams Lane, West Hurley, NY 12491

Peter Dyson Ltd., 29-31 Church St., Honley, Huddersfield, Yorksh. HD7 2AH, England (accessories f. antique gun coll.)

E-Z Tool Co., P.O. Box 3186, 25 N.W. 44th Ave., Des Moines, IA 50313 (lathe taper attachment)

Edmund Scientific Co., 101 E. Glouster Pike, Barrington, NJ 08007

Emco-Lux, 2050 Fairwood Ave., P.O. Box 07861, Columbus, OH 43207/614-445-8328

Forster Products, Inc., 82 E. Lanark Ave., Lanark, IL 61046/815-493-6360

Francis Tool Co., (f'ly Keith Francis Inc.), 1020 W. Catching Slough Rd., Coos Bay, OR 97420/593-269-2021 (reamers)

G. R. S. Corp., P.O. Box 748, Emporia, KS 66801/316-343-1084 (Grarermeister)

Gilmore Pattern Works, P.O. Box 50084, Tulsa, OK 74150/918-245-9627 (Wagner safe-T-planer)

Glendo Corp., P.O. Box 1153, Emporia, KS 66801/316-343-1084 (Accu-Finish tool)

Gold Lode, Inc., 1305 Remington Rd., Suite A, Schaumburg, IL 60195 (gold inlay kit)

Gopher Shooter's Supply, Box 278, Faribault, MN 55021 (screwdrivers, etc.)

Grace Metal Prod., 115 Ames St., Elk Rapids, MI 49629 (screw drivers, drifts)

Gunline Tools, Box 478, Placentia, CA 92670/714-528-5252

Gun-Tec, P.O. Box 8125, W. Palm Beach, Fl 33407

Half Moon Rifle Shop, 490 Halfmoon Rd., Columbia Falls, MT 59912/406-892-4409 (hex screws)

Henriksen Tool Co., Inc., P.O. Box 668, Phoenix, OR 97535/503-535-2309 (reamers)

Huey Gun Cases (Marvin Huey), Box 98, Reed's Spring, MO 65737/417-538-4233 (high grade English ebony tools)

Paul Jaeger Inc., 211 Leedom St., Jenkintown, PA 19046

Jeffredo Gunsight Co., 1629 Via Monserate, Fallbrook, CA 92028 (trap buttplate)

John's Rifle Shop, 25 NW 44th Ave., Des Moines, IA 50313/515-288-8680

K&D Grinding Co., P.O. Box 1766, Alexandria, LA 71301/318-487-0823 (cust. tools f. pistolsmiths)

Kasenit Co., Inc., 3 King St., Mahwah, NJ 07430/201-529-3663 (surface hrdng. comp.)

Terry K. Kopp, Highway 13, Lexington, MO 64067/816-359-2636 (stock rubbing compound)

J. Korzinek, RD#2, Box 73, Canton, PA 17724/717-673-8512 (stainl. steel bluing; broch. $1.50)

John G. Lawson, (The Sight Shop) 1802 E. Columbia Ave., Tacoma, WA 98404/206-474-5465

Lea Mfg. Co., 237 E. Aurora St., Waterbury, CT 06720/203-753-5116

Lightwood (Fieldsport) Ltd., Britannia Rd., Banbury, Oxfordsh. OX16 8TD, England

Lock's Phila. Gun Exch., 6700 Rowland Ave., Philadelphia, PA 19149/215-332-6225

John McClure, 4549 Alamo Dr., San Diego, CA 92115 (electric checkering tool)

McIntrye Tools, P.O. Box 491/State Road #1144, Troy, NC 27371/919-572-2603 (shotgun bbl. facing tool)

Michaels of Oregon Co., P.O. Box 13010, Portland, OR 97213/503-255-6890

Viggo Miller, P.O. Box 4181, Omaha, NE 68104 (trigger attachment)

Miller Single Trigger Mfg. Co., R.D. 1, Box 99, Millersburg, PA 17061/717-692-3704

Frank Mittermeier, 3577 E. Tremont, New York, NY 10465

Moderntools, 1671 W. McNab Rd., Ft. Lauderdale, FL 33309/305-979-3900

N&J Sales, Lime Kiln Rd., Northford, CT 06472/203-484-0247 (screwdrivers)

Karl A. Neise, Inc., 1671 W. McNab Rd., Ft. Lauderdale, FL 33309/305-979-3900

Palmgren Prods., Chicago Tool & Eng. Co., 8383 South Chicago Ave., Chicago, IL 60167/312-721-9675 (vises, etc.)

Panavise Prods., Inc., 2850 E. 29th St., Long Beach, CA 90806/213-595-7621

C.R. Pedersen & Son, 2717 S. Pere Marquette, Ludington, MI 49431/616-843-2061

Pilkington Gun Co., P.O. Box 1296, Mukogee, OK 74401/918-683-9418 (Q.D. scope mt.)

Richland Arms Co., 321 W. Adrian St., Blissfield, MI 49228

Riley's Supply Co., 116 No. Main St., Avilla, IN 46710/219-897-2351 (Niedner buttplates, grip caps)

A.G. Russell, 1705 Hiway 71N, Springdale, AR 72764 (Arkansas oilstones)

Schaffner Mfg. Co., Emsworth, Pittsburgh, PA 15202 (polishing kits)

SGW, Inc. (formerly Schuetzen Gun Works), 624 Old Pacific Hwy, S.E. Olympia, WA 98503/206-456-3471

Shaw's, 9447 W. Lilac Rd., Escondido, CA 92025/714-728-7070

Shooters Specialty Shop, 5146 E. Pima, Tucson, AZ 85712/602-325-3346

L.S. Starrett Co., 121 Crescent St., Athol, MA 01331/617-249-3551

Texas Platers Supply Co., 2453 W. Five Mile Parkway, Dallas, TX 75233 (plating kit)

Timney Mfg. Inc., 3106 W. Thomas Rd., Phoenix, AZ 85017/602-269-6937

Stan de Treville, Box 33021, San Diego, CA 92103/714-298-3393 (checkering patterns)

Turner Co., Div. Cleanweld Prods., Inc., 821 Park Ave., Sycamore, IL 60178/815-895-4545

Twin City Steel Treating Co., inc. 1114 S. 3rd, Minneapolis, MN 55415 (heat treating)

Will-Burt Co., 169 So. Main, Orrville, OH 44667 (vises)

Williams Gun Sight Co., 7389 Lapeer Rd., Davison, MI 48423

Wilson Arms Co., 63 Leetes Island Rd., Branford, CT 06405

Wisconsin Platers Supply Co. (See Texas Platers)

W.C. Wolff Co., Box 232, Ardmore, PA 19003 (springs)

Woodcraft Supply Corp., 313 Montvale, Woburn, MA 01801